全国职业院校职教出海系列教材

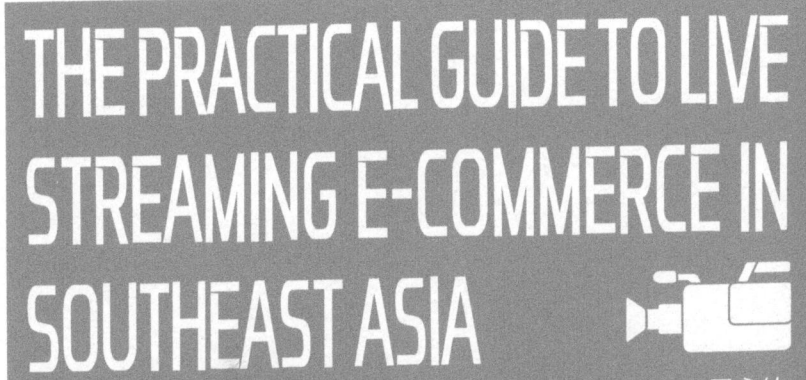

THE PRACTICAL GUIDE TO LIVE STREAMING E-COMMERCE IN SOUTHEAST ASIA
(CHINESE-ENGLISH EDITION)

主 编 弓永钦
　　　　李新龙

东南亚直播电商实务

汉英版

企业管理出版社
ENTERPRISE MANAGEMENT PUBLISHING HOUSE

图书在版编目（CIP）数据

东南亚直播电商实务：汉、英 / 弓永钦，李新龙主编 . -- 北京：企业管理出版社，2024. 11. -- ISBN 978-7-5164-3159-7

Ⅰ . F713.365.2

中国国家版本馆CIP数据核字第2024EW8907号

书　　　名	东南亚直播电商实务（汉英版）
书　　　号	ISBN 978-7-5164-3159-7
作　　　者	弓永钦　李新龙
策　　　划	寇俊玲
责任编辑	耳海燕　寇俊玲
出版发行	企业管理出版社
经　　　销	新华书店
地　　　址	北京市海淀区紫竹院南路17号　　邮　　编：100048
网　　　址	http://www.emph.cn　　电子信箱：1142937578@qq.com
电　　　话	编辑部（010）68701408　发行部（010）68417763　68414644
印　　　刷	北京亿友数字印刷有限公司
版　　　次	2024年11月第1版
印　　　次	2024年11月第1次印刷
开　　　本	710毫米×1000毫米　1/16
印　　　张	11.75
字　　　数	267千字
定　　　价	43.00元

版权所有　翻印必究　·　印装有误　负责调换

前　言

东南亚市场是全球增长最快的电商市场之一。随着互联网普及率的提高和智能手机使用率的增加，在线购物和直播带货在东南亚国家日益普及。根据美国市场研究机构 eMarketer 发布的数据显示，在 2023 年全球零售电商市场增速排名中，东南亚地区增速达 18.6%，位居第一。北京劳动保障职业学院响应国家"一带一路"倡议，从 2018 年开始，就在马来西亚、泰国等东南亚国家培养电子商务专业人才。近几年，直播电商在中国和世界范围内蓬勃发展，关于直播电商的教材也逐步问世，然而目前还没有一部专门针对东南亚国家直播电商人才培养的教材出版。为了配合北京劳动保障职业学院在东南亚地区的教学和培训活动，也为了帮助出海的中资企业培养本土直播电商人才，北京劳动保障职业学院专业教师与厦门颜值立方信息科技有限公司的企业专家组成编写团队，联合打造了这部中英双语的东南亚直播电商教材，以供培养东南亚直播电商人才之用。本书也可供以英语为交流语言的人士学习直播电商技能之用，或电商专业师生和从业人士学习专业英语之用。

本书采用项目化教学编写体例，以一名电子商务专业毕业生在东南亚开展直播电商的全套业务流程为主线，将一个完整的直播电商项目分解设计成一系列实训任务，旨在全面提升学生在东南亚市场开展直播电商的知识水平和技能。读者可以和书中的电子商务毕业生一起学习理论知识，完成直播实操，直至掌握全套直播电商流程。

本书包含 5 个项目、15 个任务，每个项目包括项目概述、项目目标、任务导入、任务目标和任务流程，提供清晰的学习路径和目标指引。任务设计覆盖了东南亚直播电商的各个环节，包括市场调研、选品、直播脚本编写、直播内容策划、设备准备、直播间搭建、直播操作、数据分析和复盘等。每个任务都结合实际工作场景，提供详细的步骤和操作指南，读者可以在完成任务的过程中，系统地学习和应用所学知识。

本书特色如下。

一、以电子商务专业毕业生参与直播电商项目为情境

本书以一名电子商务专业毕业生参与东南亚直播电商项目为情境，设计了一系列真实的项目任务，帮助读者在模拟真实工作环境中学习和实践，提高了学习的趣味性和实用性。

二、以工作过程为主线，体现项目导向、任务驱动

本书采用了以东南亚直播电商相关岗位实际工作流程为主线的编写方式，项目任务紧密围绕实际工作任务展开，确保读者能够在模拟真实的工作情境中学习和应用相关知

识。每个项目均设置了具体的任务，读者通过完成这些任务，可逐步掌握直播电商的核心技能。

三、校企合作，共同编写

本书由学校专业教师与跨境电商企业专家合作编写，充分体现了学术理论与行业实践相结合的优势。企业的参与确保了内容的实用性和前沿性，带来了当前东南亚直播电商行业的最新发展趋势和实践经验。

四、理论与实践相结合

在编写过程中，本书注重理论知识与实际操作有机结合。每个项目任务不仅涵盖了必要的理论知识，还提供了详细的操作步骤。通过这种理论与实践相结合的方式，读者能够在掌握基本理论的同时积累丰富的实践经验。

五、中英双语对照

本书是为东南亚直播电商人才培养专门打造的教材，考虑到受众的国际化特征，采用了中英双语部分对照的方式。无论以中文还是以英文为交流语言的读者都可以把它作为直播电商技能学习的教材。以学习专业英语为目的的读者也可以选择本教材，在掌握直播电商技能的同时提高专业英语水平。

本书由北京劳动保障职业学院弓永钦、厦门颜值立方信息科技有限公司李新龙共同担任主编并统筹编写，编写过程参阅、借鉴了国内外与直播电商相关的网站、书刊资料和研究成果，得到了厦门颜值立方信息科技有限公司的大力支持，在此表示感谢！

由于编者水平有限，书中难免存在疏漏与不当之处，望相关专业人士和广大读者批评指正。

编者
2024 年 6 月

目 录

※ **项目1　认识东南亚直播电商 / 001**
　　任务1　调研东南亚直播市场 / 001
　　　　子任务1　了解直播电商的概念 / 002
　　　　子任务2　分析东南亚直播电商市场的兴起与发展 / 005
　　　　子任务3　认识东南亚的主要国家及其直播市场的特点 / 010
　　　　子任务4　分析东南亚直播电商的目标用户 / 013
　　任务2　选择直播平台 / 018
　　　　子任务1　了解东南亚直播平台的类型 / 018
　　　　子任务2　调研东南亚主流直播平台 / 020
　　　　子任务3　选择合适的直播平台 / 024
　　任务3　选择直播商品 / 027
　　　　子任务1　进行直播选品 / 028
　　　　子任务2　进行直播排品、组品 / 034

※ **项目2　进行直播前的准备 / 039**
　　任务1　组建直播团队 / 039
　　　　子任务1　确定直播团队成员 / 040
　　　　子任务2　组建一个直播团队 / 045
　　任务2　策划直播活动 / 050
　　　　子任务1　明确直播目标 / 051
　　　　子任务2　确定直播主题 / 054
　　　　子任务3　设计直播互动 / 057
　　　　子任务4　策划直播方案 / 061
　　任务3　创作直播内容 / 065
　　　　子任务1　提炼产品卖点 / 065
　　　　子任务2　确定直播封面与标题 / 068
　　　　子任务3　设计直播话术 / 071
　　　　子任务4　编写直播脚本 / 078
　　任务4　搭建直播间 / 082
　　　　子任务1　选择直播设备 / 082
　　　　子任务2　布置直播间灯光 / 089
　　　　子任务3　布置直播间场景 / 094
　　任务5　开展直播预热 / 103
　　　　子任务1　制作预热视频 / 104

　　　　　子任务 2　制作直播预热图文 / 108
　　　　　子任务 3　进行直播预热宣传 / 111

※　**项目 3　使用 Shopee 平台进行直播 / 115**
　　任务 1　学习 Shopee Live 的开播流程 / 115
　　任务 2　学习 Shopee Live 直播营销工具 / 119

※　**项目 4　使用 TikTok 平台进行直播 / 125**
　　任务 1　开启 TikTok Live 直播 / 125
　　任务 2　完成 TikTok Live 直播工具设置 / 131
　　任务 3　开展 TikTok Live 直播推广 / 135

※　**项目 5　直播数据分析与复盘 / 139**
　　任务 1　获取平台直播数据 / 139
　　　　　子任务 1　获取 TikTok 平台直播数据 / 140
　　　　　子任务 2　获取 Shopee 平台直播数据 / 145
　　任务 2　进行数据分析与直播复盘 / 150
　　　　　子任务 1　直播数据统计 / 151
　　　　　子任务 2　直播数据分析方法 / 154
　　　　　子任务 3　直播数据分析实操案例 / 157
　　　　　子任务 4　直播复盘 / 166

※　**课后习题答案 / 175**
※　**参考文献 / 179**

项目1　认识东南亚直播电商

项目概述

随着数字化进程的加速，直播电商作为连接消费者与品牌的新兴渠道，显示出巨大的潜力。作为全球电子商务的重要组成部分，直播电商正在迅速改变国际贸易的模式。这种模式结合了传统电商的便利性与现代直播技术的互动性，有效地促进了卖家与买家之间的沟通，增强了用户的购物体验，并显著提高了交易的效率与成功率。

东南亚地区以其快速增长的互联网用户群和日益扩大的中产阶级消费者基础，正在成为直播电商的热点区域。

项目目标

¤ 知识目标
1. 了解东南亚的主要国家及其直播市场特点
2. 了解东南亚直播电商目标用户
3. 了解东南亚主流直播平台
4. 了解东南亚用户需求

¤ 技能目标
1. 能够进行东南亚直播电商市场分析
2. 能够进行东南亚直播电商受众分析
3. 能够为直播选择适合的平台
4. 能够合理选择直播商品

¤ 素养目标
1. 培养学生实事求是的工作态度和精益求精的工匠精神
2. 能够传播积极的内容和价值观，注重社会责任和道德价值
3. 能够尊重消费者的文化价值观，建立品牌的好感度和忠诚度

任务 1　调研东南亚直播市场

任务导入

电子商务专业毕业生 Peter 加入了一家名为"StreamASEAN"的新兴东南亚直播电商公司，该公司计划扩大其在东南亚的市场份额。作为公司的新成员，Peter 的第一个任务是进行深入的市场分析，帮助公司更好地理解当前的东南亚市场动态和潜在增长机会。这项调研将对公司后续的直播电商决策起到至关重要的作用。

在本任务中，Peter 将调研东南亚的直播市场，进行深入的市场分析，并撰写东南亚直播电商的受众分析报告。

任务目标

¤ 知识目标
1. 了解直播电商的概念
2. 了解东南亚直播电商的兴起与发展
3. 了解东南亚的主要国家及其直播市场特点
4. 了解东南亚直播电商目标用户

¤ 技能目标
1. 能够进行东南亚直播电商市场分析
2. 能够进行东南亚直播电商受众分析

¤ 素养目标
提高观察和分析实际案例的能力

任务流程

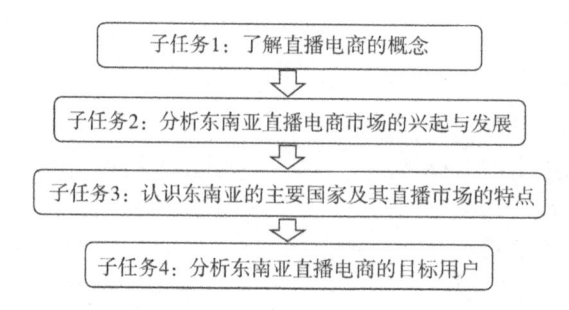

```
子任务1：了解直播电商的概念
        ↓
子任务2：分析东南亚直播电商市场的兴起与发展
        ↓
子任务3：认识东南亚的主要国家及其直播市场的特点
        ↓
子任务4：分析东南亚直播电商的目标用户
```

子任务1 了解直播电商的概念

学习过程

近年来，直播电商异军突起，改变了传统的商品交易方式，成为贸易领域中极具竞争力的新引擎。作为直播电商公司的一员，Peter首先需要对直播电商的概念有所了解。Peter对直播电商知识的搜集如下。

一、直播电商的概念

直播电商是指通过站内平台或站外社交媒体平台对商家产品进行实时介绍、展播的过程。直播电商作为互联网经济时代的商业产物，是网络营销领域新兴的营销概念。电商发展初期，产品的营销主要以文字介绍、图片展示、短视频等方式进行。随着数字经济技术的推广和运用，直播的方式越来越被大众所追捧。

世界著名的全球管理咨询公司麦肯锡认为，2016年阿里巴巴旗下淘宝直播的出现标志着销售行业进入了新篇章。在中国直播电商的带领下，西方的品牌商、零售商、商场等纷纷开始设立自己的直播频道。一方面，直播的方式可以让受众更加清晰、直观地接收关注对象的信息。另一方面，直播可以调动人体感官，让观众获得更多的参与感，场景带入性强，最终实现高转化率。同时，直播解决了购物过程中的信任问题，缩短了购物流程和时间。

二、直播电商的三要素

直播电商为电商行业注入了新的活力，但仍旧离不开电商中"人""货""场"三要素的结合。三者共同作用，决定了直播活动的吸引力和效果。

（一）人

人指直播观众与主播。直播观众是直播的基础要素，直接决定着一场直播的效果，主播负责吸引和维持观众的注意力，以及推动观众的购买行为，是直播中的关键人物。一个优秀的主播不仅需要具备良好的沟通技巧，具有个人魅力，还要对产品有足够的了解，能够准确传达商品卖点。此外，主播的个性应与品牌形象和目标受众相契合，才能在直播过程中让观众建立信任感和亲近感。

（二）货

货指在直播间销售的商品。"货"直接关系到整场直播的成败。选品时，直播团队需要考虑产品的市场需求、品质、价格定位及其在特定市场中的竞争力。优选的产品应具备独特性或创新性，能够激发目标客户的购买欲望。同时，产品的呈现方式也需要创造性，如通过现场演示、使用案例或与消费者互动来展示产品的功能和效果。

（三）场

场指直播场景。直播场景是为连接"人"和"货"而设计的。直播团队在进行直播场景布局时，需要重点考虑搭建怎样的直播场景更有助于主播与用户实时互动，并能激发用户的购买欲望，促使用户产生购买行为。直播间的布置与直播营销的商品密切相关，布局合理的直播间才能使直播营销更有感染力和说服力。

三、直播电商的特点

（一）强互动性

直播电商的消费场景具有良好的互动性。主播在向直播观众介绍商品时可以通过在镜头前试用商品，让直播观众直观地感受到商品的使用效果，这能大幅提升用户的购物体验。同时，直播观众也可以在直播间进行互动发言，参与到直播中。这种参与和互动有利于提升直播观众对商品和品牌的信任感，从而促使他们做出购买决策。

（二）强 IP 属性

主播具有很强的 IP 属性，在观众心中有着独特的标签。对于观众来说，主播不仅仅是一个为他们推荐商品的人，更是他们的情感寄托，是他们心中值得信赖的人设形象，因而用户自愿去购买主播推荐的商品。

（三）去中心化

在直播电商生态链中，主播数量众多且类型多样，很多主播不仅在电商平台拥有公域流量，还在其他媒体平台拥有自己的私域流量。与传统电商相比，直播电商具有较强的去中心化的特点，为更多的主播提供了运营个人 IP 的可能性。

任务操作

学习完上述基础知识，为更加深入地了解什么是直播电商，Peter 需要完成如下操作。

☞ **步骤一　选择一个东南亚直播电商卖家**

在网上选择并关注一个东南亚直播电商卖家，可以通过搜索引擎、社交媒体、直播平台等途径找到合适的卖家。

☞ **步骤二　观看卖家的直播**

观看该卖家的直播，试着分析该直播间的"人""货""场"特点，并将相关信息填写在表1-1中。填写的具体内容说明如下。

（1）东南亚直播电商卖家：填写卖家名称。
（2）国家：填写国家名称。
（3）直播产品：填写直播中展示的主要产品。
（4）主播：分析主播的表现，例如语言能力、亲和力、专业度等。
（5）直播间布景：描述直播间的布置，例如背景、道具、灯光、氛围等。
（6）分析总结：总结该卖家直播间的优点和不足，提出改进建议。

表1-1　东南亚电商卖家直播记录

项目	具体内容
东南亚直播电商卖家	
国家	
直播产品	
主播	
直播间布景	
分析总结	

Learning Process

1. Concept of Live Streaming E-commerce

Live streaming e-commerce refers to the process of introducing and displaying real-time products through internal platforms or external social media platforms. As a commercial product of the era of Internet economy, it is an emerging marketing concept in online marketing. The formats include text live stream, image live stream and video live stream, and have become increasingly popular with the advancement of digital economy technology.

McKinsey, a world-renowned global management consultancy, thinks the arrival of Alibaba's Taobao Live in 2016 marked the opening of a new chapter in sales. Following China's lead in live streaming e-commerce, western brand merchants and retailers began establishing their live streaming channels. Live stream allows audiences to receive information more clearly and intuitively, enhances the shopping experience, improves conversion rates, and addresses trust issues in the shopping process.

2. Three Key Elements

The success of live streaming e-commerce relies on the combination of three key elements: "people", "goods", and "scenes".

2.1 People

"People" refers to users and hosts. Users are the foundational element of a live stream and directly determine its effectiveness. Hosts are key figures in live marketing, responsible for attracting and maintaining viewers' attention and driving purchasing behavior. A good host needs excellent communication skills, product knowledge, and a personality that aligns with the brand image and target audience to build trust and rapport during the live stream.

2.2 Goods

"Goods" refers to the products sold during the live stream. When selecting products, it is essential to consider market demand, quality, price positioning, and competitiveness in the specific market. Ideally, products should be unique or innovative to stimulate the target customers' desire to purchase. Creative presentation methods, such as live demonstrations, use cases, or consumer interactions, are also crucial.

2.3 Scenes

"Scenes" refers to the live streaming environment. The design of the live streaming scene should facilitate real-time interaction between the host and users, evoke the desire to purchase, and encourage buying behavior. The setup should be closely related to the marketing products, as a well-arranged scene enhances the appeal and persuasive power of live marketing.

3. Characteristics

3.1 High Interactivity

Live streaming e-commerce offers excellent interactivity. Hosts can try products live, allowing users to see the results directly, and thus significantly enhancing the shopping experience. Users can also interact with the host about product information. Such participation and interaction can help increase the users' trust in the products and brands, which can facilitate purchase decisions.

3.2 Strong IP Attribute

Hosts have a strong IP attribute, creating a unique image in users' minds. For users, hosts are not only persons who recommend products for them, but also their emotional support, and the image of a trustworthy person in their hearts. Therefore, users voluntarily buy products recommended by hosts.

3.3 Decentralization

The live streaming e-commerce ecosystem features numerous and diverse hosts, many of whom have both public traffic on e-commerce platforms and private traffic on other media platforms. Compared to traditional e-commerce, live streaming e-commerce is more decentralized, providing more opportunities for hosts to develop their personal IP.

Task Operations

Step 1: Choose a Southeast Asian Live Streaming E-commerce Seller

Select and follow a Southeast Asian live streaming e-commerce seller online. You can find suitable sellers through search engines, social media, and live streaming platforms.

Step 2: Watch the Seller's Live Stream

Watch the seller's live stream and try to analyze the characteristics of the "people", "goods", and "scenes" in the live stream.

子任务2　分析东南亚直播电商市场的兴起与发展

学习过程

随着东南亚电商的蓬勃发展，各种电商形态也逐渐涌现，比如直播电商已成为电商行业发展的重要趋势。

在此任务中，Peter 需要了解东南亚直播电商的发展现状及其得以发展的原因，于是 Peter 做了如下探索。

一、东南亚直播电商现状

（一）东南亚直播电商发展概况

东南亚是热门的电商市场，是增长快、潜力大的蓝海市场。根据市场研究公司 eMarketer 发布的《2023 年全球零售电商预测报告》显示，东南亚将是全球电商市场规模增速的冠军，2023 年东南亚电商销售额预计增长 18.6%，远超全球其他电商市场，如图 1-1 所示。

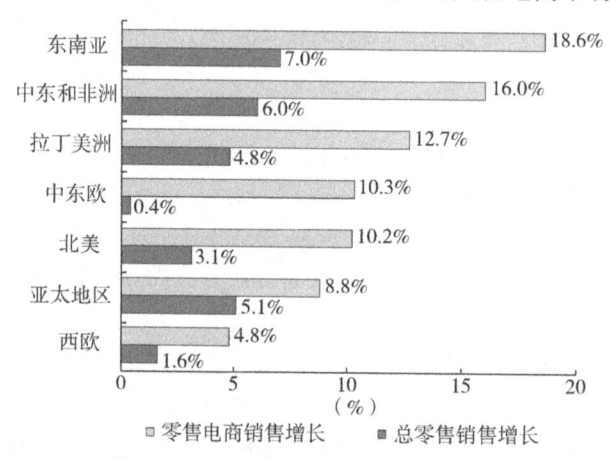

图 1-1　2023 年全球电商销售额预测

图片来源：《2023 年全球零售电商预测报告》。

根据谷歌、淡马锡、贝恩公司联合发布的《2023 年东南亚数字经济报告》显示，东南亚电商市场依旧处于高速增长阶段，2023 年印度尼西亚的电子商务 GMV（Gross Merchandise Volume，商品交易总额）约为 620 亿美元，泰国约为 220 亿美元，越南和菲律宾均约为 160 亿美元，马来西亚约为 130 亿美元，新加坡约为 80 亿美元。东南亚电子商务 GMV 在 2023 年达到 1390 亿美元，预计将在 2025 年达到 1860 亿美元，增长率为 16%。

作为电商发展增速最大的地区，以直播电商为例的新型电商模式在东南亚也得到了较好的发展。东南亚物流巨头 Ninja Van 发布的调查报告称，尽管直播销售在该地区仍然是一个相对"新鲜"的工具，但已经有近三分之一的受访卖家尝试过直播带货。根据 Cube Asia（新加坡在线零售洞察公司）调查显示，2022 年东南亚直播电商的 GMV 已达到 130 亿美元，并且呈现快速增长趋势，预计 2025 年可达到 186 亿美元，如图 1-2 所示。

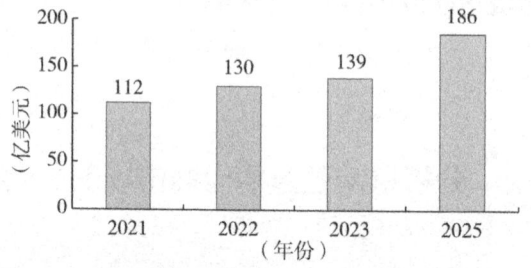

图 1-2　东南亚直播电商 GMV（单位：亿美元）

数据来源：《2023 年东南亚数字经济报告》。

（二）东南亚各国直播电商发展概况

东南亚主要国家直播电商发展概况见表1-2。

表1-2 东南亚主要国家直播电商发展概况

国家	直播电商发展概况
印度尼西亚	东南亚第一大电商市场，2021年，TikTok Shop推出了印度尼西亚小店，在印度尼西亚尝试开通直播电商功能，获得了强大的用户流量，其中90%的用户对广告有高水平接受度
泰国	东南亚第二大电商市场，电子商务发展和支付基础设施较为发达。据泰国电子商务协会称，直播电商占泰国社交媒体市场价值的38%，预计2025年将达到34.5亿美元
越南	东南亚第三大电商市场，直播带货在越南非常受欢迎，市场潜力巨大。根据Coc Coc平台的调查显示，77%的越南受访者曾观看过直播，其中71%的人在观看直播时进行了购物。2024年第一季度，有95%的越南在线消费者有直播购物经历，每月直播带货的场次超过250万场
菲律宾	东南亚第三大电商市场，直播带货的热门国家之一，用户喜欢观看视频直播娱乐，60%的品牌采用直播带货吸引客户
马来西亚	消费者已经接受直播电商作为一种新的购物方式，Shopee Live平台迎来了流量和销量的双重爆发。2023年"双十一大促销"购物节期间，借助Shopee Live的巨大流量，马来西亚卖家的订单成功增加了82倍
新加坡	拥有良好的电商基础设施，新兴技术市场已发展成熟，63%的新加坡消费者了解并乐于使用直播购物

二、影响东南亚直播电商发展的因素

（一）直播电商基础设施较为成熟

基础设施包括第三方支付、物流、供应链等，为直播电商提供了有利条件。电商公司可以更轻松地将商品送到客户手中，提高了服务的可及性。

（二）互联网用户数量庞大

东南亚地区的互联网用户数量庞大，互联网渗透率高，为直播电商提供了巨大的市场。约有6亿人口分布在这个地区，平均年龄为30岁，GDP增速保持在5%，人均GDP约为5000美元，75%的人口可以上网，这为发展直播电商创造了极佳的机会。根据探谋（TMO）发布的《2024年东南亚电子商务市场洞察报告》，东南亚五国具体人口、市场概况如表1-3所示。

表1-3 2024年东南亚五国人口、市场概况

国家	人口	GDP	人均GDP	2024年电商销售额（全年预估）	电商销售额年度同比增长
印度尼西亚	2.79亿	1.5万亿美元	4073美元	505.1亿美元	+11.2%
菲律宾	1.182亿	4715.2亿美元	3527.98美元	148.7亿美元	+15.1%
马来西亚	3449万	4455.2亿美元	11371.97美元	80.9亿美元	+14.8%
泰国	7185万	5489.9亿美元	6278.17美元	195.3亿美元	+13.9%
越南	9919万	4658.1亿美元	3655.46美元	140.2亿美元	+14.9%

数据来源：《2024年东南亚电子商务市场洞察报告》。

任务操作

学习完上述基础知识，Peter需要完成如下操作。

☞ 步骤一 选择国家

选择一个东南亚国家，例如越南、泰国、马来西亚等，调研该国家直播电商兴起与发展的历程。

可以通过以下途径获取信息。

（1）搜索引擎。
（2）专业数据公司发布的市场报告。
（3）当地相关的新闻和行业报道。

☞ **步骤二　整理结果**

整理调研结果，并将其填写在表1-4中。
调研东南亚国家直播电商的兴起和发展历程，可以关注以下几个方面。
（1）初期发展：直播电商的引入时间和初期发展情况。
（2）关键事件：推动直播电商发展的重要事件或政策。
（3）市场影响：直播电商对当地电商市场的影响。
（4）主要平台：主要的直播电商平台及发展情况。
（5）用户反馈：用户对直播电商的接受程度。

表1-4　_____（国家）直播电商发展历程

时间	发展情况

Learning Process

1. Current State of Live Streaming E-commerce in Southeast Asia

1.1 Development Overview

Southeast Asia is a hot spot for e-commerce, and is recognized as a rapidly growing and high-potential market. According to eMarketer's "Global Retail E-commerce Forecast 2023", Southeast Asia is projected to lead global e-commerce market growth rates, with its e-commerce sales expected to grow by 18.6% in 2023, as shown in Figure 1-1 (please see the Chinese section).

According to the "E-conomy SEA 2023", Southeast Asia's e-commerce market continues to grow rapidly. In 2023, Indonesia's e-commerce GMV is approximately \$62 billion, Thailand's about \$22 billion, Vietnam's and the Philippines' around \$16 billion each, Malaysia's about \$13 billion, and Singapore's about \$8 billion. The total GMV in Southeast Asia is expected to reach \$139 billion in 2023 and \$186 billion by 2025, growing by 16%.

As the region with the highest growth rate in e-commerce development, the new e-commerce model, taking live streaming e-commerce as an example, has also achieved good development in Southeast Asia. According to a survey report released by Southeast Asian logistics giant Ninja Van, although live streaming sales are still a relatively new tool in the region, nearly one-third of the sellers surveyed have tried live streaming sales. According to a survey by Cube Asia, a Singapore-based online retail insights company, the GMV of live streaming e-commerce in Southeast Asia has reached \$13 billion in 2022 and is showing a rapid growth trend. It is expected to reach \$18.6 billion by 2025, as shown in Figure 1-2 (please see the Chinese section).

1.2 Development Status

The development status of major Southeast Asian countries is shown in Table 1-1.

Table 1-1: Development Overview in Major Southeast Asian Countries

Country	Development Overview
Indonesia	Indonesia is the largest e-commerce market in Southeast Asia. In 2021, TikTok Shop attempted to open live streaming e-commerce functions in Indonesia, gaining strong user traffic. 90% of users have a high level of acceptance of advertisements
Thailand	Thailand is the second largest e-commerce market in Southeast Asia, with well-developed e-commerce conditions and payment infrastructure. According to the Thai E-commerce Association, live streaming e-commerce accounts for 38% of the social media market value in Thailand and is expected to reach $3.45 billion by 2025
Vietnam	Vietnam is the third largest e-commerce market in Southeast Asia, and live streaming e-commerce is very popular in Vietnam with huge market potential. According to a survey conducted by Coc Coc, 77% of Vietnamese respondents have watched live streams, and 71% of them have made purchases while watching live streams. In the first quarter of 2024, 95% of Vietnamese online consumers have experienced live shopping, with over 2.5 million live streaming sales per month
The Philippines	The Philippines is the third largest e-commerce market in Southeast Asia and one of the popular countries for live streaming sales. Users enjoy watching live streams for entertainment, and 60% of brands use live streaming sales to attract customers
Malaysia	Malaysian consumers have accepted live streaming e-commerce as a new way of shopping, and Shopee Live has experienced a dual surge in traffic and sales. During the "11.11 Great Promotion" shopping festival in 2023, thanks to the huge traffic of Shopee Live, the orders of Malaysian sellers successfully increased by 82 times
Singapore	Singapore has good e-commerce infrastructure and a mature emerging technology market. 63% of Singaporean consumers are aware of and willing to use live shopping

2. Factors Influencing the Development of Live Streaming E-commerce in Southeast Asia

2.1 Mature Infrastructure

The development of third-party payment systems, logistics, and supply chains in Southeast Asia provides favorable conditions for live streaming e-commerce, making it easier for e-commerce companies to deliver products to customers.

2.2 Large Internet User Base

Southeast Asia has a large population with high Internet penetration. With around 600 million people, an average age of 30, a GDP growth rate of 5%, and a per capita GDP of about $5000, 75% of the population has Internet access, creating excellent opportunities for mobile internet development. According to "Southeast Asia E-commerce Outlook 2024" released by TMO, the population and market overview of the five Southeast Asian countries is shown in Table 1-2.

Table 1-2: Population and Market Overview of Five Southeast Asian Countries in 2024

Country	Population	GDP	Per Capita GDP	2024 E-commerce Sales (Annual Estimate)	E-commerce Sales Annual Growth
Indonesia	279 million	$1.5 trillion	$4,073	$50.51 billion	+11.2%
The Philippines	118.2 million	$471.52 billion	$3,527.98	$14.87 billion	+15.1%
Malaysia	34.49 million	$445.52 billion	$11,371.97	$8.09 billion	+14.8%
Thailand	71.85 million	$548.99 billion	$6,278.17	$19.53 billion	+13.9%
Vietnam	99.19 million	$465.81 billion	$3,655.46	$14.02 billion	+14.9%

Task Operations

Step 1: Select a Country

Select a Southeast Asian country, such as Vietnam, Thailand, Malaysia and research the rise and development of live streaming e-commerce in that country.

Information can be obtained through the following channels.

(1) Search engines.

(2) Market reports published by professional data companies.

(3) Relevant local news and industry reports.

Step 2: Organize the Survey Results

Organize the survey results.

Research content includes the following aspects.

(1) Early Development: The introduction stage and initial development of live streaming e-commerce.

(2) Key Events: Important events or policies that promoted the development of live streaming e-commerce.

(3) Market Impact: The impact of live streaming e-commerce on the local e-commerce market.

(4) Main Platforms: The main live streaming e-commerce platforms and their development status.

(5) User Feedback: The acceptance and feedback of users towards live streaming e-commerce.

子任务3　认识东南亚的主要国家及其直播市场的特点

学习过程

在此任务中，Peter 需要完成他在 StreamASEAN 直播电商公司的任务，了解东南亚主要国家、东南亚国家直播电商市场的特点以及东南亚直播电商市场的调研方法。

一、了解东南亚主要国家

东南亚（Southeast Asia，缩写 SEA）位于亚洲东南部，包括中南半岛和马来群岛两大部分。东南亚地区共有 11 个国家：缅甸、泰国、柬埔寨、老挝、越南、菲律宾、马来西亚、新加坡、文莱、印度尼西亚、东帝汶，面积约 457 万平方千米。该地区的 6 个最大经济体分别是印度尼西亚、马来西亚、新加坡、菲律宾、泰国和越南。

二、东南亚国家直播电商市场的特点

东南亚国家直播市场主要存在以下特点。

（一）直播模式尚不成熟

东南亚目前的主要直播模式是社交媒体的网红主播在电商平台进行带货，有点像一次性商业活动，缺乏系统性的直播带货模式。

（二）消费增长潜力可观

人口优势是影响东南亚经济持续增长的重要因素。此外，人口结构呈现年轻化趋势，尤其是印度尼西亚、马来西亚、菲律宾和越南四国，35 岁以下人口占比超过 50%，消费增长潜力可观。

（三）主播素质参差不齐

由于MCN（Multi-channel Network，多频道网络）机构或公会不成熟，东南亚直播平台的主播素质参差不齐，而且以颜值主播和才艺主播为主，专业的带货主播较少。

（四）直播内容单一

东南亚直播内容显得较为单调，无论是聊天、才艺、游戏，还是直播带货，内容均缺乏创新。随着行业发展，内容创作或许能得到大幅提升。

三、东南亚直播电商市场的调研方法

（一）确定调研目的和问题

调研目的是了解东南亚直播电商市场的整体状态，以及定位特定细分市场，根据调研目的设计细致的问题。

（二）收集基础数据

收集一些东南亚国家的大数据变量，包括人口、出口额、市场概况、用户规模、直播电商渗透率、直播电商发展政策背景、消费水平等数据，识别潜在市场。

（三）了解市场趋势

了解东南亚市场的发展趋势，发掘优势产业以及规避可能出现的负面因素。

（四）分析竞争对手

了解市场上其他直播电商企业的销售渠道和商业模式，分析转化率、客服水平、物流水平、支付水平等指标，全方位地了解市场渗透情况。

（五）案例分析

总结一些成功或失败案例，了解背后的市场需求、商业模式、用户洞察等。

（六）形成分析报告

整理并分析收集到的所有数据信息，证实调研结论的合理性，可通过图表进行深入分析，为电商企业在业务拓展中制定合适的市场战略打下坚实的基础。

任务操作

学习完上述知识，Peter需要完成如下操作。

☞ 步骤一　选择调研国家

选择一个国家，对该国的直播电商市场情况进行调研。市场调研团队选择_____（东南亚国家）进行市场调研。

☞ 步骤二　收集基础数据

从直播电商市场概况、用户规模、市场渗透率、直播电商发展政策背景、主要直播电商平台、物流水平、支付手段等角度对所选国家直播电商市场进行调研，并填写在表1-5中。

表1-5　_____（国家）直播电商市场调研

调研国家	
直播电商市场概况	
直播电商发展政策背景	
用户规模	
市场渗透率	
物流水平	
支付手段	

续表

主要直播电商平台	
其他	

☞ **步骤三　分析竞争对手**

选择一个或几个东南亚直播电商企业，对其进行调研分析，并填写在表1-6中。

表1-6　＿＿＿＿＿＿＿＿（国家）东南亚直播电商企业调研

东南亚直播电商企业	分析指标	分析结果

☞ **步骤四　分析调研结果**

分析调研结果，并根据调研情况形成该国的直播电商市场分析报告。

Learning Process

1. Understand Major Southeast Asian Countries

Southeast Asia (SEA) is located in the southeastern part of Asia, including the Indochina Peninsula and the Malay Archipelago. There are a total of 11 countries in Southeast Asia: Myanmar, Thailand, Cambodia, Laos, Vietnam, the Philippines, Malaysia, Singapore, Brunei, Indonesia, and Timor-Leste, with an area of approximately 4.57 million square kilometers. The six largest economies in the region are Indonesia, Malaysia, Singapore, the Philippines, Thailand, and Vietnam.

2. Characteristics of the Live Streaming E-commerce Market in Southeast Asian Countries

The live streaming markets in Southeast Asia have the following characteristics.

2.1　Basic Live Streaming Models

In many Southeast Asian countries, social media influencers conduct live streaming sales on e-commerce platforms. The live streaming models in these regions are still relatively basic.

2.2　Significant Consumption Growth Potential

The demographic advantage is a key factor influencing the continuous economic growth in Southeast Asia. Additionally, the population is trending younger, particularly in Indonesia, Malaysia, the Philippines, and Vietnam, where over 50% of the population is under 35 years old. This demographic trend suggests a considerable potential for consumption growth.

2.3　Varied Quality of Influencers

Due to the immaturity of MCN institutions or guilds, the quality of hosts on Southeast Asian live streaming platforms varies greatly, with a focus on beautiful and talent hosts, and a shortage of professional influencers.

2.4　Monotonous Live Streaming Content

Southeast Asian live streaming content appears relatively monotonous, lacking innovation in chat, talent, gaming, and live streaming sales. With the development of the industry, content creation may be greatly improved.

3. Methods for Researching the Live Streaming Market in Southeast Asia

3.1 Define Research Purpose and Questions

Clearly define the research purpose and questions to understand the overall state of the live streaming e-commerce market in Southeast Asia and identify specific segments.

3.2 Collect Basic Data

Gather data on various factors such as population, export volume, market overview, user scale, live streaming e-commerce penetration rate, policy background, and consumption levels to identify potential markets.

3.3 Understand Market Trends

Learn from the experiences and lessons of Southeast Asia's e-commerce and identify potential trends, uncover advantageous businesses, and avoid possible negative factors.

3.4 Analyze Competitors

Study the sales channels and business models of other live streaming e-commerce companies in the market, analyzing indicators such as conversion rates, customer service levels, logistics levels, and payment levels to understand market penetration.

3.5 Case Analysis

Summarize successful or failed cases to understand the underlying market demands, business models, and user insights.

Prepare an Analysis Report: Organize all collected data and information, perform in-depth analysis using charts, and confirm the rationality of the research conclusions.

Task Operations

Step 1: Choose a Country for Research

Select a country to research the live streaming e-commerce market. The market research team selects _____ for market research.

Step 2: Collect Basic Data

Research the chosen country's live streaming e-commerce market from the following aspects: market overview, user scale, live streaming e-commerce penetration rate, development policy background, main live streaming e-commerce platforms, logistics level, and payment methods.

Step 3: Analyze Competitors

Survey and analyze other live streaming e-commerce companies in Southeast Asia.

Step 4: Analyze Research Results

Analyze the research results and create an analysis report on the live streaming e-commerce market in the selected country.

子任务 4　分析东南亚直播电商的目标用户

学习过程

对东南亚直播市场有了初步的了解之后，Peter 应了解影响东南亚直播电商目标用户的因素，为后续在东南亚地区开启直播打下基础。Peter 需要了解的知识如下。

影响直播电商目标用户的因素，包括环境、个人和企业三个方面。从各种影响因素来看，网民人均收入、网民数量和网民学历水平与网络消费总量存在正相关，而网民人均上网时间则与网络消费总量存在负相关。

一、环境因素

（一）网民人均收入

网民人均收入对网络消费总量有显著的正面影响。经济基础影响消费水平和消费方式，因此网络消费总量与电商消费者的人均收入密切相关。

（二）网民数量

随着网民数量的逐年增加，网络消费总量也呈现出增长趋势。同时随着网络消费观念被普遍接受、国民整体经济状况的提升、计算机价格的低廉化、网络宽带的大力普及，各国（地区）有许多收入水平不高的网民也参与到网络消费中来，造就了如今电商市场的繁荣。

（三）网民学历水平

网民学历水平与网络消费总额呈正相关。一般来讲，网民受教育程度越高，网络消费能力越强，网络消费的层次越高。若网民整体学历水平能提高，其带来的网络消费效应将更大。

（四）网民人均上网时间

网民人均上网时间与网络消费总额存在负相关。从逻辑上看，上网经验越丰富，其参与网络消费的可能性就越大，但应注意到一个问题，那就是如今上网已成为人们消遣娱乐、了解外界信息的一项基本活动，而大部分网民上网并不是为了购物。因此，网民人均上网时间的增加，只能说明互联网世界的生活越来越丰富，网民的大部分时间用于除网络购物以外的其他网络应用。不过这些年网络购物用户规模增幅一直较大，网上支付、网上银行等商务类应用的重要性进一步提升，更多的传统经济活动已经步入移动互联网时代，可以预见今后的网民人均上网时间与网络消费总量的负相关程度会减轻，也有可能呈现正相关。

二、个人因素

（一）年龄

不同年龄的消费者的关注点是不相同的。首先，关注的网站类型不同。其次，对网站内容的关注点不同，例如同样一个企业网站，成年人比较关注这个网站给予的产品价值，而青少年关注的可能是网站提供的活动。

（二）性别

男性消费者和女性消费者在对网络产品的需求以及网络消费行为习惯等方面都存在差异，营销人员应该把握两者的特点，并将其作为设计网络营销策略的考虑因素。

（三）职业

不同职业的消费者所感兴趣的网站不同，信息来源也会有所不同。专业性越强的网站，聚集对应职业人群的能力就越强，那么网络营销就要有针对性地在适合的网站投放广告。

（四）受教育程度与经济收入

由于受教育程度与经济收入有较强的正相关，因此应将两个因素放在一起考虑。消费者的受教育程度越高，在了解和掌握互联网知识方面的困难就越小，也就越容易接受网络购物的观念和方式；越是受过良好的教育，网络购物频率就越高。

（五）生活方式

不同国家（地区）的消费者的消费理念是不同的，在生活用品、书籍、娱乐等方面的消费支出比例不同，上网的时间、地点、频率以及浏览偏好等也存在明显差异。此外，消费者的购买行为受到动机、知觉、信念和态度等主要心理因素的影响。在进行电商营销时，需考虑到各国（地区）消费者的生活方式和当地的风俗习惯。

（六）个性

个性是指一个人的心理特征。不同个性的消费者的消费习惯和偏好也不同。例如，外向的消费者会比较关注运动、旅游、交友等网络资讯；而内向的消费者会倾向于文学、艺术类的网络资讯。追随型或依赖性强的消费者会更容易受到企业在网络上的营销因素的影响，易于接受广告，也较容易对品牌产生忠诚；而独立和理性的消费者则会更积极地收集各种资讯，不轻易相信广告，对企业的营销因素敏感度低。

三、企业因素

（一）支付

电商企业提供的网上支付手段的多样性、方便性、安全性，在很大程度上影响消费者的消费行为。

（二）配送

完善的物流配送系统是实物商品网络营销的一个关键点，也是电商消费者十分看重的地方。良好的物流配送系统可以提供安全、快速的配送服务，提高电商消费者的满意度。反之，很多国家（地区）的物流配送系统还不够完善，影响了本国（地区）电商的发展。

（三）营销策略

电商企业出色的营销策略对电商消费者的行为会产生积极的影响。在电商平台上，企业的营销策略可以更加多样化，从而对电商消费者产生更加深刻的影响。

（四）网站设计

网站设计对消费者的影响主要通过内容设置、界面是否友好和是否方便快速等方面体现。一个有效率的网站设计应当能够促使消费者产生某种购物习惯。

（五）客户服务

电商营销的客户服务不仅包含了传统营销的客户服务的内容，还更加注重电商企业为客户提供的资讯与信息交流。提供服务的方式可以有很多种，如常见问题交流、E-mail 信息交流、提供呼叫中心服务等。很多时候售后的退换货服务直接影响电商消费者的购买决策。

任务操作

学习完上述知识，Peter 需要完成如下操作。

步骤一 调研东南亚直播电商的目标用户

对所选东南亚国家的直播电商目标用户进行调研，并根据调研结果完成表 1-7。

表 1-7 _____（国家）目标用户调研

1. 环境因素	网民人均收入	
	网民数量	
	网民学历水平	
	网民人均上网时间	

续表

2. 个人因素	年龄	
	性别	
	职业	
	受教育程度与经济收入	
	生活方式	
	个性	
3. 企业因素	支付	
	配送	
	营销策略	
	网站设计	
	客户服务	

☞ 步骤二　撰写受众分析报告

请帮助 Peter 完成他在 StreamASEAN 直播电商公司的任务，撰写完成一份所选国家的受众分析报告。

Learning Process

The factors affecting target users of live streams include environmental, personal and corporate aspects.

1. Environmental Factors

1.1 Per Capita Income of Internet Users

It significantly positively affects the total amount of online consumption.

1.2 Number of Internet Users

As the number of Internet users increases, the total online consumption also increases.

1.3 Education Level of Internet Users

It is positively correlated with total online consumption.

1.4 Average Internet Usage Time

It is negatively correlated with total online consumption, but this relationship may turn positive as online shopping continues to grow.

2. Personal Factors

2.1 Age

Different age groups focus on different aspects of websites.

2.2 Gender

Male and female consumers have different needs and consumption behaviors.

2.3 Occupation

Consumers in different professions have varying interests and information sources.

2.4 Education Level and Income

Higher education levels make it easier for consumers to accept online shopping.

2.5 Lifestyle

Different countries have varying consumption concepts and behaviors.

2.6 Personality

Consumers with different personalities have different consumption habits and preferences.

3. Corporate Factors

3.1 Payment

The diversity, convenience, and security of online payment methods influence consumer behavior.

3.2 Distribution

A well-developed logistics system is crucial for e-commerce.

3.3 Marketing Strategies

Excellent marketing strategies have a positive impact on consumer behavior.

3.4 Website Design

Effective website design influences consumers through content setting and user-friendliness.

3.5 Customer Service

It includes traditional customer service and emphasizes information exchange.

Task Operations

Step 1: Research Target Users for Live Streaming E-commerce in Southeast Asia

Conduct research on the target users of live streaming e-commerce in the selected Southeast Asian country.

Step 2: Write an Audience Analysis Report

Write an audience analysis report for the selected country.

课后习题

1. （多选题）以下哪些属于影响直播电商目标用户的因素？
A. 营销策略　　　　　　　　　　B. 生活方式
C. 年龄　　　　　　　　　　　　D. 网民人均上网时间

2. （单选题）在进行东南亚直播电商市场调研时，哪项不是分析的主要焦点？
A. 市场渗透率　　　　　　　　　B. 用户规模
C. 电商发展政策背景　　　　　　D. 产品生产成本

3. 请简述：在进行东南亚直播电商市场调研时，为什么了解市场趋势是重要的步骤？

Exercises

1. (Multiple Choice) Which of the following are factors that influence the target users of live streaming e-commerce?
A. Marketing strategies　　　　　B. Lifestyle
C. Age　　　　　　　　　　　　D. Average Internet usage time

2. (Single Choice) When you research the live streaming e-commerce market in Southeast Asia, which item is not a primary focus of the analysis?
A. Market penetration rate　　　B. User scale
C. E-commerce development policy background　　D. Product production cost

3. Please briefly explain why understanding market trends is an important step when you

research the live streaming e-commerce market in Southeast Asia.

任务 ② 选择直播平台

任务导入

直播平台是直播产业链中重要的组成部分，是直播内容的输入和输出渠道。为了在东南亚市场中取得成功，选择一个合适的直播平台至关重要。完成对东南亚直播电商市场的调研后，StreamASEAN 直播电商公司希望能对东南亚的主流直播平台有系统的了解，以便选择适合公司开展东南亚直播业务的平台，于是公司向 Peter 下达任务：为公司选择最适合的东南亚直播平台。

在本任务中，Peter 将详细了解东南亚直播平台的类型及主流直播平台，分析各平台的优缺点，并学习如何根据公司的需求和市场特点选择最适合的直播平台。

任务目标

¤ 知识目标
1. 了解东南亚直播平台的类型
2. 了解东南亚主流直播平台

¤ 技能目标
1. 能够为直播选择直播平台
2. 能够进行东南亚直播电商受众分析

¤ 素养目标
培养学生分析决策和判断能力

任务流程

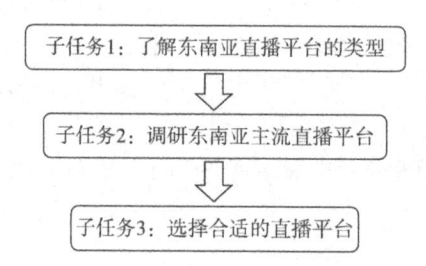

子任务1：了解东南亚直播平台的类型
↓
子任务2：调研东南亚主流直播平台
↓
子任务3：选择合适的直播平台

子任务 1 了解东南亚直播平台的类型

学习过程

直播平台是直播营销产业链中不可或缺的一部分，它为直播提供了内容输入和输出的渠道。目前东南亚电商主流的直播平台可以分为社交和内容直播平台、电子商务直播平台和自主直播电商平台。

每种直播平台的目标用户不一样，直播平台的类型也不一样，因此在选择直播平台时，Peter 应先了解直播平台的类型及其输入输出内容的特点，这样才能选出适合自己的直播平台。

一、社交和内容直播平台

社交和内容直播平台是指上线直播业务的社交平台。这类平台原本以用户社交为主，在增添直播功能后，平台上的用户除了可以实时与他人分享生活方式、发布即时信息外，还可以开通直播、观看直播等。东南亚常见的社交和内容平台主要有 Facebook、Instagram、TikTok 等，见图 1-3。

图 1-3　Facebook、Instagram、TikTok 社交和内容直播平台图标

二、电子商务直播平台

电子商务直播平台指的是推出直播业务的传统电商平台，商家借助平台内的技术资源进行产品直播来实现商品销售，用户可以边观看直播边购买商品。电子商务直播平台具有很强的营销性，东南亚两个占主导地位的电子商务平台分别是 Lazada 和 Shopee，见图 1-4。

图 1-4　Lazada、Shopee 电子商务直播平台图标

三、自主直播电商平台

一些拥有电子商务业务的大型品牌和零售商自建了实时销售环境，以提高参与度和转化率。自主直播电商平台拥有自主权，直接连接消费者和卖家，不受制于任何平台，卖家自己掌握制定规则，灵活性强，最主要的是可以塑造品牌，建立品牌壁垒和产生品牌溢价，有利于稳定长期的发展。东南亚常见的自主直播电商平台有 Zalora、优衣库泰国等，见图 1-5。

图 1-5　Zalora 自主直播电商平台图标

任务操作

学习完上述知识，Peter 需要完成如下操作。

对东南亚的直播电商平台进行调研，并将调研结果填写在表 1-8 中。

表 1-8　东南亚直播平台分类

平台类型	平台名称	平台简介
社交和内容直播平台		
电子商务直播平台		
自主直播电商平台		

平台名称：填写各直播平台的名称，包括社交和内容直播平台、电子商务直播平台和自主直播电商平台三种。

平台简介：简要介绍平台的主要特点、目标市场、用户基础等信息。

Learning Process

1. Social and Content Live Streaming Platforms

Social and content live streaming platforms refer to social platforms that have incorporated live streaming features. Initially focusing on user interaction, these platforms now allow users to share their lives, post updates, and engage in live stream, both as broadcasters and viewers. Common social and content platforms in Southeast Asia include Facebook, Instagram, and TikTok, as shown in Figure 1-3 (please see the Chinese section).

2. E-commerce Live Streaming Platforms

E-commerce live streaming platforms are traditional e-commerce platforms that have introduced live streaming capabilities. Merchants use the platform's technical resources to live stream to facilitate real-time sales. Users can watch the live streams and purchase products simultaneously. These platforms are highly market-oriented, with Shopee and Lazada being the dominant e-commerce live streaming platforms in Southeast Asia, as shown in Figure 1-4 (please see the Chinese section).

3. Proprietary Live Streaming E-commerce Platforms

Some large brands and retailers with e-commerce operations have created their own live streaming environments to enhance engagement and conversion rates. Proprietary live streaming e-commerce platforms offer full autonomy, directly connecting consumers with sellers without being restricted by external platforms. This flexibility allows merchants to set their own rules, build brand identity, create brand barriers, and generate brand premiums, which is beneficial for long-term development. Common proprietary live streaming e-commerce platforms in Southeast Asia include Zalora, and Uniqlo Thailand as shown in Figure 1-5 (please see the Chinese section).

Task Operations

Research live streaming e-commerce platforms in Southeast Asia and fill in a form with the research results.

Platform Name: Fill in the names of each live streaming platform. This includes three types: social and content live streaming platforms, e-commerce live streaming platforms, and proprietary live streaming e-commerce platforms.

Platform Overview: Briefly introduce the main features, target market, user base, and other relevant information of each platform.

子任务2　调研东南亚主流直播平台

学习过程

随着直播行业的飞速发展，直播平台如雨后春笋般涌现出来，部分平台以其自身特有的优势，快速占领东南亚市场，成为主流平台。在了解了东南亚的平台类型之后，Peter 需要调研东南亚占据主流地位的直播平台，并分析这些平台具有的优势和劣势，为后续的选择直播平台做准备。Peter 对目前东南亚主流直播平台了解如下。

一、东南亚的主流直播平台

东南亚具有众多的直播平台，根据东南亚头部物流服务商 Ninja Van 2023 年关于各平台受欢迎程度的研究数据显示，Shopee 以 27% 的占比领先，其次是 Facebook，占比为 25.5%，紧随其后的是 TikTok，占比为 22.5%，而 Lazada 则以 15% 的占比位列第四。图 1-6 详细展示了东南亚主流直播平台的消费者偏好占比。

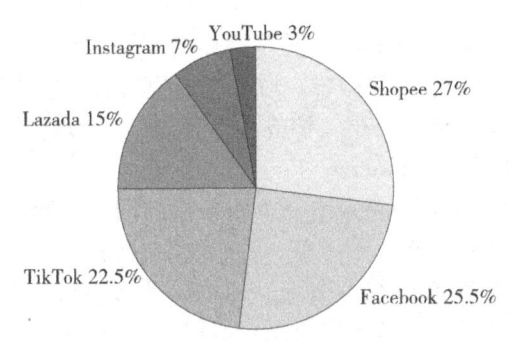

图 1-6　东南亚主流直播平台

数据来源：《东南亚直播电商报告》。

二、东南亚不同国家的主流直播电商平台

在不同国家，各个直播电商平台的受欢迎程度存在差异。从图 1-7 可以看出，排名前三位的，新加坡的直播电商平台的受欢迎程度依次是 Shopee、Facebook、TikTok，马来西亚的直播电商平台的受欢迎程度依次是 Shopee、Facebook、TikTok，印度尼西亚的直播电商平台的受欢迎程度依次是 TikTok、Shopee、Lazada，菲律宾的直播电商平台的受欢迎程度依次是 Shopee、Facebook、Lazada，泰国的直播电商平台的受欢迎程度依次是 Facebook、TikTok、Shopee，越南的直播电商平台的受欢迎程度依次是 Facebook、Shopee、TikTok。

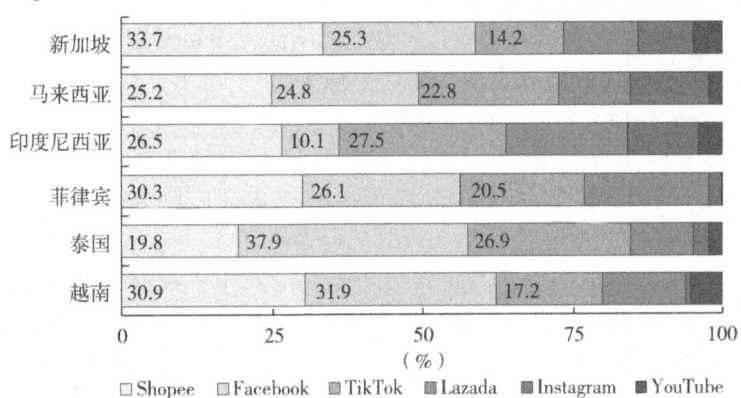

图 1-7　东南亚不同国家主流直播电商平台的受欢迎程度

图片来源：《东南亚直播电商报告》。

三、认识东南亚主流直播平台

（一）Shopee 直播平台——Shopee Live

Shopee 诞生于 2015 年，由有东南亚"小腾讯"之称的 SEA 创立。Shopee 在短短两年内风靡东南亚，覆盖新加坡、马来西亚、菲律宾、印度尼西亚、泰国、越南等市场，同时在中国的深圳、上海和香港设立跨境业务办公室。在接下来的时间里先后击败了由阿里巴巴注资的 Lazada 和地区电商巨头 Tokopedia。

2019 年，Shopee 推出 Shopee Live，具有直播带货功能，主播以直播的方式向购物者推广自己的商店和产品。实时直播会话的卖方，应用内商店页面上将会显示一个"Shopee Live"标签。

Shopee Live 直播功能可以带来海量流量，让商品在极短时间内实现高曝光和快出单。其中美容护肤、3C 电子、时装服饰、时尚配饰是四大直播热门品类，相当多的产品通过 Shopee Live，实现从 0 单到万单，抑或从"日出千单"到"时出千单"的质变。

（二）Lazada 直播平台——LazLive

Lazada 于 2012 年 3 月推出，是东南亚首屈一指的网上购物平台，中文名为来赞达，Lazada 在印度尼西亚、马来西亚、菲律宾、新加坡、泰国以及越南均设有分支机构，同时在韩国、英国、俄罗斯等地设有办事处。Lazada 平台主要经营 3C 电子、家居用品、玩具、时尚服饰、运动器材等产品，平台成立不到 7 年的时间，就一跃成为东南亚最大的电子商务平台。

2019 年，Lazada 正式推出直播平台 LazLive，允许卖家和用户在线进行实时互动，并提供详细的产品演示和同时购买商品的功能。2021 年"双十一"期间，LazLive 平台通过直播实现了 GMV 同比增长 187%，疫情期间，LazLive 直播服务产生的 GMV 实现了环比 45% 的增长。

（三）TikTok 直播平台——TikTok Live

2016 年，TikTok 由字节跳动集团推出，最初以"抖音"为名在中国市场推广，随后于 2017 年下半年出海，面向国际市场，更名为"TikTok"。TikTok 推出后短时间内风靡全球，曾多次登上美国、印度、德国、法国、日本、印度尼西亚和俄罗斯等地 App Store 或 Google Play 总榜首位。2021 年，TikTok 月活跃用户数量突破 10 亿大关。平台总下载量已超过 30 亿次，覆盖全球 150 多个国家和地区。

2017 年，TikTok 上线 TikTok Live，具有直播功能，内容创作者可以通过该功能在平台进行直播，并允许创作者通过直播与受众实时互动。

（四）Facebook 直播平台——Facebook Live

Facebook 属于社交媒体范畴，是东南亚第二大受欢迎的直播电商渠道。尽管 Facebook 没有端到端的直播电商解决方案，但它在东南亚广泛流行，使其成为直播电商探索的一个不可忽视的重要渠道。

Facebook 于 2018 年 12 月推出直播带货功能，2020 年正式推出可以直接点击商品详情完成购买的 Live Shopping 功能，但目前取消该点击功能，将重心重新转回短视频业务。由 Facebook 部分品牌更名而来的 Meta 公司计划独立推出直播产品 Super。

任务操作

学习完上述知识后，Peter 需要完成以下操作步骤。

☞ **步骤一　明确调研目标**

了解东南亚各主流直播平台的特点、用户群体和市场定位。

☞ **步骤二　了解信息收集渠道**

信息收集渠道有如下途径参考。

（一）搜索引擎

使用Google、Bing等搜索引擎，查找有关各直播平台的最新信息和数据。

（二）专业数据公司

参考尼尔森、艾瑞咨询等专业数据公司的市场研究报告，获取市场分析数据。

（三）官方平台

访问各直播平台的官方网站，查阅其帮助文档和使用指南，了解平台功能和用户特征。

☞ **步骤三　填写调研结果**

将收集到的信息和数据整理后，填写在表1-9中。

表1-9　东南亚直播平台分析

直播平台	平台概述	平台人群画像
Shopee		
Lazada		
TikTok		
Facebook		

Learning Process

1. Main Live Streaming Platforms in Southeast Asia

According to a 2023 study by Ninja Van on platform popularity, Shopee leads with a 27.0% share, followed by Facebook at 25.5%, TikTok at 22.5%, and Lazada at 15%, as shown in Figure 1-6 (please see the Chinese section).

2. Popular Live Streaming E-commerce Platforms in Different Countries

The popularity of live streaming e-commerce platforms varies in different countries, as shown in Figure 1-7 (please see the Chinese section).

Singapore: Shopee, Facebook, TikTok.

Malaysia: Shopee, Facebook, TikTok.

Indonesia: TikTok, Shopee, Lazada.

The Philippines: Shopee, Facebook, Lazada.

Thailand: Facebook, TikTok, Shopee.

Vietnam: Facebook, Shopee, TikTok.

3. Overview of Main Live Streaming Platforms in Southeast Asia

3.1 Shopee Live

Founded in 2015, Shopee launched Shopee Live in 2019, covering multiple markets and focusing on popular categories like beauty, electronics, and fashion.

3.2 LazLive

Established in 2012, Lazada launched LazLive in 2019, enabling real-time interaction between sellers and users. LazLive saw a 187% GMV increase during the "Double Eleven" sale in 2021.

3.3 TikTok Live

Launched in 2016, TikTok covers over 150 countries and regions. Creators can interact with audiences in real time through TikTok Live.

3.4 Facebook Live

Facebook introduced its live streaming feature in 2018, and added Live Shopping in 2020. Currently, it focuses on short videos and plans to launch a separate live streaming product, Super.

Task Operations

Step 1: Define Research Objectives

Understand the characteristics, user demographics, and market positioning of the main live streaming platforms in Southeast Asia.

Step 2: Find Channels of Information Collection

The channels of information collection include the following.

2.1 Search Engines

Use search engines such as Google and Bing to find the latest information and data about each live streaming platform.

2.2 Professional Data Company Reports

Refer to market research reports from professional data companies like Nielsen and iResearch to obtain detailed market analysis data.

2.3 Official Websites

Visit the official websites of each live streaming platform, and review their help files and user guides to understand platform functions and user characteristics.

Step 3: Fill in the Research Results

Organize the collected information and data, and fill in a form.

子任务3　选择合适的直播平台

学习过程

在了解了东南亚主流直播平台之后，Peter需要完成StreamASEAN直播电商公司下达的任务：选择合适的东南亚直播电商平台。在此之前，Peter需要学习直播平台选择的技巧。

一、用户规模

选择直播平台时，应特别关注平台的用户规模。用户规模是指该平台上活跃用户的数量，用户规模越大，直播内容就可能被更多的观众看见，带来更高的流量和更大的曝光度。对于希望扩大品牌影响力或增加销售额的企业来说，选择用户规模较大的平台，可为其直播业务的发展提供坚实的保障。

二、用户画像

用户画像是指平台用户的基本特征和行为习惯，包括年龄、性别、地域分布、兴趣爱好、消费习惯等。由于不同直播间的直播内容和销售商品不同，选择一个用户画像与其目标受众相匹配的平台至关重要。因此，深入分析各个直播平台的用户画像，有助于选择最适合的直播平台，提高直播的效果。

三、入驻门槛

不同的直播平台对新入驻商家的要求各不相同，有的平台门槛较低，几乎任何个人或企业都可以轻松入驻，而有的平台则需要商家提供营业执照、一定的营业额证明等。个人或企业在选择直播平台时，应考虑自身的条件和资源，以确保能够满足平台的入驻要求。高门槛的平台可能带来更高质量的用户和更多的商业机会，但同时也可能限制了一些资源有限的中小企业的选择。

四、平台调性

平台调性是指平台对外展示的主要风格和形象。例如，一些平台注重年轻化和娱乐化，适合时尚、美妆等产品的直播，而另一些平台则更注重专业性和商务性，适合科技产品或B2B（Business-to-Business，企业与企业之间）业务的直播。因此，个人或企业在选择直播平台时，应根据自身品牌的定位和风格选择调性相符的平台，以便更好地传达品牌信息，吸引目标用户。

五、流量获取方式

目前，直播平台主要有两种流量获取方式：公域流量和私域流量。公域流量是指平台通过推荐算法、搜索引擎和社交媒体等渠道吸引的新用户，这种方式可以帮助商家快速增加曝光度和吸引新观众；私域流量则是通过商家自有渠道吸引的用户，这种方式可以帮助商家建立长期稳定的用户群体。个人或企业在选择直播平台时，应了解平台主要的流量获取方式，以便制定相应的营销策略，最大限度地提高直播的效果。

任务操作

学习完上述直播平台选择技巧，Peter需要完成如下操作。

☞ 步骤一　东南亚直播平台调研

（1）选择一个东南亚国家进行直播平台调研。
（2）调研四个主要直播平台：Shopee、Lazada、TikTok 和 Facebook。
（3）使用在线报告、平台文档和其他可信来源收集信息。
（4）将调查结果填写在表1-10中。

表1-10　_____（国家）主流直播平台调研

直播平台	用户规模	用户画像	入驻门槛	平台调性	流量获取方式
Shopee					
Lazada					
TikTok					
Facebook					

（5）调研内容概述。

用户规模：平台的用户数量及其活跃度。
用户画像：平台用户的年龄、性别、地域等基本信息。
入驻门槛：平台对入驻商家的要求和条件。
平台调性：平台的品牌形象和用户体验。

流量获取方式：平台如何吸引流量和用户。

☞ **步骤二　选择直播平台**

（1）根据东南亚国家市场调研及直播平台分析结果，为 StreamASEAN 直播电商公司选择直播电商平台：_____（直播电商平台名称）。

（2）准备一个简短的演示（3~5分钟），展示选择的平台并阐述选择的理由。

Learning Process

There are many tips for choosing a live streaming platform.

1. User Scale

When selecting a live streaming platform, individuals or businesses should consider the platform's user scale. The larger the user base is, the greater the potential traffic will be. A large user scale can provide a guarantee for the subsequent development of live streaming business.

2. User Profile

Since the live streaming content and products sold by individuals or businesses vary, it is necessary to analyze the user profile of the platform when choosing a live streaming platform.

3. Entry Threshold

Different live streaming platforms have varying entry thresholds. Due to the differing conditions and resources of individuals or businesses, the entry threshold can somewhat limit the choice of live streaming platforms.

4. Platform Tone

The platform tone refers to the main and most unique style that the platform presents externally.

5. Traffic Acquisition Methods

Currently, there are two main traffic acquisition methods on live streaming platforms: one tends to acquire traffic from the public domain, and the other tends to acquire traffic from the private domain.

Task Operations

Step 1: Research on Live Streaming Platforms in Southeast Asia

Conduct research on the main live streaming platforms in the selected country through online reports, questionnaires, and other resources.

（1）Select a Southeast Asian country for live streaming platform research.

（2）Each group will research four main live streaming platforms: Shopee, Lazada, TikTok, and Facebook.

（3）Use online reports, platform documentation, and other credible sources to gather information.

（4）Overview of research content.

User Scale: The number of users on the platform and their activity level.

User Profile: Basic information about platform users, including age, gender, and region.

Entry Threshold：The requirements and conditions for merchants to join the platform.
Platform Tone：The brand image and user experience of the platform.
Traffic Acquisition Methods：How the platform attracts traffic and users.

Step 2：Select a Live Streaming Platform

Based on the market research of Southeast Asian countries and the analysis results of live streaming platforms, select a live streaming e-commerce platform：_____（Live Streaming E-commerce Platform）.

课后习题

1.（单选题）哪个平台属于东南亚的电子商务类别的直播平台？
　A. Facebook　　　　　　　　　　B. Instagram
　C. Shopee　　　　　　　　　　　D. Zalora
2.（单选题）哪个直播平台在东南亚受到消费者的追捧程度最高？
　A. Shopee　　　　　　　　　　　B. Facebook
　C. TikTok　　　　　　　　　　　D. Lazada
3. 请简述：选择直播平台时，应考虑哪几个重要因素？

Exercises

1.（Single Choice）Which platform belongs to the e-commerce category of live streaming platforms in Southeast Asia?
　A. Facebook　　　　　　　　　　B. Instagram
　C. Shopee　　　　　　　　　　　D. Zalora
2.（Single Choice）Which live streaming platform is the most popular among consumers in Southeast Asia?
　A. Shopee　　　　　　　　　　　B. Facebook
　C. TikTok　　　　　　　　　　　D. Lazada
3. Briefly describe the important factors to consider when you choose a live streaming platform.

任务 3　选择直播商品

任务导入

俗话说："七分选品，三分运营。"对于电商企业而言，直播选品不仅是产品销售的过程，更是展示企业价值观和建立国际品牌形象的关键。在完成了直播平台的选择后，StreamASEAN 直播电商公司向 Peter 下达工作任务：为即将进行的直播选择商品，确定店铺商品类目，并选择五个商品，用于东南亚直播电商。

在这次选品任务中，Peter 需要了解直播选品的知识、技巧，精心筛选出既符合东南亚目标市场需求又能反映公司品牌形象的产品。

任务目标

¤ 知识目标

1. 了解选品及组品的技巧
2. 了解选品工具的使用

¤ 技能目标

1. 能够分析选品依据
2. 能够使用选品工具进行选品

¤ 素养目标

培养学生的法律意识和规则意识,确保所有产品遵循所在国及目标市场国的相关法律与规定

任务流程

子任务1:进行直播选品
⬇
子任务2:进行直播排品、组品

子任务1　进行直播选品

学习过程

选品是电商成功的关键因素之一。好的选品不仅能吸引客户,还能显著提高转化率和利润率。然而,在繁多的产品和不断变化的市场趋势中找到那些"赢家"产品绝非易事。因此,掌握使用专业选品工具的技能显得尤为重要。

在此任务中,Peter 需要了解直播选品的依据,并使用适用于东南亚直播的选品工具。Peter 对相关知识了解如下。

一、确定选品依据

(一)根据粉丝画像选品

先分析直播账号的粉丝画像,了解粉丝群体的性别、年龄、地域分布,以及兴趣、购物偏好等属性特征,然后在选品时根据粉丝的属性特征挑选符合粉丝需求的商品。

(二)根据市场趋势选品

根据市场趋势选择直播商品,可以查阅与直播人设匹配的行业领域的市场调查研究报告,也可以订阅有关市场趋势的媒体内容,时刻关注新发展、新趋势。

(三)根据直播人设定位选品

根据直播人设定位进行选品不仅是一种原则,也是具体的方法。例如,美妆达人可以选择与化妆、护肤等有关联的商品,如口红、粉底、眉笔、化妆刷等。

(四)根据商品热度选品

主播可以选择一些当前比较热门的商品,这样既可以增加直播间的流量和人气,又可以增加直播间的销量。

【注意】选品需要符合以下选品原则。

(1) 符合主播人设：主播及其团队选择的商品要和主播的人设定位相匹配。

(2) 商品性价比高：性价比高的商品不管在哪个直播电商平台都更有优势。

(3) 优先考虑热销商品：在直播选品时，要重点考虑近段时间的热销商品，特别是在近30天内热销的商品。

(4) 商品要亲自试用：为了保证商品质量，主播及其团队在选品时要亲自试用商品，排除质量低劣的商品，这样才能让用户买得放心、用得安心。

二、使用选品工具进行选品

FastMoss（Fast, Analytical, Smart, Targeted, Market-Oriented Selection Strategy）是专注于TikTok平台的数据分析工具，还是一种有效的直播选品工具。使用FastMoss可以确保直播团队在选品过程中考虑到市场需求、粉丝偏好和商品热度等多个因素。

Google Trends是一款主要用来计算某个搜索词相对于其他搜索词的走势比较的工具，提供相对的搜索量和地域信息，用来判断关键词在谷歌网页搜索中的趋势走向。

Jungle Scout是亚马逊卖家广泛使用的一个工具，虽然主要针对亚马逊，但其市场分析和产品研究功能也适用于理解东南亚市场的趋势和消费者需求。它提供的产品追踪、销售估算和关键词研究功能都是进行有效选品的关键。

Helium 10是一款功能强大的电商工具套件，提供一系列功能，包括关键词研究、市场趋势分析、竞争情报等，帮助卖家优化产品列表和增加销售。尽管同样以亚马逊为主，但它的市场分析工具可以帮助理解东南亚消费者的行为。

任务操作

学习完上述基础知识，Peter需要完成公司的选品任务。以下Peter选用FastMoss、Google Trends分别进行选品数据分析，需要完成如下操作。

☞ 步骤一　使用第三方选品工具选品

Peter可任选以下两种选品工具之一进行直播选品。

（一）使用FastMoss进行选品

1. 登录平台

登录https：//www.fastmoss.com/，进入FastMoss官网，输入账号和密码，点击"登录（Log In）"按钮。如果没有账号，点击"注册（Sign Up）"进行注册，并在页面左上角选择国家处，选择东南亚国家。

2. 输入搜索关键词

在搜索框中输入感兴趣的产品或关键词。例如，如果想销售运动鞋，可以输入"运动鞋（Sneakers）"或更具体的品牌或类型，如"跑步鞋（Running Shoes）"。

点击"爆款商品（Top-Selling Products）"，即可查看近7天销量高且环比增长率高的商品，见图1-8。

3. 搜索榜单

FastMoss的商品工具栏还提供热销榜、热推榜、新品榜等各类榜单，协助卖家进行选品。

4. 查看商品详情

点击榜单上的商品，即可进入商品详情页，详情页中可以查看商品详情信息，包括

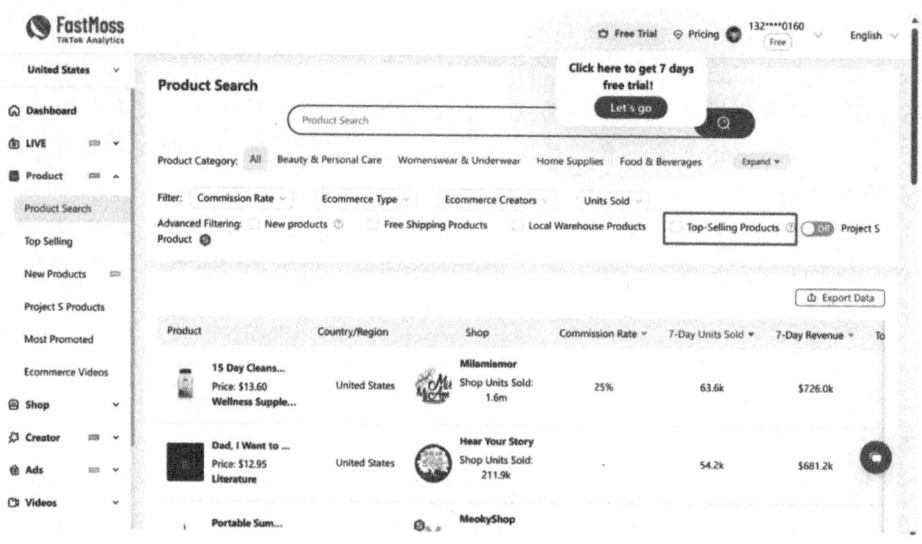

图1-8 点击"爆款商品（Top-Selling Products）"

封面、标题、价格等，也可以查看商品的销售数据。

（二）使用 Google Trends 进行选品

使用 Google Trends 进行选品是一种有效的方法，可以了解消费者兴趣的时间性变化和地理分布，从而做出更明智的选品决策。下面是使用 Google Trends 进行选品的步骤。

1. 访问 Google Trends

打开 Google Trends 网站（https：//www.trends.google.com）。这个工具是免费的，可以直接在浏览器中访问。

2. 输入搜索关键词

在搜索框中输入感兴趣的产品或关键词。例如，如果想销售运动鞋，可以输入"运动鞋（Sneakers）"或更具体的品牌或类型，如"跑步鞋（Running Shoes）"。

3. 设定地理和时间范围

根据市场定位，选择适当的地理位置（如特定国家或地区）和时间范围（可以是过去几个月、一年或更长时间）。通过这个功能可以了解在特定区域和时间内，相关产品的搜索趋势。

4. 分析趋势数据

查看生成的趋势图表，分析关键词的搜索频率随时间的变化。高峰期可能表明较高的消费者兴趣，而低谷期则可能表示兴趣下降，见图1-9。

5. 比较相关关键词

使用"比较（Compare）"功能添加其他相关关键词进行比较。

例如，比较"跑步鞋（Running Shoes）"与"足球鞋（Soccer Shoes）"的搜索趋势，看看哪种类型的运动鞋更受欢迎，见图1-10。

6. 检查地域兴趣

查看"地域兴趣（Interest by Region）"部分，了解哪些地区对哪些产品更感兴趣。这可以帮助定位市场推广活动和库存分布。

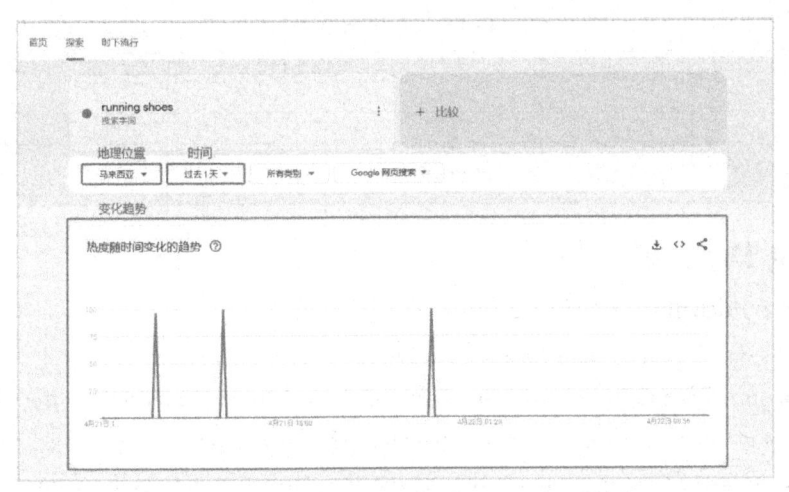

图 1-9　设定地理和时间范围后的分析趋势数据

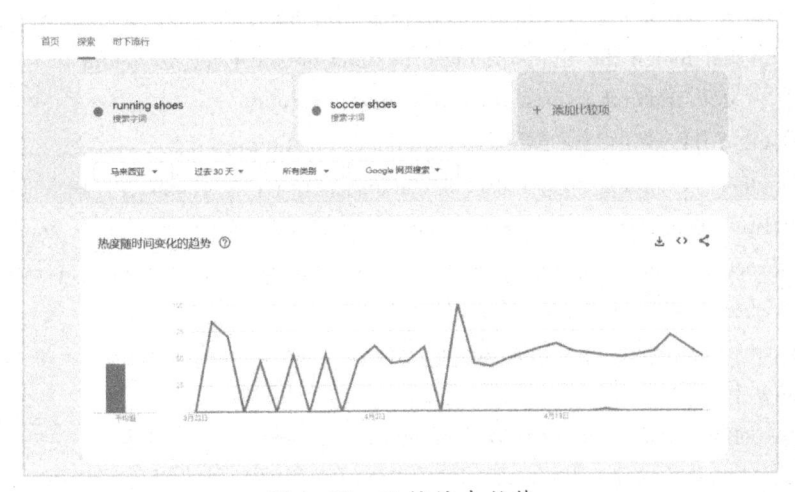

图 1-10　比较搜索趋势

图片来源：Google Trends。

7. 搜索热度和相关查询

浏览"搜索热度（Search Popularity）"和"相关查询（Related Queries）"部分，这里会显示不同子区域的搜索热度及与搜索关键词相关的热门话题和查询。这些数据可以帮助卖家发现市场上的新趋势或潜在的细分市场。

8. 应用数据到选品决策

根据从 Google Trends 得到的洞见，确定哪些产品有较高的市场需求和增长潜力。结合其他市场研究和供应链信息，做出最终的选品决策。

【注意】市场趋势是动态变化的，定期回访 Google Trends，更新你的数据，确保你的选品策略保持与当前市场趋势的一致性。

☞ 步骤二　选择直播商品

结合选品依据，及利用直播选品工具选品等方法，选择出五个将用于直播的商品，并填写在表 1-11 中。

表 1-11　直播商品选择

类目	一级类目	二级类目	商品

Learning Process

1. Determining Selection Criteria

1.1 Selection Based on Fan Profile

Analyze the fan profile of the live streaming account to understand the demographic characteristics of the fan base, such as gender, age, geographic distribution, interests and shopping preferences. Choose products that match the attributes and needs of the fans.

1.2 Selection Based on Market Trends

To select live streaming products according to market trends, review industry market research reports that match the live streaming persona or subscribe to media content related to market trends to stay updated on new developments and trends.

1.3 Selection Based on Live Streaming Persona Positioning

Select products according to the live streaming persona positioning, which is not only a principle but also a specific method. For example, a beauty influencer can choose products related to makeup and skincare, such as lipsticks, foundation, eyebrow pencils, and makeup brushes.

1.4 Selection Based on Product Popularity

Choose currently popular products to increase the traffic and popularity of the live stream, and boost sales.

Note: Selection should adhere to the following principles.

Match the Live Streaming Persona: The selected products should match the positioning of the live streaming persona.

High Cost-Performance Ratio: Products with a high cost-performance ratio have an advantage on any live streaming e-commerce platform.

Prioritize Hot-Selling Products: Focus on recently hot-selling products, especially those trending in the last 30 days.

Personal Product Testing: To ensure product quality, the host and their team should personally test the products to eliminate inferior quality items, ensuring that users can purchase with confidence.

2. Using Selection Tools for Product Selection

FastMoss (Fast, Analytical, Smart, Targeted, Market-Oriented Selection Strategy) is a data analysis tool for the TikTok platform, designed specifically for selecting live streaming products. This tool assists e-commerce teams in systematically and efficiently choosing products. Using the FastMoss ensures that the product selection process considers various factors such as market demand, fan preferences, and product popularity.

Google Trends is a tool primarily used to compare the trend of a specific search term relative to other search terms. It provides relative search volumes and geographical information, helping to identify keyword trends in Google web searches.

Jungle Scout is a widely used tool by Amazon sellers. Although it primarily targets Amazon, its market analysis and product research features are also applicable for understanding trends and consumer needs in the Southeast Asian market. Key features include product tracking, sales estimates, and keyword research, all of which are crucial for effective product selection.

Helium 10 is another powerful suite of e-commerce tools that offers a range of functionalities, including keyword research, market trend analysis, and competitive intelligence. These tools help sellers optimize product listings and increase sales. While Helium 10 is also primarily focused on Amazon, its market analysis tools can help understand consumer behavior in the Southeast Asian market.

Task Operations

Step 1: Selecting Products by Using Third-Party Tools

Choose one of the following product selection tools for live streaming product selection.

1.1 Using FastMoss for Product Selection

(1) Log in to the Platform: Visit FastMoss. Enter your username and password, and then click the "Log In" button. If you don't have an account, click "Sign Up" to create one. In the top left corner, select a Southeast Asian country.

(2) Enter Search Keywords: In the search box, type in the product or keywords you're interested in. For example, if you want to sell sneakers, type "Sneakers" or more specific terms like "Running Shoes".

Click on "Top-Selling Products" to view products with high sales and growth rates over the past 7 days, as shown in Figure 1-8 (please see the Chinese section).

(3) Explore Additional Rankings: The FastMoss product toolbar offers various rankings, including "Top Selling", "Most Promoted", and "New Products" lists, to assist sellers in product selection.

(4) View Product Details: Click on a product from the ranking lists to go to the product detail page. Here, you can see product details, including the cover image, title, and price, as well as sales data.

1.2 Using Google Trends for Product Selection

Using Google Trends helps understand consumer interest trends and geographical distribution, aiding in making informed product selection decisions. Here are the steps.

(1) Visit Google Trends: Open Google Trends, which is free to use in your browser.

(2) Enter Search Keywords: In the search box, type in the product or keywords you're interested in. For example, for sneakers, type "Sneakers" or more specific terms such as "Running Shoes".

(3) Set Geographical and Time Range: Choose the appropriate geographical location

(specific country or region) and time range (past few months, a year, or longer) based on your market positioning.

(4) Analyze Trend Data: Examine the generated trend charts and analyze how search frequency changes over time. Peaks indicate high consumer interest, while troughs suggest declining interest, as shown in Figure 1-9 (please see the Chinese section).

(5) Compare Related Keywords: Use the "Compare" feature to add other relevant keywords for comparison. For instance, compare "Running Shoes" with "Soccer Shoes" to see which type is more popular, as shown in Figure 1-10 (please see the Chinese section).

(6) Check Regional Interest: View the "Interest by Region" section to understand which areas have a higher interest in your product. It helps you target your marketing efforts and inventory distribution.

(7) Search Popularity and Related Queries: Browse the "Search Popularity" "Related Queries" section to see popular related topics and queries. This can help identify new trends or potential niche markets.

(8) Apply Data to Product Selection: Use insights from Google Trends to identify products with high market demand and growth potential. Combine this data with other market research and supply chain information to make final decisions of product selection.

Note: Market trends are dynamic. Regularly revisit Google Trends to update your data and ensure your product selection strategy aligns with current market trends.

Step 2: Choose Live Streaming Products

Based on the selection criteria and the methods outlined above, select five products for the live stream.

子任务2　进行直播排品、组品

学习过程

有效的选品策略能够直接吸引目标客户群体，增加交易的转化率，并显著提升利润率。因此，面对复杂多变的全球市场和庞杂的产品种类，如何精准地筛选出具有市场潜力的产品，并通过合理的组品策略将它们有效地推向市场，是每个电商人士必须面对的挑战。

在此任务中，Peter需要学习如何制定高效的排品、组品策略，Peter对相关知识了解如下。

一、直播商品的类型

（一）引流款

引流款指为了给平台或者店铺及商品带来流量的商品（利润预期在0%至1%），折扣空间可以设置在30%至50%，在直播开始后的15分钟上架，数量占比为10%，以超低价格，配合一些营销功能在直播间迅速聚拢一些人气。例如在"黑色星期五"这种节日，引流款可以为店铺带来巨大的流量。

（二）利润款

利润款顾名思义就是指利润来源的盈利商品，这类商品流量不多，但是利润高。利润款商品会在直播间人气最高时上架，一般都是高流量、高曝光的当季爆款。利润款应适用于目标群体中某一类特定的小众群体，这些人追求个性，所以这部分商品突出的卖点及特点必须符合这一部分小众群体的心理。

（三）爆款

爆款指直播间卖得比较火爆、深受观众喜欢的商品。其价格不像引流款商品那样低，但是会给直播间带来大量订单和用户。

（四）常规款

常规款是销量中规中矩、比较常见的商品，上架这些商品最主要的原因是让直播间产品数量丰富，不断给客户刺激感，保证客户留存率。

（五）新款

新款指最新上市的商品，这种款式的商品一般相对于之前的款式的商品，有着更加新鲜、时尚、性能更好等特征，更能满足人们的需求。一般这种款式的商品比较常见于季节交替时，或者商家以前的商品已经吸引不到客户，急需新的款项吸引留住客户时。

（六）形象款

形象款指凸显直播间形象气质、给人留下深刻印象的商品。形象款应该选择一些高品质、高调性、高客单价的极小众产品。

根据平台的销售情况，不断调整优化，了解竞争对手在这些品类上的动态，关注对手的 SKU（Stock Keeping Unit，最小存货单位）变化、价格变化，随时保持竞争。

二、直播电商组品策略

（一）引流款+利润款

一场直播的盈利主要看利润款的销量，但是一般来说，利润款肯定是客单价比较高的商品，并非所有人都有意愿和有能力购买。

因此，商家如果想通过利润款获取利润，那么直播间必须有大量的观众来进行一定比例的转换。这个时候就必须有一些引流款给直播间引进流量，并且通过这些引流款提高直播间观众的停留时长、互动、评论以及商品点击、商品下单等各项指标。

（二）引流款+爆款+利润款依次循环

带货直播间通常对观众观看时长有一定要求，引流款、爆款等不同款式的商品上架可以不断提振观众信心，从而更大程度留住客户。

直播间先以引流款制造氛围，再通过预告以及爆款拉动观众的兴奋感，从而带动观众互动、评论、商品下单、点击等活动，提高直播间流量池。同时通过一些小活动循序渐进提高爆款以及利润款的转化率，从而提高利润款的购买量。最终在观众热情消失前，利用引流款再次制造气氛，从而保证观众新鲜度的良好循环。

一个好的组品方案可以为直播间最大化提升用户停留、GMV 以及 UV（Unique Visitors，独立访客）价值，从而达到提升直播间权重、沉淀精准用户的目标。

任务操作

学习完上述知识，Peter 需要完成如下操作。

☞ **步骤一　进行商品规划**

(1) 引流款：价格较低、折扣力度大的商品，以吸引观众进入直播间。

(2) 利润款：利润较高的商品，在直播间人气高峰时段推销。

(3) 爆款：热门商品，预计在直播中会有较高销量。

(4) 常规款：销售稳定、常见的商品，丰富直播间商品种类。

(5) 新款：最新上市的商品，吸引对新产品感兴趣的观众。

(6) 形象款：高品质、高价格的商品，提升直播间的整体形象。

☞ **步骤二　填写直播商品组品清单**

将所选择的商品按照上述分类填写在表1-12中。

表1-12　直播商品选品组品清单

序号	分类	产品名称	直播间定价	组品策略	利润率	图片
1	引流款					
2	利润款					
3	爆款					
4	常规款					
5	新款					
6	形象款					

Learning Process

1. Types of Live Streaming Products

1.1 Traffic Products

These products aim to bring traffic to the platform or store with a profit expectation of 0% to 1%. The discount range is typically set between 30% and 50%, and the products are listed after the live stream starts 15 minutes, accounting for about 10% of the total. They are sold at very low prices to quickly gather popularity in the live streaming room. For example, at events like "Black Friday", traffic products can bring massive traffic to the store.

1.2 Profit Products

These are the primary profit-generating products, with fewer views but higher profit margins. Profit products are listed when the popularity of live stream is at its peak. They are usually high-traffic, high-exposure seasonal bestsellers. They cater to a specific niche within the target audience, so the product's selling points and features must align with this niche's preferences.

1.3 Bestsellers

These are popular products that sell well and are liked by viewers in the live stream. Their prices are not as low as traffic products but they generate a large number of orders and attract many users.

1.4 Regular Products

These are commonly seen products with moderate sales. The main purpose of listing these products is to enrich the variety in the live streaming room, continuously stimulate customers, and ensure customer retention.

1.5 New Products

The latest products that are generally fresher, more fashionable, and have better performance compared to previous versions. These products are common during seasonal transitions or when new items are needed to attract and retain customers if older products no longer do.

1.6 Image Products

These highlight the live streaming room's image and style, leaving a deep impression. Image products should be high-quality, high-end, and high-priced niche products.

Adjust and optimize product mix strategy according to the platform's sales performance, keep track of competitors' dynamics in these categories, and monitor SKU (Stock Keeping Unit) and price changes to maintain competitiveness.

2. Live Streaming E-commerce Product Mix Strategy

2.1 Traffic Products for Audience Growth + Profit Products

The main profit from a live stream depends on the number of profit products sold. Since profit products are typically high-priced, not everyone is willing or able to buy them. Therefore, to attract a large audience for conversion, traffic products are used to draw in viewers, and enhance viewer retention, interaction, comments, and data on product clicks and orders.

2.2 Traffic Products + Bestsellers + Profit Products in Cycles

Live stream often requires a certain duration. The combination of different types of products keeps viewers engaged, and increases the live stream's watch time and interaction. Start with traffic products to create an atmosphere, followed by bestsellers to excite viewers, driving interaction and orders, thus boosting the live stream's traffic. Gradually increase the conversion rate of bestsellers and profit products through small activities. When viewer enthusiasm wanes, use traffic products again to create a new atmosphere, ensuring a continuous fresh experience for viewers.

A good product mix strategy can maximize user retention, GMV (Gross Merchandise Volume), and UV (Unique Visitors) value, enhancing the live stream's weight and retaining precise users.

Task Operations

Step 1: Classify the Products

Traffic-Generating Products: Low-priced products with significant discounts to attract viewers to the live stream.

Profit Products: High-profit products to promote during peak viewership times in the live stream.

Best-Selling Products: Popular products are expected to have high sales during the live stream.

Regular Products: Common products with stable sales to enrich the variety of products in the live stream.

New Products: Newly launched products to attract viewers interested in new items.

Image Products: High-quality, high-priced products to enhance the overall image of the live stream.

Step 2: Fill in a Live Streaming Product Listing Form

According to the above categories, fill in a form with the selected products.

课后习题

1. （多选题）以下哪些属于直播商品的类型？
   A. 引流款　　　　　　　　　　B. 常规款
   C. 新款　　　　　　　　　　　D. 爆款

2. （单选题）引流款商品在直播销售策略中的主要作用是什么？
   A. 提供最高利润率　　　　　　B. 聚集人气并增加流量
   C. 直接提高销售额　　　　　　D. 凸显直播间形象

3. （单选题）利润款商品通常在什么时候上架？
   A. 直播开始时　　　　　　　　B. 直播人气最高时
   C. 直播即将结束时　　　　　　D. 直播后 15 分钟内

Exercises

1. (Multiple Choice) Which of the following belong to the types of live streaming products?
   A. Traffic Product　　　　　　B. Regular Product
   C. New Product　　　　　　　D. Bestseller

2. (Single Choice) What is the main purpose of traffic products in live streaming sales strategies?
   A. Providing the highest profit margin
   B. Gathering popularity and increasing traffic
   C. Directly increasing sales revenue
   D. Highlighting the live stream's image

3. (Single Choice) When are profit products typically listed?
   A. At the beginning of the live stream
   B. When the live stream has the highest popularity
   C. Towards the end of the live stream
   D. Within 15 minutes after the live stream begins

项目 2　进行直播前的准备

项目概述

东南亚地区凭借其快速增长的互联网用户群和不断壮大的中产阶级消费者基础，已经成为直播电商的热点区域。在这样一个多元化且具有巨大潜力的市场中，仔细策划直播的每一个环节，从技术准备到内容创造，都是成功的关键。为确保直播电商在竞争日益激烈的东南亚市场取得成功，进行周密的直播前准备工作显得至关重要。这些准备活动不仅包括直播团队的精心组建和直播间的专业搭建，还涵盖了对直播内容的深入策划和直播活动的全面预热。这一系列的准备工作旨在创建一个专业、互动性强的直播环境，不仅能够吸引观众参与，还能有效提升观众的购买意愿。

项目目标

¤ 知识目标
1. 了解直播团队的结构及岗位职责
2. 了解直播活动及内容的策划方法
3. 了解东南亚主流直播平台
4. 了解东南亚用户需求

¤ 技能目标
1. 能够进行直播间灯光及场景搭建
2. 能够进行直播间视频和图文预热
3. 能够完成直播团队的搭建并合理分工
4. 能够设计直播话术并撰写直播脚本

¤ 素养目标
1. 培养学生发现问题并找到有效解决方案的能力
2. 培养学生团队分工合作的意识
3. 培养学生项目管理和时间管理能力，确保活动的各个方面都能有序进行
4. 培养学生组织协调能力

任务 1　组建直播团队

任务导入

在直播产品选择完成之后，StreamASEAN 直播电商公司向 Peter 下达任务：组建一个专业且高效的直播团队。这一步对于直播活动的成功至关重要，一个优秀的团队不仅能确保直播流程的顺畅执行，还能显著提升观众的参与度和满意度，进而最大化销售效果并扩大品牌的影响力。因此，Peter 需要精心挑选团队成员，并进行周密的分工安排，

确保每一环节都能高效协同工作，共同推动直播活动向预定目标迈进。

在本任务中，Peter 将详细了解不同团队成员的角色与职责，并为即将进行的直播活动组建直播电商团队。

任务目标

¤ 知识目标

1. 了解直播团队的成员构成
2. 了解直播电商各岗位的职责
3. 了解直播设备及使用方法

¤ 技能目标

1. 能够组建直播团队
2. 能够完成直播团队内部的合理分工

¤ 素养目标

1. 在直播团队组建的过程中，能够强调诚信、互相尊重和注重公平
2. 培养团队分工合作的意识

任务流程

子任务1：确定直播团队成员
⇩
子任务2：组建一个直播团队

子任务 1　确定直播团队成员

学习过程

一个多元化且高效的团队是直播成功的关键。在组建团队的过程中，需要考虑到各种角色的职责，包括主播、助理、场控人员等。正确的团队组合不仅能够提高直播的专业度，还能让团队在直播过程中有效应对各种突发情况，确保直播活动的顺利进行。

在此任务中，Peter 需要详细了解各个角色的具体职责和所需的专业技能，确保直播团队配置最优化，以应对直播电商的各种挑战。Peter 对直播团队成员的具体职责了解如下。

一、直播团队的主要岗位及职责

（一）主播

在一场直播中，主播是出镜最多的人，承担着在镜头前讲解商品和活跃直播间氛围的任务。

（1）直播前，主播需要将直播脚本的内容、商品的特性与卖点、活动、粉丝福利等内容了然于心。只有这样，主播才能在直播过程中更好地发挥个人能力，统筹全场，流畅地进行商品介绍并与粉丝互动，引导粉丝关注和下单。

（2）直播过程中，主播需要掌控直播节奏，时刻注意自己的个人形象和直播表现，

活跃直播间的氛围，促进销售等。

（3）直播后，主播需要参与直播内容的复盘，分析和总结直播的效果，并通过微博、微信等渠道对直播进行二次宣传，或不时向粉丝分享福利，以树立个人、店铺及品牌的良好形象，提升个人、店铺及品牌的曝光度，增加粉丝的黏性。

（二）副播

副播是协助主播进行直播的人，也称为副主播或辅助主播。副播通常负责在直播间内辅助主播开展直播。副播的存在可以提高直播的互动性和观看体验，尤其是在内容丰富或需要多角度展示的直播活动中。

（三）助理

助理即直播助理，主要负责辅助主播开展直播，是直播前端运营中不常出镜的一个角色。助理的工作内容包括在开播前通过各种渠道发布直播预告，确认商品和道具的准备是否到位，在直播过程中配合场控人员提醒主播直播活动的关键时间节点。有时，助理也承担副播的工作。从表面上看，主播、副播及助理的工作主要是面向直播间内的，实际上，他们也可能会参与直播活动的整个运营环节，包括直播间的搭建、直播前的准备、直播后的数据复盘甚至是选品和制定营销策略。另外，他们也需要给直播团队提供一些信息反馈，如粉丝的需求和喜好等。

（四）场控人员

场控人员要在直播前检查直播间软硬件设备、直播账号，开播后负责管理直播间的中控台，协调商品临时的上架与下架，发布优惠信息、红包公告，进行抽奖，并实时掌握直播间数据波动，及时与主播沟通，随时根据直播间要求更改商品价格等。

（五）策划人员

策划人员主要负责撰写直播方案，包括明确直播主题、根据直播主题确定上播的商品、确定直播时长、规划每款商品的介绍时长、针对直播间内不同等级的粉丝设计不同的福利方案。

（六）运营人员

运营人员一般包括商品运营人员和活动运营人员。商品运营人员主要负责选品排品，并挖掘商品卖点，做好商品优化等；活动运营人员主要负责收集活动信息，策划直播活动方案，搭建直播间场景，做好开播准备等。

（七）数据分析人员

数据分析人员主要负责收集直播数据并对数据进行分析，根据数据分析结果提出优化建议，同时可以为直播复盘提供数据支撑。数据收集和分析的工作也可以直接由策划人员完成，策划人员通过直播数据分析反映的情况，直接对直播方案进行优化，从而避免在与数据运营沟通交流过程中产生信息损耗的情况。不过，由策划人员承担数据收集和分析的工作，会增加其工作量。

（八）客服

直播间的客服主要起辅助的作用，负责与粉丝互动并为粉丝答疑解惑，配合主播的直播，处理商品发货及售后问题。客服需要熟悉商品信息，以便向粉丝准确描述商品的卖点与优势，同时还应掌握一定的沟通技巧。

二、如何挑选合适的主播

（1）主播的外貌和气质需要和直播间的整体风格、销售的产品定位相符。同时主播需要具有个人魅力，能够在镜头前自然自信地展示自己，从而吸引和留住观众。

（2）主播需要具有较强的学习能力和学习意愿，了解东南亚市场的用户喜好和文化习惯。

（3）主播需要有较强的表现力、互动力、销售力，能够与观众积极互动，回答观众问题，处理观众的反馈，创造良好的互动氛围；能够通过有效的销售技巧促进产品销售；具备专业的产品知识，能够针对特定类目，详细、准确地讲解产品的特点和使用方法。

（4）主播需要能够使用东南亚市场的主要语言，如英语、马来语、泰语、越南语等。语言表达需要流畅，语速和语气要有节奏感，具备感染力和信服力，能够清晰地传达信息，与观众产生共鸣。

任务操作

学习完上述知识，Peter 需要通过实际的市场调研，了解当前直播电商岗位的需求，掌握直播电商行业所需的技能和岗位要求。Peter 需要完成如下操作。

☞ 步骤一　完成直播岗位市场调研

（一）搜索职位

打开浏览器，利用搜索引擎，搜索知名招聘网站，进入招聘网站首页。

在招聘网站搜索栏，输入直播电商相关岗位关键词，例如"主播""运营人员"等。

（二）收集和整理职位信息

收集和整理职位信息并填写在表 2-1 中。

表 2-1　直播岗位调研

招聘网站名称	职位数量	职位名称	岗位要求

（三）总结分析

综合所搜集到的职位信息，总结直播电商岗位需要具备的主要技能，并将总结结果填写在表 2-2 中。

表 2-2　直播岗位技能总结

岗位	具体技能

☞ 步骤二　为直播团队写一份招聘启事

公司要求 Peter 为直播团队写一份招聘启事，Peter 需要选择一个岗位，将招聘启事填写在下方。

招聘启事

为了进一步提升直播效果,现招聘一名全职主播加入我们的直播团队。

岗位：_____

岗位职责：

1. _____
2. _____
3. _____

任职要求：

1. _____
2. _____
3. _____

Learning Process

1. Main Positions and Responsibilities in a Live Streaming Team

1.1 Host

The host is the main person on camera, and is responsible for explaining products and energizing the live stream. Before the live stream, the host needs to be familiar with the script, product features, promotions, and fan benefits. During the live stream, the host should control the pace, maintain a good image and performance, and drive sales. After the live stream, the host participates in reviewing the content, analyzing the results, and promoting the live stream through social media to enhance personal, shop, and brand exposure and increase fan loyalty.

1.2 Co-host

The co-host assists the host in conducting the live stream, improving interactivity and viewing experience, especially during content-rich or multi-angle display live streams.

1.3 Live Streaming Assistant

The live streaming assistant assists the host in conducting the live stream, publishes live streaming announcements, ensures the preparation of products and props, and reminds the host of key time points. Sometimes the assistant acts as a co-host. He/She is involved in the overall live streaming operation, including setting up the live streaming room, preparation, data review after the live stream, product selection, and marketing strategy formulation.

1.4 Field Controller

The field controller adjusts software and hardware before the live stream begins, manages the control panel during the live stream, coordinates product listings, publishes discount information and announcements, conducts lotteries, and adjusts product prices as needed.

1.5 Planner

The planner writes the live streaming plan, defines the theme, selects products, determines the duration, plans the introduction time for each product, and designs benefits for fans of different levels.

1.6 Operation Staff

The operation staff consists of product operation staff and activity operation staff. Product operation staff determine the products to be listed, identify selling points, and optimize products. Activity operation staff collect activity information, plan live streaming activities, and execute the plans.

1.7 Data Analyst

The data analyst collects and analyzes live streaming data, provides optimization suggestions based on analysis, and supports live streaming review with data. Planners can also undertake data collection and analysis to directly optimize the live streaming plan, avoiding communication losses with data operations.

1.8 Customer Service Representative

The customer service representative interacts with fans, answers their questions, supports the host, and handles product delivery and after-sales issues. The customer service representative needs to be familiar with product information and have good communication skills.

2. How to Choose the Right Host

(1) The host's image and temperament should match the style of the live streaming room and the product positioning.

(2) The host should have strong learning ability and a willingness to learn, understanding the preferences and cultural habits of users in the Southeast Asian market.

(3) The host should have strong presentation skills, interaction capabilities, and sales abilities. For specific categories, they need to have professional knowledge to explain the products.

(4) The host should be able to speak the languages of the Southeast Asian market fluently, with a rhythm, infectiousness, and credibility in their speeches.

Task Operations

Step 1: Complete Live Streaming Job Market Research

1.1 Search for Positions

Open a browser and use a search engine to find well-known job search websites. Navigate to the homepage of the job search website.

In the search bar of the job search website, enter keywords related to live streaming e-commerce positions, such as "host", "operation staff", etc.

1.2 Collect and Organize Job Information

1.3 Summarize and Analyze

Synthesize the collected job information and summarize the main skills required for live streaming e-commerce positions.

Step 2: Write a Job Advertisement for the Live Streaming Team

Choose one of the positions and write a job advertisement. Fill out the job advertisement in the section below.

Recruitment Notice

Position:＿＿＿＿＿＿

Responsibilities:

1. ＿＿＿＿＿＿＿＿＿＿＿＿＿＿＿＿＿＿＿＿＿＿＿＿＿＿＿＿＿＿＿＿＿＿＿
2. ＿＿＿＿＿＿＿＿＿＿＿＿＿＿＿＿＿＿＿＿＿＿＿＿＿＿＿＿＿＿＿＿＿＿＿
3. ＿＿＿＿＿＿＿＿＿＿＿＿＿＿＿＿＿＿＿＿＿＿＿＿＿＿＿＿＿＿＿＿＿＿＿

Requirements:

1. ＿＿＿＿＿＿＿＿＿＿＿＿＿＿＿＿＿＿＿＿＿＿＿＿＿＿＿＿＿＿＿＿＿＿＿
2. ＿＿＿＿＿＿＿＿＿＿＿＿＿＿＿＿＿＿＿＿＿＿＿＿＿＿＿＿＿＿＿＿＿＿＿
3. ＿＿＿＿＿＿＿＿＿＿＿＿＿＿＿＿＿＿＿＿＿＿＿＿＿＿＿＿＿＿＿＿＿＿＿

子任务2　组建一个直播团队

学习过程

搭建一个有效的直播团队是确保直播成功的关键步骤。这个过程涉及从多个角度考虑团队成员的能力、角色分配以及工作协调。因此，Peter需要从多个角度出发，精心挑选适合的团队成员，确保每个人都能在其擅长的领域发挥最大的能力。在此之前，Peter首先需要对直播团队的结构有一定的了解。他对直播团队结构的了解如下。

一、初始阶段的直播团队

一般作为刚接触直播电商的新手，团队结构会相对简单。对运营人员的要求较高，必须是全能型人才，在直播过程中能够集运营场控人员、助理等身份于一身，且能够自如地转换角色。

只设置1名主播的缺点在于团队无法实现连续直播，而且当主播流失、生病等问题出现时，会影响直播的正常进行。

团队结构：项目负责人—直播团队（主播、运营人员）。

职责见表2-3。

表2-3　初始阶段团队职责分工

团队人员	职责分工
运营人员1人	营销任务分解，货品组成规划，品类规划，陈列规划，直播间数据运营
	策划商品权益活动、直播间权益活动、粉丝分层活动、排位赛制活动等
	编写商品脚本、活动脚本、关注话术脚本、控评话术脚本，封面场景策划，下单角标设计，负责妆容、服饰、道具等
	直播设备调试，直播软件测试，保障直播视觉效果，发券，配合表演，后台回复，数据即时记录反馈
主播1人	熟悉商品脚本、活动脚本，运用话术，做好复盘，控制直播节奏，总结情绪、表情、声音等

二、发展阶段的直播团队

发展阶段的直播团队的人数基本在4～5人，包括主播、运营人员、场控人员等岗位。如果条件允许，还可以为主播配备助理或副播，协助配合主播完成直播间的所有活动。该阶段的直播团队已经有了一段时间的实操经验，具备一定基础的有效粉丝，也拥有一定的转粉能力和销售能力。

团队结构：项目负责人—直播团队（策划人员、主播、副播、场控人员）。

职责见表2-4。

表2-4 发展阶段团队职责分工

团队人员	职责分工
主播	开播前熟悉直播流程、商品信息和直播脚本内容
策划人员	①策划商品权益活动、直播间权益活动、粉丝分层活动、排位赛制活动等 ②编写商品脚本、活动脚本、关注话术脚本、控评话术脚本，封面场景策划，下单角标设计，负责妆容、服饰、道具等
副播	协助主播介绍商品，介绍直播间福利，主播有事时担任临时主播
场控人员	直播设备调试，直播软件调试，保障直播视觉效果，发券，配合表演，后台回复，数据即时记录反馈

三、成熟阶段的直播团队

随着团队的不断发展，企业或商家可以适当壮大直播团队，团队人员更多，分工更细化，工作流程也更优化。处于该阶段的直播团队已是完备的团队，拥有较好的粉丝沉淀和直播间流量，具备稳定的销售转化能力。适合拥有较好的粉丝积累和直播间流量，能够持续稳定转化的成熟型商家。

团队结构：项目负责人—直播团队（策划人员、编导、运营人员、主播、副播、助理、场控人员、拍摄剪辑人员、客服）。

职责见表2-5。

表2-5 成熟阶段团队职责分工

团队人员		职责分工
主播团队3人	主播	开播前熟悉直播流程、商品信息和直播脚本内容
	副播	协助主播介绍商品，介绍直播间福利，主播有事时担任临时主播
	助理	准备直播商品、使用的道具等；协助配合主播工作，做主播的模特、互动对象，完成画外音互动等
策划人员1人		规划直播内容，确定直播主题，准备直播商品，做好直播前的预热宣传，规划开播时间段，做好直播间外部导流和内部用户留存等
编导1人		编写商品脚本、活动脚本、关注话术脚本、控评话术脚本，封面场景策划，下单角标设计，负责妆容、服饰、道具等
场控人员1人		做好直播设备如摄像头、灯光等相关软硬件调试；负责直播中控台的后台操作，包括直播推送，商品上架，监测直播实时数据等；接收并传达指令
运营人员2人		负责营销任务分解、货品组成、品类规划、直播间数据运营、活动宣传推广和粉丝管理等
拍摄剪辑人员1人		负责视频拍摄、剪辑（直播花絮、主播短视频，以及商品的相关信息），辅助直播工作
客服2人		配合主播与用户进行在线互动和答疑；修改商品价格，上线优惠链接，解决发货、售后等问题

任务操作

学习完上述知识，Peter最终确定组建发展阶段的直播团队，组建该直播团队需要完成如下操作。

☞ 步骤一 组成直播团队

要求：根据团队成员的兴趣和特长，选择合适的人员组成直播团队。每组应包含

4~5人,确保各个角色都能被有效分配。

☞ **步骤二　分配角色**

根据每个成员的优势和技能,将不同的角色分配给团队成员。明确每个角色的职责,确保每个成员都能清楚了解自己的任务。

☞ **步骤三　填写分工表**

将分配结果填写在表2-6中,要求确保每个团队成员明确自己的角色和职责。

表2-6　直播团队成员分工

角色	姓名	职责分工
主播		
副播		
策划人员		
场控人员		

Learning Process

1. The Initial Stage of the Live Streaming Team

In the initial stage, the team structure is relatively simple with high demands on the operation staff, who must be versatile and capable of managing various roles such as operation staff, field controller, and assistant during the live stream. The disadvantage of having only one host is the inability to ensure continuous live stream and any issues like host's turnover or illness can disrupt the live stream.

Team Structure: Project Leader-Live Streaming Team (Host, Operation Staff), as shown in Table 2-1.

Table 2-1: Responsibilities in the Initial Stage Team

Team Member	Responsibilities
Operation Staff (1 person)	Marketing task breakdown, product composition planning, category planning, display planning, live streaming data operations
	Plan product rights activities, live streaming room activities, fan segmentation activities, and ranking competition activities
	Write product scripts, activity scripts, follow-up scripts, and review control scripts, plan cover scene, design order corner mark, and is responsible for makeup, clothing, and props
	Live streaming equipment debugging, software testing, ensuring visual effects, issuing vouchers, performing, backend replies, and instant data recording
Host (1 person)	Familiarize oneself with product scripts, activity scripts, use appropriate scripts, conduct reviews, control live streaming pace, and manage emotions, expressions, and voice

2. The Development Stage of the Live Streaming Team

At the development stage, the team expands to 4-5 members including the host, operation staff, and field controller. If conditions allow, an assistant or co-host can be added to assist the host with all live streaming activities. This team has practical experience, a base of effective followers, and conversion and sales capabilities.

Team Structure: Project Leader-Live Streaming Team (Planner, Host, Co-host, Field Controller), as shown in Table 2-2.

Table 2-2: Responsibilities in the Development Stage Team

Team Member	Responsibilities
Host	Familiarize oneself with the live streaming process, product information, and live streaming script before going live
Planner	• Plan product rights activities, live streaming room activities, fan segmentation activities, and ranking competition activities • Write product scripts, activity scripts, follow-up scripts, and review control scripts, plan cover scene, design order corner mark, and is responsible for makeup, clothing, and props
Co-host	Assist the host in product introductions, explain live streaming benefits, and act as a temporary host when needed
Field Controller	Live streaming equipment debugging, software testing, ensuring visual effects, issuing vouchers, performing, backend replies, and instant data recording

3. The Mature Stage of the Live Streaming Team

As the team grows, the enterprise or merchant can expand the live streaming team to make roles more detailed and workflows optimized. A mature live streaming team has good follower retention and traffic, with stable conversion capabilities, suitable for merchants with good follower accumulation and stable live streaming traffic.

Team Structure: Project Leader-Live Streaming Team (Planner, Director, Operation Staff, Host, Co-host, Assistant, Field Controller, Filming/Editing Staff, Customer Service Representative), as shown in Table 2-3.

Table 2-3: Responsibilities in the Mature Stage Team

Team Member		Responsibilities
Host Team (3 people)	Host	Familiarize oneself with the live streaming process, product information, and live streaming script before going live
	Co-host	Assist the host in product introductions, explain live streaming benefits, and act as a temporary host when needed
	Assistant	Prepare live streaming products, use props, assist the host, act as a model, interact with the host, and perform off-screen interactions
Planner (1 person)		Plan live streaming content, determine the theme, prepare products, conduct promotions before live stream, plan time slots, and manage external and internal user retention
Director (1 person)		Write product scripts, activity scripts, follow-up scripts, and review control scripts, plan cover scene, design order corner mark, and is responsible for makeup, clothing, and props
Field Controller (1 person)		Debug live streaming equipment such as cameras and lights, manage control panel operations, push live stream, list products, monitor real-time data, and receive and transmit commands
Operation Staff (2 people)		Marketing task breakdown, product composition planning, category planning, live streaming data operations, activity promotion, and fan management
Filming/Editing Staff (1 person)		Handle video shooting and editing (live streaming highlights, short videos, product information), and assist with live streaming work
Customer Service Representative (2 people)		Interact with users online, answer questions, modify product prices, launch discount links, and handle shipping and after-sales issues

Task Operations

Step 1: Form a Live Streaming Team

Requirements: Choose suitable personnel to form the live streaming team based on the team members' interests and strengths. Each group should consist of 4-5 people, ensuring that all roles can be effectively assigned.

Step 2: Assign Roles

Assign different roles to team members according to each member's strengths and skills. Clearly define the responsibilities of each role to ensure that every member understands their tasks.

Step 3: Complete the Division of Labor Form

Fill in a form with the results of the role assignments, ensuring that every team member is clear about their role and responsibilities.

课后习题

1. （单选题）以下关于直播团队成员的描述中，哪项是错误的？
   A. 主播在直播前需要熟悉直播脚本和商品特性，以便在直播中有效地引导销售
   B. 副播主要负责在直播间内协助主播，提高直播的互动性和观看体验
   C. 场控人员在直播过程中不参与直播软硬件的调试工作
   D. 策划人员负责撰写直播方案，包括确定直播主题和商品介绍时长

2. （单选题）在直播团队的发展过程中，以下哪项描述最准确地反映了团队结构的变化？
   A. 初始阶段的团队仅需1名主播和1名运营人员，不需要其他支持人员
   B. 发展阶段的团队通常包括主播、运营人员、场控人员等4~5人，以应对增加的直播活动
   C. 成熟阶段的团队缩减人员，仅由项目负责人和1名主播组成，以提高效率
   D. 所有阶段的团队结构和职责是固定不变的，不会因发展阶段的不同而有所调整

3. 请说明在直播团队的初始阶段，为什么通常要求运营人员具备全能型的技能，以及这种要求对团队运营的影响是什么。

Exercises

1. (Single Choice) Which of the following descriptions about live streaming team members is incorrect?

   A. The host needs to be familiar with the live streaming script and product features before the live stream to effectively guide sales

   B. The co-host is mainly responsible for assisting the host in the live stream, enhancing interactivity and viewing experience

   C. The field controller do not participate in the debugging of live streaming software and hardware during the live stream

   D. The planner is responsible for writing the live streaming plan, including determining the live streaming theme and product introduction duration

2. (Single Choice) During the development of a live streaming team, which of the following descriptions most accurately reflects the changes in team structure?

A. The initial stage team only requires one host and one operation staff, with no need for other support staff

B. The development stage team usually includes 4-5 people, including the host, operation staff, and field controller, to handle increased live streaming activities

C. The mature stage team reduces personnel, consisting only of the project leader and one host to improve efficiency

D. The team structure and responsibilities remain fixed at all stages and do not change based on the development stage

3. Explain why it is usually required for operations personnel to have versatile skills in the initial stage of a live streaming team, and what impact this requirement has on team operations.

任务 ② 策划直播活动

任务导入

在这个高速发展的数字时代，一个精心策划的直播活动不仅是展示产品的舞台，更是与观众建立联系和增强品牌认知的关键机会。对于即将进行的直播，StreamASEAN 直播电商公司想要为直播观众创造一个既信息丰富又娱乐性强的体验，使每一位观众都能感受到品牌的独特价值和商品的优越性能。StreamASEAN 直播电商公司要求 Peter 所在的直播团队分工为即将到来的"黑色星期五"设计一份直播活动策划，要求完成从目标、主题到互动环节的安排，确保这场直播能有效地推动销售和品牌的扩展。

在本任务中，Peter 将明确直播目标、确定直播主题、设计直播互动环节，并为即将进行的直播活动完成直播方案的制定。

任务目标

¤ 知识目标
1. 了解直播目标的分类和制定方法
2. 了解直播主题的重要性和构思方法

¤ 技能目标
1. 能够明确直播目标和主题
2. 能够为直播设置互动环节
3. 能够为直播编写策划方案

¤ 素养目标
培养学生项目管理和时间管理能力，确保活动的各个方面都能有序进行

任务流程

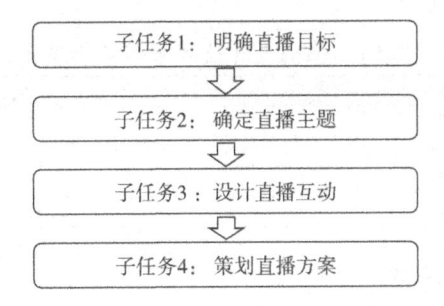

```
子任务1：明确直播目标
      ↓
子任务2：确定直播主题
      ↓
子任务3：设计直播互动
      ↓
子任务4：策划直播方案
```

子任务 1　明确直播目标

学习过程

直播目标是一场直播活动策划的核心，所有直播活动策划方案的细节都是围绕直播目标展开的。准备一场直播活动前，Peter 的直播团队首先应明确直播活动的目标。为确定直播目标，Peter 首先对直播目标的内容了解如下。

一、直播目标的分类

目标分为长期目标和短期目标。一个成熟的直播团队，往往在每年的年初或是某个时间节点，提前做好一整年或较长时间段内的运营规划，这便是长期目标。短期目标即指本场直播的具体目标，如直播在线人数的目标、新增粉丝的目标、商品销售额的目标等。

一场直播活动的目标通常包括产品和用户两个方面。围绕产品的目标大多是一些可以量化的数据，包括销售金额、下单量、购买件数等，也可以包括一些不可量化的指标，例如用户对产品的体验感受、品牌认可度、产品认可度等。围绕用户的核心目标通常是指核心用户群与直播间的关系，包括观看次数、新增粉丝数、关注数等，也包括不可量化的目标，如用户对直播间的评价、用户对直播间定位的认可等。

明确直播目标有助于个人或企业有目的、有针对性地策划与开展直播活动。直播目标主要有拉新、促活和转化三种，三者之间相互促进、紧密联系。另外，直播团队一般以一个目标为主，其他目标为辅，不贪多求全，否则会增加直播难度，导致目标难以实现。针对不同目标定位，衡量是否达成目标的考核指标不同。

（1）拉新。拉新指增加新用户。以此为目标，主要的考核指标有直播间访问用户数、直播间新增粉丝数、主播粉丝群新增粉丝数等。

（2）促活。促活指提高用户活跃度。以此为目标，主要的考核指标有直播间用户点赞数、直播间用户评论量、直播间分享率、直播间用户观看时长等。

（3）转化。转化指促进用户产生付费行为。以此为目标，主要的考核指标有商品点击率、用户购买率、商品销售额等。

❋ 案例参考

案例参考内容见表 2-7。

表 2-7 某小型直播间短期目标设置

目标制定维度	直播目标
直播间增粉数	1000 人
直播间观看人数	1 万人次
直播销售额	1000 元
品牌口碑	店铺搜索指数达到 5 星

二、直播目标制定原则

一个合理的直播目标应该是，在有限的时间内完成可以衡量的、具体的而非模糊的、可以达到的直播目标。直播运营者在明确直播目标时要遵循 SMART 原则，尽量让目标科学化、明确化、规范化。SMART 原则的具体内容如下。

（1）具体性（Specific）：指要用具体的语言清楚地说明直播要达成的目标，直播的目标要用特定的指标来衡量，不能笼统、模糊。

（2）可衡量性（Measurable）：指直播目标应是可数量化的或者可行为化的，应该有一组明确的数据来衡量目标是否达成，例如，利用此次直播使店铺的日销售额提高 20%。

（3）可实现性（Attainable）：指目标要客观，直播运营者付出努力是可以实现的，例如，上一场直播吸引了 20 万人观看，因此这一次将观看人数设定为 25 万人是可实现的。

（4）相关性（Relevant）：指直播的目标要与企业设定的其他营销目标相关，例如，很多企业会在电商平台运营网店，将某次直播的目标设定为"使网店 24 小时内的订单转化率提高 500%"。

（5）时限性（Time-Bound）：指目标的达成要有时间限制，这样目标才有督促作用，避免目标的实现被拖延，例如"从直播开始的 24 小时内，新品的销量突破 10 万件"。

任务操作

学习完上述知识，Peter 需完成如下操作。

☞ 步骤一 制定直播短期目标

应用 SMART 原则为本场直播制定直播短期目标，并填写在表 2-8 中。

表 2-8 直播间短期目标设置

目标制定维度	直播目标

☞ 步骤二 直播目标评估

根据 SMART 原则，对照表 2-9，评估所制定目标的合理性。

表 2-9 直播目标评估标准

评估项目		评估标准
目标的具体性	清晰明确	直播目标是否具体明确
	详细描述	目标是否详细描述了直播的内容、重点和期望的成果

续表

评估项目		评估标准
目标的可衡量性	设定衡量标准	直播目标是否设定了明确的衡量标准，如销售额、观看人数、互动次数等
	数据指标	目标是否可以通过具体的数据和指标进行衡量
目标的可实现性	资源范围内	直播目标是否在现有资源和能力范围内可实现
	实际情况	目标是否考虑了团队的实际情况和市场环境
目标的相关性	提升价值	目标是否有助于提升品牌价值、增加客户黏性或提升销售业绩
目标的时限性	明确时间期限	直播目标是否设定了明确的时间期限，如直播日期、时间段和持续时长

Learning Process

1. Classification of Live Streaming Goals

Live streaming goals are divided into long-term and short-term goals. Long-term goals refer to the operational plan made at the beginning of the year or a specific time point, covering the entire year or a longer period. Short-term goals refer to the specific objectives of a single live stream, such as the number of online viewers, new followers, and sales volume.

The goals of a live stream usually include both product and user aspects. Product goals are often quantifiable data such as sales amount, order quantity, and the number of items purchased, or non-quantifiable indicators such as user experience, brand recognition, and product acceptance. User goals focus on the relationship between the core user group and the live stream, including viewing frequency, new followers, and the number of follows, as well as non-quantifiable aspects like user feedback and recognition of the live stream's positioning.

Clearly defining live streaming goals helps individuals or businesses to plan and execute live streaming activities purposefully and effectively. There are three main types of live streaming goals: attracting new users, increasing user engagement, and converting users. Each type has different evaluation metrics, and the team usually focuses on one primary goal with secondary goals to avoid overcomplicating the live stream and making the objectives harder to achieve.

Attracting New Users: Increasing new users. Key metrics include the number of users visiting the live stream, new followers in the live streaming room, and new followers of the host's fan group.

Increasing User Engagement: Enhancing user activity. Key metrics include the number of likes, comments, shares, and watch time in the live streaming room.

Converting Users: Promoting user transactions. Key metrics include product click-through rate, user purchase rate, and sales volume.

❋ Reference

For the reference case, please see Table 2-4.

Table 2-4: Short-Term Goals for a Small Live Streaming Room

Goal Setting Dimension	Live Streaming Goal
Increase in the Number of Followers	1000 people
Number of Viewers	10,000 views
Sales Revenue	￥1000
Brand Reputation	Store search index reaches 5 stars

2. Principles for Setting Live Streaming Goals

A reasonable live streaming goal should be achievable, measurable, specific, and attainable within a limited time frame. When setting live streaming goals, operators should follow the SMART principle to ensure the goals are scientific, clear, and standardized. The SMART principle includes:

Specific: Clearly state the goal in specific terms, using particular indicators to measure it.

Measurable: The goal should be quantifiable or actionable, with clear data to measure its achievement, such as increasing daily sales by 20% through this live stream.

Attainable: The goal should be realistic and achievable with effort, for example, setting the number of viewers at 250,000 if the previous live stream attracted 200,000 viewers.

Relevant: The goal should be relevant to other marketing goals set by the company, such as increasing the conversion rate of online store orders by 500% within 24 hours of the live stream.

Time-Bound: The goal should have a time limit to provide a sense of urgency and prevent delays, such as achieving 100,000 sales within 24 hours from the start of the live stream.

Task Operations

Step 1: Set Live Stream Goals

Set live streaming goals using the SMART principle.

Step 2: Evaluate Live Streaming Goals

Evaluate the rationality of the set goals according to the SMART principles and Table 2-5.

Table 2-5: Live Streaming Goal Evaluation Criteria

Evaluation Item		Evaluation Criterion
Specificity of the Goal	Clear and Specific	Is the live streaming goal clear and specific
	Detailed Description	Does the goal provide a detailed description of the content, focus, and expected outcomes of the live stream
Measurability of the Goal	Setting Measurement Criteria	Does the live streaming goal have clear measurement criteria, such as sales figures, number of viewers, or interaction counts
	Data Indicators	Can the goal be measured using specific data and indicators
Achievability of the Goal	Within Resource Limits	Is the live streaming goal achievable within existing resources and capabilities
	Practicality	Does the goal consider the team's actual situation and market environment
Relevance of the Goal	Value Enhancement	Does the goal help in enhancing brand value, increasing customer engagement, or improving sales performance
Time-Boundedness of the Goal	Time Constraints	Does the live streaming goal have a clear time limit, such as the date, time slot, and duration of the live stream

子任务2　确定直播主题

学习过程

直播主题影响着直播活动的具体内容、玩法及商品的设计。直播主题除了写在直活动方案中，还常体现于直播预热海报、推文封面等宣传物料上。为确定直播主题，Peter 对直播主题的构思方法了解如下。

一、策划结合热点的直播主题

在当下的手机时代，人们每天都要接收到大量的信息，在信息的围绕下，想要抓住用户的注意，就必须结合最新的热点。直播主题的策划需注重如何与时下热点相结合，以此来吸引更多人群的关注，这是策划直播主题的一个重要方法。直播主题如果能够与热点良好结合，可以有效增加在直播平台的内容曝光度，为直播带来更多流量。同时，与热点结合的主题可以更快速吸引大量用户的目光，并带动用户对直播内容的分享和讨论，从而吸引更多人群的关注。

那么，如何结合当前热点进行直播主题的策划呢？热点的维持时间非常有限，要想成功借助热点来吸引更多用户的关注，给直播带来更多流量，需要对每个热点进行深入的思考和挖掘。

首先，每一个热点都有其背后的故事和核心内容，直播策划在结合当前热点时，要深刻挖掘热点所代表的核心内容和价值。

其次，将挖掘出的热点的核心内容和价值与直播内容深度结合，形成直播内容的亮点。

最后，即使热点内容的最热关注时间点已经过去，但是这个热点仍然会给人们带来一段时间持续的影响，在这段时间内，仍然可以二次开发热点的价值，实现再次引流。

虽然结合当前热点进行直播主题的策划可以给直播带来好的引流效果，但是也要注意选择与直播内容确实有结合点的热点进行策划，避免生硬地设计，否则会被用户冠以"蹭热度"的评价，对于直播的宣传和转化反而会带来负面影响。因此，在进行热点的选择时，一定要进行理性分析，选择适合的热点展开主题的策划，这样才能真正实现为直播引流。

二、直播主题要重点突出

同一款产品的直播，也可以策划出不同的主题。以生蚝海鲜为例，一个直播主题可以是围绕生蚝的打捞、分类、包装等生产过程展开，强调它的原产地、新鲜打捞等特点。另一个直播主题可以是围绕生蚝的制作，从清洗、取生蚝肉、配菜准备、烹饪过程、酱汁调料的制作等展示如何做出一盘美味的生蚝。两个不同的主题，都没有单纯围绕推销生蚝展开，但是给用户呈现了更加可靠的商品背后的信息或者商品的制作方法，这是对产品更立体的宣传，也能给直播间带来很好的销售转化。一个好的直播主题不仅能够给直播间带来好的流量，同时也能够有效激发用户的购物意愿，提高产品的销售。在策划直播主题时，注意一定要能够突出产品特点，既要有独特性又要贴近生活。同时，整个直播的过程也应围绕直播的主题展开，直播主题应始终贯穿于直播过程中。

（一）突出产品特点

在策划直播主题时，一定要突出产品的特点。例如，一场以某个县的农产品为主要内容的直播，主题可以突出"助农""产地原发"等特色。

（二）贴近用户日常生活

用户在直播间购买的产品大多是与自己的日常生活相关的，因此直播主题的策划也应该贴近人们的日常生活，这样更能够引起用户的兴趣。例如，夏季防晒技巧、厨房小妙招、早春通勤女装穿搭、年前购物大集锦、金牌吃货榜单等都是很贴近生活的直播主题。

任务操作

学习完上述知识，Peter 需要完成如下操作。

步骤一　构思直播主题

根据表 2-10 的维度，Peter 需构思本场直播的直播主题。

表 2-10　直播主题设置

维度	直播主题
结合热点	
突出产品特点	
贴近用户日常生活	

步骤二　选定直播主题

为本场直播选定一个直播主题：＿＿＿＿＿＿＿＿＿＿＿＿＿。

Learning Process

Live streaming themes can be conceived from the following dimensions.

1. Plan Live Streaming Themes around Hot Topics

To capture users' attention in the information age, live streaming themes need to incorporate the latest hot topics. Combining hot topics with live streaming themes can increase content exposure, attract more traffic, and encourage users sharing and discussion. When planning, it's important to deeply explore the core content and value represented by the hot topic and integrate it with the live streaming content. Even after the peak interest in a hot topic passes, it can still provide residual value and draw traffic. It's crucial to choose hot topics that naturally align with the live streaming content to avoid hitchhiking on the heat, which can negatively impact promotion and conversion.

2. Highlight the Focus in Live Streaming Themes

The live stream of the same product can have different themes. For example, with oysters, one theme could focus on the production process, emphasizing origin and freshness, while another could showcase cooking methods. Different themes can provide a multi-faceted promotion of the product, enhancing sales conversion in the live stream. A well-conceived theme can attract traffic and boost sales by highlighting product features and being relatable to daily life. The theme should run throughout the entire live stream, emphasizing the product's unique characteristics and relevance to everyday life.

2.1 Highlight Product Features

The theme should highlight the product's unique features. For example, a live stream about agricultural products from a certain county can emphasize "supporting farmers" and "origin freshness".

2.2 Relatable to Daily Life

Live streaming themes should relate to the users' daily lives to capture their interest. Examples include summer sun protection tips, kitchen hacks, early spring office wear, pre-holiday shopping guides, and gourmet rankings.

Task Operations

Step 1: Conceive a Live Streaming Theme

Conceive a live streaming theme for this session.

Step 2: Select a Live Streaming Theme

Select a live streaming theme for this session: _____.

子任务 3　设计直播互动

学习过程

　　一场成功的带货直播活动的核心虽然是产品介绍，但仅依靠此环节往往会让观众感到单调乏味，并逐渐产生疲劳。因此，为了保持直播间的活力与吸引力，Peter 考虑在策划中加入多种形式的互动活动，旨在提高观众参与度和激励消费行为，比如抽奖、发红包和秒杀等。为此，Peter 对直播间常见的直播互动玩法做出如下了解。

一、派发红包

　　派发红包是直播间提供给观众立即见效、直观的好处和利益，是主播聚集人气、与用户互动的有效方法之一。在直播期间，派发红包形式可以分为站内发放红包和站外平台发放红包。

（一）站内发放红包

　　提前向用户公布红包发放时间，引导用户将直播间分享给亲戚朋友共同进入直播间抢红包，这样不仅可以增加用户停留时间、活跃气氛，还能提升直播间的流量。

（二）站外平台发放红包

　　除了在直播平台上发放红包之外，主播可以在其他社交平台发放专属渠道的红包，并提前告知用户。这种跨平台发放红包的方法，能够帮助主播在不同平台之间完成引流，便于直播结束之后的效果发酵。

　　等到了和用户约定的时间，主播就要在平台发放红包。为了营造热闹的氛围，主播最好在发红包之前倒计时，让用户产生紧张感。

二、设计抽奖

　　直播间抽奖是主播常用的互动玩法之一，主播希望通过抽奖的方式，延长用户在直播间的停留时间，增加用户黏性，但并不是每次都能够达到理想的效果。有时抽奖环节时间过长，会打乱整个直播的节奏；有时流量会在抽奖的当下涌入直播间，但是结束后又迅速离开直播间。所以，主播把握好整体抽奖的节奏，需要遵循以下三个原则。

（一）选择抽奖奖品

　　奖品最好是直播中正在上架的商品，可以是热门款，也可以是新品。

（二）要分散抽奖次数

　　为了保持整场直播的流量，奖品不要集中一次抽完，要将抽奖环节分散在直播过程中，可以以整点为节点进行抽奖，在直播预告阶段就进行预告。

（三）把握抽奖节奏

主播要尽量通过点赞数或者弹幕数把握直播的抽奖节奏，分散抽奖，可以以整点划分，或者在点赞量达到一定的峰值时进行抽奖。

三、促销活动

制造直播间高人气和高热度的根本目的，除了提升品牌知名度之外，重点还是使流量能够快速变现。当直播间积累了一定的人气之后，巧妙地开展各种促销活动，有助于提高转化率。下面介绍几种常见的促销活动类型。

（一）优惠券促销

优惠券促销是直播带货中最常见的促销活动之一，在产品上架的同时上架优惠券，让用户先领取优惠券再购买，让他们实实在在感受到产品的优惠，刺激他们下单购买。从覆盖的品类来看，常见的优惠券基本可以划分为两种：第一种为商品优惠券，第二种为店铺优惠券。商品优惠券是指针对直播间某个商品独有的优惠类型，进入直播间的用户可享受到与店铺内不一样的优惠。而店铺优惠券则不针对某款特定的产品，而是针对整间店铺大部分产品，且即使不在特定的直播时段购物也可以使用。在专属优惠券的激励下，用户会进一步提高消费热情。

除此之外，还可以针对不同目标人群设定不同的优惠券，比如可以针对新粉赠送店铺新人福利券，可以激励老粉转化三名新粉从而获取奖励券，增加用户的黏性。

（二）满减优惠

在后台根据商品的定价设置不同的阶梯价格，让用户为了享受满减优惠政策而购买更多的产品。例如，一件产品198元，但满220元就可以减50元，那么这时用户就会为了获得满减优惠而搭配购买本场直播中客单价比较低的产品进行凑单。用户能够以更低的价格获得自己喜欢的产品，而直播间的成交额也可以得到提高。在设定满减活动时，首先可以考虑巧妙插入关联产品，让想享受优惠的用户快速找到搭配产品，从而打造"爆款"；其次，满减金额的门槛可根据直播间的客单价进行阶梯化设置。

（三）定时开售

定时开售和预售是有区别的，预售是可以直接购买的，但是发货晚；而定时开售是不可以购买的，只能预约购买。定时开售可以帮助直播进行测品，直播团队根据预约的人数来判断该产品是否受用户的喜欢。除了定时开售能够帮助测品外，给产品拍视频也能测品，直播团队根据视频的数据判断产品是否受欢迎，还可以把产品挂在直播间的2、3号链接，下播后通过点击率判断产品是否受欢迎。

四、裂变营销

裂变营销是用户想要获得某项优惠就必须按照规则将产品链接或者直播间链接分享给好友，在好友的帮助下获得优惠。这种活动在推广店铺时使用可能会吸引更多人点击产品，或者在分享的过程中让更多人对产品产生兴趣；在推广直播间时使用会为直播间带来更多的观看次数，让更多人进入直播间，增加直播间的流量。

五、打造商品的捡漏价值

在直播间展现出商品的市场价格，通过直播间改价的形式，让用户确信商品价值，产生捡漏感。通过更改库存，或者在直播间强调产品数量限制，来营造紧迫感。

六、现场烘托氛围

使用直播贴片展示直播间重点时间，还可以使用一些物料、道具、音乐来营造氛围。主播讲品时，现场工作人员给予互动，例如现场试吃、现场测试产品等。

七、控评技巧

带动直播间的评论节奏，提高直播间热度，常见话术如下：今天直播间为大家争取到了一个很低的价格，从来没有过的价格，大家想不想要，想要的回复"想要"。

任务操作

学习完上述知识，Peter 需完成如下操作。

☞ 步骤一　了解不同直播平台可设置的直播互动活动

通过查阅资料、观看示例直播或与有经验的直播团队交流，了解不同直播平台（如 TikTok、Facebook 等）提供的互动活动设置选项。例如：投票、抽奖、连麦、评论互动等。

- TikTok：投票、评论互动、礼物打赏、连麦互动。
- Facebook：投票、评论互动、分享、打赏。

☞ 步骤二　设置互动环节

根据不同直播平台可设置的互动环节，进行直播互动环节设置，并填在表 2-11 中。

表 2-11　互动环节设置

时间	互动活动

Learning Process

There are many common interactive methods in live streams.

1. Distributing Red Envelopes

Distributing red envelopes is a common interactive method in live streams to attract user participation. Red envelopes can be distributed within the platform or on external platforms.

1.1　Within the Platform

Announce the distribution time in advance and encourage users to share the live stream with friends, increasing user retention and stream traffic.

1.2　External Platforms

Distribute exclusive red envelopes on other social platforms to attract users to the live stream, enhancing the overall effect.

Conduct a countdown before distribution to create a sense of urgency.

2. Designing Lotteries

Lotteries in live streams extend user retention and increase user engagement, but the rhythm must be managed to avoid disrupting the overall flow.

2.1　Choose Prizes

Select popular or new products being showcased in the live stream.

2.2 Distribute Lottery Times

Spread out the lottery sessions throughout the live stream, either at specific intervals or based on the number of likes.

2.3 Manage Rhythm

Use likes or comments to control the timing of the lotteries.

3. Promotional Activities

Promotional activities help quickly monetize traffic and increase conversion rates.

3.1 Voucher Promotions

Offer vouchers when products are listed, including product-specific and store-wide vouchers, to stimulate purchases.

3.2 Discount Promotions

Set different price tiers to encourage users to buy more products to enjoy discounts.

3.3 Timed Sales

Help gauge product popularity by allowing users to reserve purchases, providing valuable insights for the team.

4. Viral Marketing

Users must share product or live streaming links with friends to receive discounts. This method attracts more clicks on product links or live streams, increasing viewership and traffic.

5. Creating a Sense of Bargain Value for Products

Utilize pricing strategies to highlight the market price of products, making users believe in the value of the items through price changes during the live stream. This can create a sense of urgency and the feeling of snagging a great deal. You can adjust inventory or emphasize product quantity limits during the live stream to build a sense of urgency.

6. Enhancing the Live Atmosphere

Use live streaming overlays to highlight key moments in the stream, and employ various materials, props, and music to create an engaging atmosphere. During the product presentation, have on-site staff interact, such as live taste tests or product demonstrations.

7. Comment Control Techniques

Guide the rhythm of comments to boost live streaming engagement. Common prompts include typing "want", "1", or "bought".

Script: "Today, we've secured an unprecedentedly low price for you. It's a price we've never offered before. Do you want it? If you do, type 'want' in the chat."

Task Operations

Step 1: Understand the Live Interaction Activities Available on Different Live Streaming Platforms

By researching, watching examples of live streams, or communicating with experienced live streaming teams, understand the interaction options provided by different live streaming platforms (such as TikTok, Facebook). Examples of interaction activities include polls, giveaways, co-hosting, and comment interactions.

（1）TikTok：Polls, comment interactions, gift rewards, co-hosting interactions.

（2）Facebook：Polls, comment interactions, shares, rewards.

Step 2：Set up Live Interaction Activities

Based on the interaction activities available on different live streaming platforms, set up the live interaction activities.

子任务4　策划直播方案

学习过程

直播方案一般用于直播运营团队的内部沟通，目的是让参与直播的人员熟悉直播活动的流程和分工。直播方案要简明扼要，直达主题。开展直播营销要有完整的营销思路，但仅靠思路是无法实现营销目标的。StreamASEAN直播电商公司要求Peter的直播电商运营团队将抽象的思路转换成具象的文字表达，用方案的形式呈现出来，并将其传达给参与直播的所有人员，以保证直播活动顺利进行。在撰写策划方案前，Peter了解了直播方案策划的相关知识。

一、直播方案的作用

直播营销思路是抽象的，而直播方案就是思路的具体化。直播方案便于直播活动的所有参与者准确、完整地把握直播活动的思路，落实每项任务，完成预定目标。

二、直播方案的要素

直播营销策划方案要简明扼要。一份完整的直播方案通常要具备以下内容。

（一）营销目标

明确直播需要实现的营销目标，如品牌宣传、产品推广、产品销售等，以及期望吸引的用户人数和想要取得的产品销量等。

（二）直播简介

对直播的整体思路进行简要描述，包括直播的形式、平台、特点、主题等。

（三）直播人员分工

对直播运营团队中的人员进行分工，并明确每个人的职责。

（四）直播时间节点

明确直播中的各个时间节点，包括直播前期筹备的时间点、宣传预热的时间点、直播开始的时间点、直播结束的时间点等。直播方案中需要明确体现的时间节点有两部分：直播的整体时间节点和直播中各个环节的时间节点。

第一部分是直播的整体时间节点，包括前期准备、直播现场、直播进行时、直播结束后四个模块的时间节点，直播团队确定直播的整体时间节点可以便于所有参与者对直播的工作有一个整体的印象。第二部分是直播中各个环节的时间节点，即直播团队需要明确主要环节及每个环节的开始时间和截止时间，防止由于某个环节延误而导致直播的整体延误。

（五）直播成本预算

说明整场直播活动的预算情况，以及直播中各个环节的预算，以合理控制成本。每一场直播活动都会涉及预算，整体预算情况、各环节的预算情况，都需要直播团队在直播方案中进行简要描述。一般情况下，一场直播活动可能需要以下四个方面的费用投入。

基础投入：手机、计算机、摄像机、话筒等直播硬件费用，直播间装饰费用，直播团队的薪酬，直播场地的租赁费用，直播平台店铺的开店费用。

现场福利活动：现场福利以发放红包、优惠券、实物礼品为主，如关注账号领红包、抽奖得红包、优惠券、实物礼品等。

前期宣传活动：各个宣传渠道的引流费用、宣传物料的制作费用等。

后期宣传活动：各个渠道的维护费用、推广费用，以及宣传物料制作费用等。当某个项目组可能出现预算超支的情况时，需要提前告知相关负责人，便于整体协调。

任务操作

学习完上述知识，Peter 所在的直播团队需要完成"黑色星期五"直播活动策划方案，具体操作如下。

☞ 步骤一　团队分工

按照各个成员在直播团队中的角色，进行方案任务分工。

☞ 步骤二　制定直播方案

需明确直播目标、直播时长与时间、直播宣传与互动方式等，并将直播策划方案填写在表 2-12 中。

表 2-12　直播策划方案

直播目标	
直播简介	
方案项目	基本信息
直播主题	
直播简述	
人员分工	
时间节点	
预算估计	
直播互动方式	

☞ 步骤三　将整合的直播方案制作成 PPT

☞ 步骤四　进行方案汇报

汇报时间 5~10 分钟。汇报后接受提问，并进行答辩。方案内容将根据表 2-13 进行评估。

表 2-13　方案评估标准

评估项目	评估标准
直播方案的清晰度和详细程度	直播方案包含明确的目标、详细的执行步骤、时间安排和预算评估
创意和互动策略	直播互动环节设计合理，方式多样，能够有效地增加观众的参与度
团队协作和角色分配	每个团队成员的角色分配明确
演示效果	演示过程流畅，能够有效地展示直播方案的内容及亮点

Learning Process

1. The Role of a Live Streaming Plan

A live streaming marketing plan transforms abstract marketing ideas into concrete strategies, enabling all participants to accurately and comprehensively grasp the live stream's objectives, implement each task, and achieve the predetermined goals.

2. Elements of a Live Streaming Plan

A complete live streaming plan should be concise and typically include the following elements.

2.1 Marketing Goals

Define the marketing objectives to be achieved by the live stream, such as brand promotion, product marketing, sales targets, and the expected number of users and product sales.

2.2 Live Streaming Overview

Provide a brief description of the overall concept of the live stream, including its format, platform, features, and theme.

2.3 Division of Responsibilities

Specify the roles and responsibilities of each member of the live streaming team.

2.4 Live Streaming Timeline

Clearly outline the various time points in the live stream, including preparation, promotional activities, start time, and end time. The timeline consists of two parts: the overall timeline and the specific timelines for each segment, ensuring each stage proceeds on time and preventing delays.

2.5 Budget for the Live Stream

Describe the budget for the entire live streaming event and for each segment to ensure cost control. The budget typically covers the following aspects.

Basic Investment: Costs for hardware such as phones, computers, cameras, microphones, as well as decoration of the live streaming room, team salaries, venue rental, and the cost of opening a store on a live streaming platform.

On-site Benefits: Red envelopes, vouchers, and physical gifts, such as rewards for following or participating in lotteries.

Pre-promotion Activities: Costs for channeling traffic through various promotional channels and creating promotional materials.

Post-promotion Activities: Maintenance and promotion costs for various channels and production costs for promotional materials. If any project group exceeds its budget, the relevant responsible person should be notified in advance to facilitate overall coordination.

Task Operations

Write a live streaming plan for the "Black Friday" promotion.

Step 1: Team Division of Writing Tasks

Divide tasks of writing according to the roles of each member in the live streaming team.

Step 2: Develop a Live Streaming Plan

Clearly define the objectives, duration, promotion, and interactive methods.

Step 3: Create a PowerPoint Presentation for the Integrated Live Streaming Plan

Step 4: Present the Plan

The presentation should last 5-10 minutes. After the presentation, answer questions and engage in a discussion. The content of the plan will be evaluated according to Table 2-6.

Table 2-6: Plan Evaluation Criteria

Evaluation Item	Evaluation Criterion
Clarity and Detail of the Plan	The live streaming plan includes clear objectives, detailed execution steps, a timeline, and a budget assessment
Creativity and Interaction Strategy	The design of the interaction segment is reasonable and diverse, effectively increasing audience engagement
Team Collaboration and Role Assignment	Each team member's role is clearly defined
Presentation Effectiveness	The presentation is smooth and effectively showcases the content and highlights of the live streaming plan

课后习题

1. （多选题）一份直播方案需要包括哪些内容？
   A. 营销目标　　　　　　　　B. 直播简介
   C. 直播人员分工　　　　　　D. 直播成本预算

2. （单选题）关于直播间派发红包的策略，以下哪一项描述是正确的？
   A. 站内发放红包应该随机进行，无需提前告知观众
   B. 站外平台发放红包不利于增加直播平台的流量
   C. 主播应在约定时间发放红包，并在发放前进行倒计时，增加观众的期待感
   D. 发放红包的主要目的是减少直播间的观众数量

3. 在策划直播主题时，如何有效地结合当前热点以提高直播的观众参与度和流量？

Exercises

1. (Multiple Choice) What should be included in a live streaming plan?
   A. Marketing goals　　　　　　　B. Live streaming overview
   C. Team roles and responsibilities　　D. Live streaming budget

2. (Single Choice) Which of the following statements about the strategy of distributing red envelopes in a live streaming room is correct?

   A. Red envelopes distributed within the platform should be random and do not need to be announced in advance

   B. Distributing red envelopes on external platforms does not help increase traffic to the live streaming platform

   C. The host should distribute red envelopes at the agreed time and conduct a countdown beforehand to increase the audience's anticipation

   D. The main purpose of distributing red envelopes is to reduce the number of viewers in the live streaming room

3. How can current hot topics be effectively incorporated into live streaming themes to increase audience engagement and traffic?

任务 3　创作直播内容

任务导入

直播不仅仅是一种技术应用，更是一种全新的沟通艺术，能够即时连接世界各地的观众。直播不只是展示产品的平台，还是一个与观众建立真实联系的桥梁。StreamASEAN 直播电商公司即将举办"黑色星期五"直播活动，传达产品的独特价值和展示商品优越性，要求 Peter 所在的直播团队在直播开始之前完成直播内容创作。

在本任务中，Peter 将提炼产品卖点，确定直播话术、标题和封面，并为即将进行的直播撰写直播脚本。

任务目标

¤ 知识目标
1. 了解提炼直播产品卖点的方法
2. 了解直播话术的设计要点

¤ 技能目标
1. 能够制作直播封面与标题
2. 能够编写直播脚本
3. 能够使用 AI 写作工具设计直播脚本

¤ 素养目标
培养快速应变和处理直播中突发情况的能力

任务流程

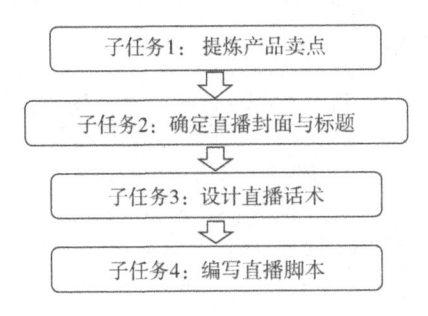

```
子任务1：提炼产品卖点
        ↓
子任务2：确定直播封面与标题
        ↓
子任务3：设计直播话术
        ↓
子任务4：编写直播脚本
```

子任务 1　提炼产品卖点

学习过程

对于直播电商而言，产品是关键的要素，而展示产品的好方法就是展示产品的卖点。常用的提炼产品卖点的方法有 FAB 法则和产品属性提炼法。接下来，Peter 需要完成直播产品卖点的提炼。在此之前，Peter 对直播产品卖点提炼的方法了解如下。

一、FAB 法则

FAB 法则，即属性（Feature）、作用（Advantage）和益处（Benefit）法则，是一种说服性的销售技巧，常用于提炼产品卖点。实际上，也可以简单地将 FAB 法则理解为以下几点，见表 2-14。

表 2-14　使用 FAB 法则提炼产品卖点的方法

组成	具体内容
属性	产品的特征、特点，主要从产品的属性、功能等角度进行挖掘，例如：超薄、体积小、防水等
作用	产品的优点及作用，根据产品的特色和用户关心的问题进行挖掘，例如：方便携带、耐用
益处	产品能带给用户的利益，需以用户利益为中心，激发其购买欲望，例如：带来视听享受、价格低

二、产品属性提炼法

与 FAB 法则相较，产品属性提炼法则依据产品的不同属性维度来系统性地分析并提炼产品卖点。这种方法可以更细致地发掘产品的核心价值和潜在优势，具体可以分为以下几个方面。见表 2-15。

（一）产品价值属性

产品价值属性指产品的使用价值，是产品本身具有的能够满足受众需求的属性。

（二）产品形式属性

产品形式属性指产品使用价值得以实现的形式或目标市场对某一特定需求的满足形式，包括质量、外形、手感、重量、体积、包装等。

（三）产品期望属性

产品期望属性指产品满足受众期望的一系列条件。不同的受众有不同的期望，例如，除了洗涤、甩干外，有些受众还希望洗衣机具有烘干、消毒等功能。

（四）产品延伸属性

产品延伸属性指超出产品基本功能之外的附加价值，如品牌形象、用户服务、附加的保证或保险等。这些属性可以提升产品的吸引力，增加消费者的忠诚度，有助于在竞争激烈的市场中区分同类产品。

表 2-15　使用产品属性提炼法提炼产品卖点

组成	具体内容
价值属性	产品核心的价值，例如：节能电器减少电费开支
形式属性	外观上的描述，例如：现代设计适合任何家居装饰
期望属性	消费者期望产品具备的特质，例如：高效率、低噪声
延伸属性	附加功能或服务，例如：五年保修期

任务操作

学习完上述知识，Peter 需完成如下操作。

☞ 步骤一　使用 FAB 法则提炼产品卖点

根据即将用于直播的产品的相关产品信息，使用 FAB 法则提炼它的卖点，并填写在表 2-16 中。

表2-16 使用FAB法则提炼直播产品的卖点

组成	具体内容
属性	
作用	
益处	

☞ **步骤二 使用产品属性提炼法提炼产品卖点**

根据即将用于直播的产品的相关产品信息，使用产品属性提炼法提炼它的卖点，并填写在表2-17中。

表2-17 使用产品属性提炼法提炼直播产品的卖点

组成	具体内容
价值属性	
形式属性	
期望属性	
延伸属性	

Learning Process

1. FAB Method

The FAB method extracts product selling points using Features, Advantages, and Benefits.

F (Feature): Characteristics and attributes of the product, such as being ultra-thin or waterproof.

A (Advantage): The advantages these features bring, such as portability and durability.

B (Benefit): The specific benefits these advantages provide to the user, such as providing an audio-visual experience or being cost-effective.

2. Product Attribute Extraction Method

The Product Attribute Extraction Method systematically extracts product selling points by analyzing different attribute dimensions of the product. It includes the following aspects.

2.1 Product Value Attribute

The utility value of the product, such as "energy-saving appliances reduce electricity costs."

2.2 Product Form Attribute

The form in which the utility of the product is realized, such as quality, appearance, and texture.

2.3 Product Expectation Attribute

The conditions under which the product meets audience's expectations, such as high efficiency and low noise.

2.4 Product Extension Attribute

Additional value beyond the basic function of the product, such as brand image and customer service.

Task Operations

Step 1: Extract Product Selling Points Using the FAB Method

Based on the relevant product information for the upcoming live stream, extract its selling points using the FAB Method.

Step 2：Extract Product Selling Points Using the Product Attribute Extraction Method

Based on the relevant product information for the upcoming live stream, extract its selling points using the Product Attribute Extraction Method.

子任务2　确定直播封面与标题

学习过程

用户在决定是否观看直播时，首先会注意直播封面与标题。直播封面可直观体现直播内容，好的直播封面具有明显的引流效果。制作直播封面和拟定标题前，Peter应先了解制作直播封面和拟定标题的方法。

一、制作直播封面

（一）直播封面的形式

一种直播封面设计以人物为主体，封面中的人物可以是品牌形象代言人、商品模特或主播。以人物为主体的封面应选择具有一定知名度的人物，更能引起用户的关注。

另一种直播封面设计以商品为主体，即在封面中展示直播推荐的商品。此时，图片应直观立体，让用户能够直接观察到商品的细节、特点等。

（二）制作直播封面的要求

封面图是用户形成对直播间第一印象的重要途径，一个足够吸引人的封面图可以为直播间带来流量。打造优质的直播封面图要注意以下几点。

1. 保持美观、清晰

封面图保持美观、干净、整洁，除了官方提供的角标、贴图等带有促销元素的内容以外，不能添加任何文字和其他贴图，否则会显得杂乱无章，影响用户阅读，导致用户在看到封面图的第一眼就划走。

2. 色彩要适当

直播封面图的色彩要鲜艳，但不要过分华丽，能体现直播主题即可。坚决杜绝任何形式的"牛皮癣"，否则会影响重要内容的呈现效果。另外，由于直播封面图的背景本身就是白色，如果封面图中仍然选择白色背景，就会导致图片不够突出、醒目，很难吸引用户，所以封面图中的背景禁用白色。

3. 图片尺寸合理

在制作直播封面时，一定要注意图片的大小。如果图片太小了，呈现出来的内容可能会不太清晰。遇到图片不够清晰的情况，直播运营者最好重新制作图片，甚至是重新拍摄，因为画面的清晰度将直接影响用户对封面图片和直播内容的感受。一般来说，各大直播平台对于直播封面图片的大小都有一定的要求。

4. 要考虑固定信息的展现

封面图的固定信息包括左上角的直播观看人数和右下角的点赞量，封面图的重要内容要避开左上角和右下角，以免与直播观看人数、点赞量等构成部分相互干扰，影响观看体验。

5. 符合直播主题

封面图要契合直播主题，让用户在看到直播封面图时就能了解直播的大致内容，进而决定是否要进入直播间。例如，主播在工厂直播实地看货，封面图要选择工厂、车间等实景图；主播在柜台或摊位直播，封面图要选择柜台或摊位实拍图；主播在直播间介绍商品，封面图最好不用模特或主播的人像图片，而是选择精美的商品细节图。

6. 符合直播平台规则

许多直播平台都有自己的规则，有的直播平台甚至将这些规则整理成文档进行展示。对于直播运营者来说，要想更好地运营直播账号，就应该遵循平台的规则。直播运营者可以从规则中找出与直播封面相关的内容，并在选择直播封面时将相关规则作为重要的参考依据。

二、拟定直播标题

（一）标题的作用

标题的核心作用有两点：一是给用户看，吸引用户点击和观看直播；二是给平台看，以获得平台更多的流量推荐。能让人眼前一亮的标题可以吸引更多用户观看直播，也更容易获得平台的推荐。

（二）拟定标题的常用策略

1. 借助名人效应

名人是大众所关注的对象，很多广告都借助了名人效应，直播标题也可以借助名人效应，如名人同款、名人直播带货、名人直播专场等。

2. 设置疑问

在标题中设置疑问，激发用户的好奇心，增强用户的点击欲望。

3. 利益化

标题可以直接指明直播利益点，以此来吸引用户观看。

4. 制造紧迫感

在标题中添加"数量有限"等字样，以制造紧迫感、紧缺感，促使用户立刻采取行动。

5. 借助热点

热点事件容易引起人们的关注，如节日等，基于热点拟定标题，可以通过大众对热点的关注，引导用户观看直播。

6. 解决用户需求

在标题中注明用户在生活或工作中所遇到的烦恼和困难，或者相关的解决方案，能够解决用户需求，引起他们的关注。

任务操作

学习完上述知识，Peter 需要根据以下步骤制作直播封面和拟定标题。

☞ **步骤一　制作直播封面**

使用 Photoshop 为即将开展的直播活动设计直播封面。

☞ **步骤二　拟定直播标题**

根据本场直播已知的信息，Peter 需要根据标题策略撰写标题，并填写在表 2-18 中。

表2-18　直播标题

策略	标题
借助名人效应	
设置疑问	
利益化	
制造紧迫感	
借助热点	
解决用户需求	

从表格中为本场直播选择一个最合适的标题：_____

Learning Process

1. Creating Live Streaming Covers

1.1 Forms of Live Streaming Covers

Live streaming cover designs can feature either people or products. When using people, choose well-known individuals to attract attention, and show them interacting with the product. When using products, clearly display the product details and features.

1.2 Requirements for Creating Live Streaming Covers

Aesthetic and Clear: The cover image should be attractive, clean, and tidy, avoiding excessive text and stickers.

Appropriate Colors: Colors should be bright but not overly flashy; avoid using a white background.

Reasonable Image Size: Ensure that the image size is appropriate and the content is clear.

Display of Fixed Information: Avoid placing important content in the top left and bottom right corners where fixed information appears.

Align with Live Streaming Theme: The cover should match the live streaming theme, making clear what the stream is about at a glance.

Follow Platform Rules: The cover must comply with the rules of the live streaming platform.

2. Designing Live Streaming Titles

2.1 Role of Titles

The core functions of a title are to attract users to click and watch the live stream and to gain more traffic recommendations from the platform.

2.2 Common Strategies for Designing Titles

Leveraging Celebrity Effect: Use the influence of celebrities, such as "celebrity-endorsed" or "celebrity live stream".

Posing Questions: Include questions in the title to arouse curiosity.

Highlighting Benefits: Clearly state the benefits of the live stream to attract viewers.

Creating Urgency: Add phrases like "limited quantity" to create a sense of urgency.

Using Hot Topics: Design titles around trending events to attract attention.

Addressing User Needs: Mention problems or solutions that users might encounter in their lives or work to draw their attention.

Task Operations

Step 1: Creating Live Streaming Covers
Use Photoshop to design a live streaming cover for the upcoming live stream event.

Step 2: Designing Live Streaming Titles
Based on the known information about the live stream, write titles using the title strategies.

子任务 3　设计直播话术

学习过程

对于主播而言，话术水平直接影响在直播时销售商品的有效性，直播营销话术是商品特性、功效和材料的口语表达，是主播吸引和留住用户的手段。为了在直播开场吸引更多用户观看直播，方便在正式开播时推销商品，Peter 决定从设计直播话术入手，建立用户对直播间的期待值，为直播间积攒人气。在此之前，Peter 需要对直播话术了解如下。

一、了解直播流程

在直播的前 5 分钟，主播应自我介绍，拉近与观众的距离。主动与进入直播间的粉丝互动，欢迎新观众并感谢老粉丝的支持。通过简要介绍店铺、公司和品牌的历史和故事，增强观众的信任感。此外，可以利用直播间的抽奖活动来吸引更多观众，增加粉丝停留时间和新粉的关注。在接下来的 5 到 15 分钟内，主播高频率讲解产品的特点和优势，并说明当前的优惠活动，包括抢购时间和限量信息，同时通过互动问题或活动引导观众参与。在直播 15 到 20 分钟时，进入产品介绍环节，每个产品的讲解时间为 5 到 10 分钟。介绍产品基本信息、福利和发放优惠券，邀请商家或品牌方参与产品试用演示和推荐，并安排秒杀活动，提供限时优惠。通过设定互动目标，如点赞数或评论数，达到目标后进行抽奖，活跃直播间氛围并稳定观众数量。最后，主播应感谢观众的参与和互动，表达感激之情，并预告下次直播的时间和主要内容，鼓励观众继续关注和参与。直播流程时间见表 2-19。

表 2-19　直播流程时间表

时间段	活动内容	具体操作
0~5 分钟	自我介绍、粉丝互动、品牌介绍、抽奖吸引流量	主播互动、抽奖
5~15 分钟	讲解产品及优惠信息	介绍产品特点，说明优惠活动，引导互动
15~20 分钟	产品介绍环节	介绍产品基本信息、福利讲解、优惠券发放、产品试用演示、秒杀活动
全程	点赞、互动达到一定频率抽奖	设置互动目标，进行抽奖
最后	感谢粉丝，预告下次直播	表达感激之情，宣布下次直播信息

二、直播话术的设计要点

（一）开场话术

1. 欢迎类话术

在直播开场的 1~5 分钟，主播应热情和老观众打招呼，并欢迎新观众，可以通过读取观众的用户名来个性化问候，例如："您好×××，欢迎来到官方直播间。"

（1）明确欢迎对象。欢迎单个用户时，可直接通过"用户名称+欢迎语"的方式表达；欢迎所有用户时，可直接用概括性的词语称呼用户，并加上欢迎语欢迎用户到来，如"欢迎大家""欢迎朋友们"。

（2）重视用户体验。通过"用户名称+欢迎语+提问式"的方式对用户提问，让用户评论、回答或分享故事，表现主播对用户的关注、重视，例如："欢迎，您的名字好熟悉，您看过我们的直播几次了？"

（3）话术要富有感染力。设计欢迎话术时，要表现语气语调的变化和力度，欢迎用户时要使用热情的语气，语调要高昂，让用户第一时间感受到主播良好的精神状态，延长观看的时间。

2. 引导互动

引导观众进行互动，如点赞或留言，可以提高直播间活跃度。例如："大家好，欢迎来到直播间。如果喜欢的话，记得点个'关注'，点击小红心支持一下。"

3. 商品和促销预告

开场时，给出商品和促销预告，将用户留在直播间中，例如："今晚购买商品的粉丝都有机会获得主播赠送的礼物。"同时，策划抽奖或其他互动活动，增加观众的参与感，例如："不多说，我们开始抽奖，输入口令'××××'参与。"

（二）暖场话术

1. 围绕直播主题

将直播主题以关键词的方式呈现。主播可以反复提及这些关键词，加深用户对直播间的印象。

2. 保留悬念

通常会用"神秘""重磅"等词突出商品的价值，话术要保留悬念，可采取含蓄、委婉的表达方式，并选用概括性的词对商品进行大致描述，适当保留一些商品的特色和福利。

（三）互动留人话术

直播间留人和互动相辅相成，主播需通过提供福利和及时互动来提高观众留存率。主要策略包括以下内容。

1. 留人话术

主播应定期提供福利以吸引和留住观众，例如每5~10分钟发放福利，并引导观众关注直播间，例如："12点整我们开始抽免单名额，快关注加入粉丝团参与抽奖，并可领取10元优惠券。"

2. 互动话术

主播应当扮演客服角色，及时回答观众问题，耐心解答同一问题，以确保互动质量。例如回复："好的，我马上为您试穿这条裙子和小西装。"

除了回答观众的问题外，主播还可以引导直播间的观众参与互动，包括评论、点赞、点击购物车或商品、加入粉丝团等。主播可以通过以下方式来引导观众在评论区进行有效互动。

（1）提问式：所提出问题的答案只能是肯定的或否定的，观众用几个字就可以表明观点，例如："这款口红你们用过吗？""刚才分享的小技巧大家学会了吗？"

（2）选择式：主播通过抛出选择题引导观众参与互动，并从中获得反馈，例如："想要A款的打出'1'，想要B款的打出'2'。"

（3）刷屏式：观众参与互动并发言，会让新来的观众感受到直播间的活跃度，产生对直播内容的好奇心，例如："想要这款商品的朋友请在评论区打出'想要'两个字。"

在整场直播中，主播每隔5~10分钟就要提醒观众参与互动。

（四）商品介绍话术

商品介绍话术关键在于突出商品的卖点和优势，这对提高直播的商品转化率至关重要。主播首先可以通过特定词语描述商品的特色和基本信息，针对不同品类的商品，主播要注意用词的准确性、描述的合理性。

（五）促进成交话术

到了成交阶段，很多观众可能会犹豫不决，仍存有疑虑。要想打消观众的疑虑，刺激观众快速做出购买决策，主播在使用促进成交话术时要讲究以下技巧。

1. 增强信任感

主播在介绍商品的时候可以运用多种方法来增强观众对商品的信任感。例如，主播在介绍商品时讲一些自己的家人、工作人员使用商品的经历；在直播间展示自己的购买订单，证明某款商品是"自用款"，且是自己重复购买的商品；在直播间现场试用商品，分享使用体验与效果，验证商品的功能。同时，主播还要描述商品对观众的价值，双管齐下，刺激观众的购买欲望。

2. 设置价格锚点

主播要善于为商品设置价格锚点，用对比价格影响观众对商品最初价格的评估。

3. 营造紧迫感

很多观众在下单时会犹豫不决，这时主播就要用促进成交话术来刺激观众的购买欲望。促进成交话术的关键是营造抢购的氛围，增加观众的紧迫感，向观众发出行动指令，让他们抓住机会尽快购买。例如："这款商品数量有限，还剩最后100件，如果你看中了一定要及时下单，不然一会儿就抢不到了。""仅有今天购买这款商品的朋友才能享受到'买2送1'的福利，明天活动结束，价格会恢复到以前的水平，希望喜欢这款商品的朋友抓紧时间购买。"

（六）直播下播话术

在直播结束时，主播要友好、礼貌地与观众告别，对观众的支持和守护表示感谢，同时预告下一场直播的时间、要介绍的商品和提供的福利，甚至直接告知观众某款商品具体的上架时间，方便一些不能一直坚守在直播间的观众购买。常见的直播下播话术如下。

1. 总结型直播结束话术

概括性较强，主要用于回顾整场直播商品，为用户简单介绍主推商品，推荐热卖商品，反复强调商品的优惠力度，并通过描述商品销量和抢购速度等，吸引新用户赶紧下单，提醒已经下单的用户尽快付款。

2. 预告型直播结束话术

主要是将下次直播的某些信息提前告知用户，提前为下一次直播积累热度。这类话术中通常包括下次直播要售卖的商品、优惠、福利或嘉宾阵容等信息，以提高下次直播的吸引力，引起用户的期待。

3. 感谢型直播结束话术

用于主播表达对用户观看、关注直播及点赞、评论、转发等互动行为的感谢，如"非常感谢大家今天的陪伴和观看"。

✻ 案例参考

开场

问候（1分钟）

大家好，欢迎大家来到我（主播名）的直播间"XXXX"。嗨，你好（观众姓名），谢谢你来到我的直播间！你好啊！

今日福利（2分钟）

今天给大家带来2024年X品牌X电子产品的闪购活动，超大折扣力度500元，原价1999元，现在只要1499元。直播间其他更多电子产品优惠力度高达400元。直播快结束时，将为关注我直播间的粉丝送上价值299元的大礼。点击立即关注，记得不要离开直播间哦！

下单指南（1分钟）

在TikTok Shop购买优惠商品超级方便！只要点击屏幕左下方的"购物车"，点击"立即购买"，然后通过电子钱包/银行转账付款即可。

商品介绍和玩法

基本信息（5~10分钟）

想吃油炸食品，又害怕胆固醇？为你准备了X品牌的最新空气炸锅，大容量4.5升。我用它烤过一个大蛋糕，发现用起来刚刚好！功率800瓦，再也不用为电费担心啦！全网最低价，原价188元，现在只要89元！

问答（1分钟）

需要发货到砂拉越（Sarawak）？没问题，领取包邮券吧！也可以看看所在地区是否支持货到付款。

提醒用户下单（2分钟）

好的，5分钟后将恢复原价……还有2分钟……别忘了完成付款！

直播间玩法（3~5分钟）

照我们之前说的，现在所有的空气炸锅都卖完了，那就让我们用空气炸锅来一个自由烹饪挑战赛吧！

结尾

问答（5~10分钟）

今天直播以后我会干些什么？可能会去……

提醒用户完成付款（2分钟）

哇，时间过得真快，今天的直播马上就要结束了。大家都完成支付了吗？如果错过了今天的超值优惠，那可实在是太糟糕了。

预告（1分钟）

感谢大家今天下单、点赞、观看、留言、分享、参与赠品活动。每周一到周五晚上六点起，我们的直播和你不见不散。别忘了设置提醒，快来赢得更多超值优惠吧！

可以在这里看到直播时间表，记得关注账号、领取奖品、设好提醒，我们下次直播不见不散。拜拜！

案例来源：TikTok平台。

三、使用 AI 写作工具设计直播话术

（一）AI 写作工具的概念

AI 写作工具是一种利用人工智能技术，特别是自然语言处理（Natural Language Processing，简称 NLP）能力，来辅助或增强写作过程的软件。这类工具可以自动生成文本、提供写作建议、检查语法和拼写错误，以及优化文本的风格和语调。

（二）AI 写作工具的作用

1. 提高写作效率

AI 写作工具可以快速生成文本，帮助用户节省编写初稿所需的时间。它们能够自动完成语句，提供多种写作建议，从而加速写作流程。

2. 提高文本质量

AI 工具可以提供语法和拼写检查，帮助用户纠正写作中的错误。它们还能提供风格和语调的建议，使文本更加符合特定的读者群体或发布平台的要求。

3. 激发内容创意

AI 写作工具能够生成创意写作提示，帮助用户克服写作障碍，激发新的内容创意。用户可以利用 AI 工具探索不同的写作风格和角度，拓展思维方式。

4. 生成个性化内容

根据用户的特定需求，AI 工具可以帮助定制个性化的文本，如营销邮件、社交媒体帖子或个人简历。这些工具能根据历史数据和用户偏好进行学习，不断优化输出结果。

（三）常见 AI 写作工具

目前市面上有众多 AI 写作工具，包括 ChatGPT、JOJO AI、Grammarly、QuillBot、Copy.ai 等，这些工具各有特色，用户可以根据自己的具体需要选择合适的 AI 写作工具来辅助自己的写作活动。

任务操作

学习完上述知识，Peter 可以自己编写完成直播话术，也可以选择一款 AI 写作工具。

以下以 JOJO AI 这款 AI 写作工具为例撰写直播脚本，Peter 需完成如下操作。

☞ 步骤一　输入需求

打开写作工具。在输入框输入："设计 5 条用于＿＿＿＿直播的开场话术。"见图 2-1。

图 2-1　输入直播话术

☞ 步骤二　生成话术

AI 自动生成 5 条通用话术，例如针对运动鞋直播间，JOJO AI 将自动生成以下 5 条直播话术，见图 2-2。

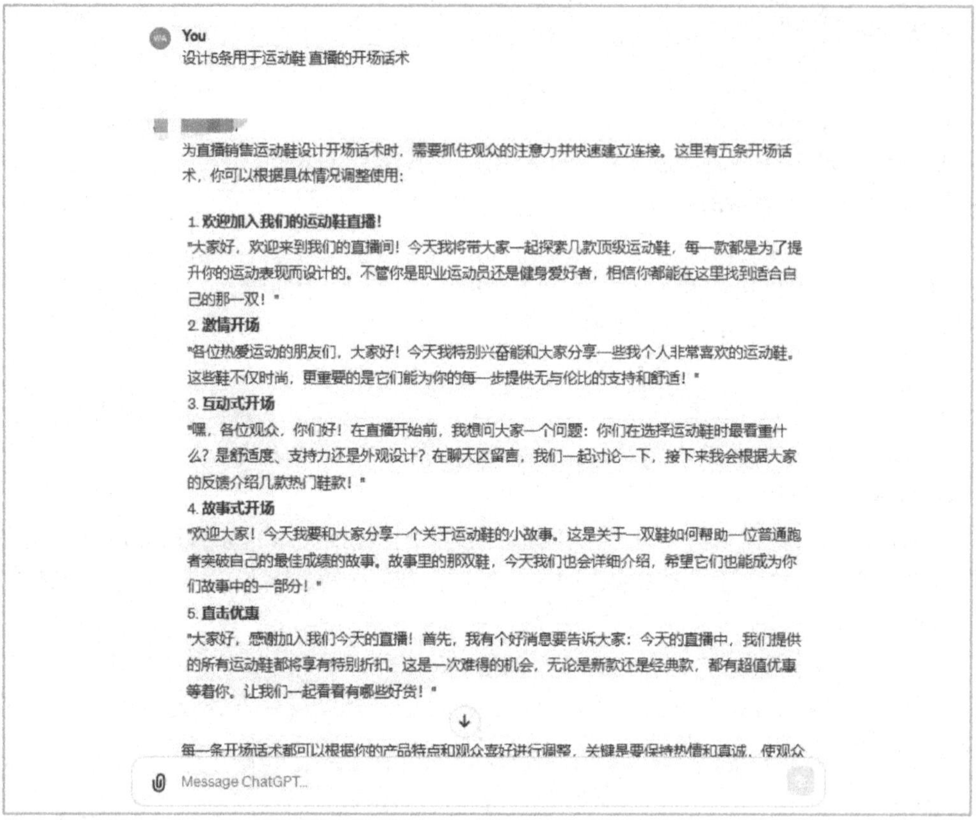

图 2-2　AI 提供的话术参考

☞ 步骤三　整理直播话术

分别在输入框输入"设计欢迎话术""设计暖场话术""设计推销话术""设计互动留人话术""设计下播话术"。之后将话术进行修改及整理，将设计完成的直播话术填写在表 2-20 中。

表 2-20　直播话术

话术	选用话术
欢迎话术	
暖场话术	
推销话术	
互动留人话术	
下播话术	

☞ 步骤四　练习直播话术

使用直播市场当地语言或英语，做直播话术的练习。

Learning Process

1. Understand the Live Streaming Process

The live streaming schedule is shown in Table 2-7.

Table 2-7: Live Streaming Schedule

Time Period	Activity	Specific Actions
0-5 Minutes	Self-introduction, fan interaction, brand introduction, and prize draw to attract traffic	Host interaction, prize draw
5-15 Minutes	Product and discount information presentation	Introduce product features, explain discount activities, and guide interaction
15-20 Minutes	Product introduction session	Basic product information introduction, benefits explanation, voucher distribution, product trial demonstration, and flash sale
Entire Duration	Likes and interactions to a certain frequency for prize draws	Set interaction targets; conduct prize draws
End	Thank fans; announce the next live stream	Express gratitude; announce next live streaming details

2. Key Points for Designing Live Streaming Scripts

2.1 Opening Scripts

Welcome Scripts: The host should warmly greet both new and returning viewers in the first 1-5 minutes. Personalized greetings using viewers' usernames enhance user experience, with an enthusiastic tone and high pitch to engage viewers.

Encourage Interaction: Ask viewers to like or comment to boost engagement.

Product and Promotion Previews: Announce product previews and promotions to retain viewers in the live stream.

2.2 Warm-up Scripts

Focus on the Live Streaming Theme: Use keywords related to the theme repeatedly to reinforce viewer memory.

Maintain Suspense: Use words like "mystery" and "blockbuster" to keep viewers curious.

2.3 Engagement and Retention Scripts

Retention Scripts: Offer regular benefits every 5-10 minutes to attract and retain viewers.

Interaction Scripts: Act as a customer service representative, answer questions patiently, and encourage interaction through questions, choices, and calls to action.

2.4 Product Introduction Scripts

Highlight selling points and advantages of the product to increase conversion rates.

2.5 Sales Promotion Scripts

Build Trust: Share personal or family experiences with the product, show purchase orders, and demonstrate the product live.

Set Price Anchors: Influence viewers' price evaluation by setting comparative prices.

Create Urgency: Use limited quantities and time-sensitive offers to prompt immediate purchases.

2.6 Closing Scripts

Summary: Review the main products and emphasize the discounts.

Preview: Provide information about the next live stream to build anticipation.

Gratitude: Thank viewers for watching and interacting.

3. Using AI Writing Tools to Design Live Streaming Scripts

3.1 Concept of AI Writing Tools

Software utilizing artificial intelligence, particularly natural language processing (NLP), to assist or enhance the writing process.

3.2 Functions of AI Writing Tools

Improve Writing Efficiency: Quickly generate text, provide writing suggestions, and speed up the writing process.

Enhance Text Quality: Offer grammar and spelling checks, and optimize text style and tone.

Inspire Content Ideas: Generate creative writing prompts to overcome writer's block.

Personalize Content: Customize texts based on user needs, such as marketing emails or social media posts.

3.3 Common AI Writing Tools

ChatGPT, JOJO AI, Grammarly, QuillBot, and Copy.ai, each with unique features to suit different writing needs.

Task Operations

Use JOJO AI writing tool to create live streaming scripts.

Step 1: Input Keywords

Open the writing tool and input: "Design 5 opening scripts for a live stream.", as shown in Figure 2-1 (please see the Chinese section).

Step 2: Generate Scripts

The AI will automatically generate 5 general scripts. For example, for a sneaker live stream, JOJO AI will generate the following 5 scripts, as shown in Figure 2-2 (please see the Chinese section).

Step 3: Organize the Live Streaming Scripts

Input separately in the text box to design warm-up scripts, sales scripts, engagement and retention scripts, and closing scripts. Modify and organize the scripts.

Step 4: Practice the Live Streaming Scripts

Practice the live streaming scripts in the local language or in English.

子任务4 编写直播脚本

学习过程

直播脚本是影响直播活动成功与否的关键因素之一。直播脚本能够提前规划直播内容和活动，梳理直播流程，把控直播节奏，使直播活动按照直播团队预想的方向有序进行。因此，在正式进行直播之前，StreamASEAN 直播电商公司要求 Peter 所在的直播团队设计一份直播脚本。Peter 了解了如下直播脚本的相关知识。

一、直播脚本的含义

直播脚本是指直播场景的脚本化处理,整个直播过程,包括主播在开播前后所有要做的事情都可以通过直播脚本来实现。有了脚本后,直播团队可以有效地应对在直播过程中的突发情况,也能更好地把握住直播"主动权"。

二、直播脚本的分类

在直播电商中,直播脚本分为单品直播脚本和整场直播脚本。

(一)单品直播脚本

单品直播脚本是介绍单个产品的脚本,以单个商品为单位,规范商品的解说,突出商品卖点,一般包含商品的品牌介绍、商品的功能和用途、商品价格等。

由于一场直播一般会持续2~6个小时,大多数直播间都会推荐多款产品。每一款产品定制一份简略的单品直播脚本,以表格的形式,将产品的卖点和优惠活动标示清楚,可以防止主播在介绍产品时手忙脚乱,混淆不清,也能帮助主播精准、有效地给直播间粉丝传递产品的特征和价格优势。

单品直播脚本一般包括品牌介绍、卖点介绍、利益点强调、促销活动和催单话术等,注意凸显价格优势,及时回答粉丝问题,见表2-21。

表2-21 单品直播脚本范例

序号	商品名称	商品图片	品牌信息	品牌介绍	利益点	市场价	直播活动价	优惠模式

(二)整场直播脚本

整场直播脚本是针对整场直播过程编写的脚本。在直播带货过程中,优秀的直播脚本一定要考虑到细枝末节,让主播从上播到下播都有条不紊,让人员、道具都得到充分的调配。因此,直播脚本需细化每一个直播现场环节,规划出标准化直播现场流程,包括详细的时间节点以及在该时间节点内主播要做的事和说的话。见表2-22。

表2-22 整场直播脚本范例

直播脚本的要素	内容说明
直播时间	明确直播开始到结束的时间
直播地点	XX直播室
商品数量	写明用于直播的产品名称及每种产品的数量
主播介绍	主播的名字及主播的特点
人员分工	明确直播参与人员的职责,如主播负责讲解商品、演示商品功能、引导粉丝关注和下单等;助理负责与粉丝互动、回复粉丝问题等;场控人员/客服负责商品的上下架、修改商品价格、发货与售后
预告文案	撰写直播预告文案
注意事项	说明直播的注意事项
直播流程	直播流程应该规划详细的时间节点,说明开场预热商品讲解、粉丝互动、结束预告等环节的具体内容

任务操作

学习完上述知识,Peter所在的直播团队需要为即将进行的直播设计一份整场直播脚本,具体操作步骤如下。

☞ **步骤一　明确直播要素**

明确直播时间、地点、商品数量及人员分工。

☞ **步骤二　明确直播流程**

明确直播流程，并将直播各要素填写在表 2-23 中。

表 2-23　整场直播脚本

直播时间	
直播地点	
商品数量	
主播介绍	
人员分工	
预告文案	
注意事项	

直播流程			
时间段	流程规划	人员分工		
^	^	主播（话术）	助理	场控人员

Learning Process

1. Definition of a Live Streaming Script

A live streaming script refers to the script-based management of live streaming scenarios. It encompasses all activities the host must perform before, during, and after the live stream. By using scripted programming for live streaming functions, the activities can proceed in an orderly manner. A script helps handle unexpected situations and maintain control throughout the live stream.

2. Types of Live Streaming Scripts

In live streaming e-commerce, scripts are categorized into single product scripts and whole session scripts.

2.1 Single Product Live Streaming Script

A single product live streaming script is tailored for individual products, standardizing the presentation and highlighting the product's key selling points. It includes brand introduction, product features, usage, and pricing. For most live streams, which typically last 2–6 hours and feature multiple products, each product should have a concise script presented in a table format to prevent confusion and ensure accurate communication of product features and price advantages.

2.2 Whole Session Live Streaming Script

A comprehensive live streaming script must consider all details, ensuring the host manages the session smoothly from start to finish. This script should outline every stage of the live stream, and specify timeframes and the tasks and dialogues the host needs to perform, as shown in Table 2-8.

Table 2-8: Example of Whole Session Live Streaming Script

Script Elements	Description
Live Streaming Time	Specify the start and end times of the live stream
Live Streaming Location	××Live Streaming Room
Number of Products	List the names and quantities of the products featured in the live stream
Host Introduction	Include the host's name and characteristics
Personnel Responsibilities	Define the roles and duties of participants, such as the host handling product descriptions and guiding viewers to make purchases, assistants managing interactions and responses, and support staff overseeing product listing, price adjustments, shipping, and after-sales services
Preview Script	Write the preview script for the following live streams
Precautions	Note any important considerations for the live stream
Live Streaming Process	Plan detailed timeframes for each stage, specifying activities such as opening warm-ups, product descriptions, viewer interactions, and closing announcements

Task Operations

Step 1: Determine the Live Streaming Elements

Determine the live streaming time, location, number of products, and personnel assignments.

Step 2: Outline the Live Streaming Process

课后习题

1.（单选题）在使用FAB法则描述一个产品时，以下哪项最准确地代表了"B"即益处（Benefit）的概念？（ ）

A. 产品由耐用的材料制成　　　　　　B. 产品能够提升工作效率

C. 产品让使用者感觉更自信　　　　　D. 产品具有防水功能

2.（多选题）在编写直播脚本时，哪些元素是至关重要的？（ ）

A. 详细的产品介绍时间节点　　　　　B. 主播的即兴发言时间

C. 预定的互动环节和观众提问时间　　D. 道具和背景布置的细节

3. 请简述制作直播封面时应考虑的三个重要因素，并解释为什么这些因素对吸引观众至关重要。

Exercises

1. (Single Choice) When you use the FAB method to describe a product, which of the following most accurately represents the concept of "B" or Benefit?

A. The product is made of durable materials

B. The product can improve work efficiency

C. The product makes the user feel more confident

D. The product is waterproof

2. (Multiple Choice) Which elements are crucial when creating a live streaming script?

A. Detailed timeframes for product introductions

B. Time for the host's impromptu speeches

C. Scheduled interaction and audience Q&A time

D. Details on props and background setup

3. Briefly describe three important factors to consider when you create a live streaming cover image and explain why these factors are crucial for attracting viewers.

任务 4　搭建直播间

任务导入

设计并搭建专业直播间，通过高质量的直播展示可以提升企业的品牌形象和增加产品销售。StreamASEAN 直播电商公司向 Peter 所在的直播团队下达任务：搭建直播间，并要求直播间须符合国际化标准，便于吸引并维护东南亚及其他地区的客户群体。

在本任务中，Peter 将通过精确的设备选择、场景布置和光源配置，确保直播间的专业标准与品牌相符，从而吸引更广泛的国际客户。

任务目标

¤ 知识目标
1. 了解直播设备
2. 了解直播间灯光和场景布置的方法和要求

¤ 技能目标
1. 能够进行直播间灯光布置
2. 能够进行直播间场景布置
3. 能够制作直播间素材

¤ 素养目标
培养学生面对技术故障能迅速诊断问题并找到有效解决方案的能力

任务流程

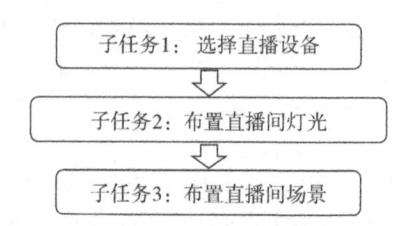

```
子任务1：选择直播设备
      ↓
子任务2：布置直播间灯光
      ↓
子任务3：布置直播间场景
```

子任务 1　选择直播设备

学习过程

选择合适的设备是直播成功的关键因素，将直接影响到直播的画质、声音清晰度和传输流畅性。在直播间搭建前，Peter 需要选择合适的直播设备，在此之前，Peter 对直播设备进行如下了解。

一、直播间基础设备

（一）计算机

计算机用于 PC 直播、直播后台管理、脚本设计、修图、视频剪辑等。如果没有特殊需求（如游戏直播等），购买主流配置的笔记本电脑即可，但接口要足够丰富，以满足外部设备的连接需求。主播在选择计算机时也可参考一些专业网站，然后根据自己的需求和预算进行选择。

（二）视频设备

直播视频设备可以根据直播要求选择手机摄像头或者使用专业相机设备。

1. 直播手机

手机直播的主要设备，适用于室内直播和室外直播。建议选择支持1080P以上高清摄像头、内存不低于4GB的手机完成直播。

2. 摄像头

用电脑直播时，外接摄像头需要选择能够支持4K分辨率、具备自动对焦和光学防抖功能的高清摄像头，确保在各种光照环境下都能捕捉到清晰、稳定的画面，见图2-3。

（三）稳定设备

包括手机支架、三脚架和手持云台稳定器等，用于固定手机、摄像头、话筒等设备，以保证直播画面稳定，尤其在移动拍摄或长时间录制时保持画面稳定，见图2-4。

（四）音频设备

1. 声卡

选用多频道输入和具备高质量音频输出的外接专业声卡，以适应复杂的直播音频处理需求，见图2-5。

图2-3 摄像头 　　图2-4 直播稳定设备 　　图2-5 声卡

2. 收音设备

用于直播收音，提供清晰的语音捕捉功能，适应直播间内的活动，具备优秀的噪声抑制技术。

3. 耳机

耳机可以让主播在直播时监听自己的声音，从而更好地控制自己的音调、分辨伴奏等。

4. 话筒

直播时的音质直接影响着直播的质量，所以话筒的选择非常重要。目前常用的话筒主要分为动圈话筒和电容话筒。动圈话筒声音清晰、真实，但收集的声音饱满度差。电容话筒收音能力强，音效饱满圆润，听起来愉悦舒适，没有尖锐的高音带来的突兀感，但容易形成"喷麦"。见图2-6。

图2-6 领夹话筒

（五）网络设备

如果网络速度慢或者网络稳定性较差，直播画面的加载速度就会过慢，导致画面卡顿，影响用户的观看体验。因此，直播团队应使用网速较快的网络设备，以保证直播画面的流畅性与稳定性。建议升级网络带宽，带宽达到 30M 以上。

（六）灯光设备

在室内直播时，需要进行产品细节展示。因为自然光线不太充足，因此室内直播时多用前置摄像头，补光就显得尤为重要。补光灯主要为直播间打光，提供辅助光线，以得到较好的光影效果。补光灯的类型主要包括环形灯与柔光灯。直播间灯光设备见图 2-7。

图 2-7　直播间灯光设备

1. 环形灯

环形灯是一种非常受欢迎的照明工具，尤其在美容摄影、视频博客、自拍和其他多种拍摄场景中有广泛应用。它的独特之处在于其环形设计，这种设计能够产生均匀的光线，最大限度地减少阴影，让主播面部特征更加突出。

常见的环形灯有直播美颜灯、球形补光灯等。

2. 柔光箱

柔光箱是摄影和视频制作中常用的照明附件，主要作用是软化灯光，减少阴影的硬度，提高光线在场景中的均匀分布。通过改变柔光箱与光源的距离，可以控制光线的软硬和覆盖范围。柔光箱提供的光线比较集中，方向性好，易于控制光线的落点。除了常见的方形和矩形，柔光箱还有八边形（俗称章鱼灯）和条形等形状。

3. 柔光球

柔光球是一种摄影和视频照明配件，用于软化光源发出的光线。在直播环境中使用柔光球可以显著改善画质，使得光线更加柔和、均匀，减少阴影和过于强烈的高光，对于提升视频质量和观看体验非常有帮助。柔光球兼容多种光源，包括闪光灯、LED 灯等，使用可调节亮度的灯具，以便根据不同的直播场景和环境光线条件进行调整。

（七）提词设备

直播间提词设备，常称为电视提词器，是专为帮助主播或演讲者在直播中顺畅呈现演讲内容而设计的设备。这种设备通常安装在摄像机前，通过将屏幕上的文字反射到透明玻璃上，让摄像机背后的人能够看到文字而摄像机捕捉不到文字。在选择直播间提词设备时，需要考虑其显示的清晰度、设备的兼容性以及是否适合直播场景的移动性需求。提词设备的类型包括传统的安装在镜头前的提词器、便携式平板提词器，以及可以直接安装在各类摄像机上的摄像头提词器，各有其适用的专业新闻报道、移动直播和户外直播等不同场景。选择合适的提词设备可以显著提升直播的专业度和流畅性。提词器见图 2-8。

图 2-8　提词器

（八）直播道具

直播道具是用于增强直播呈现效果的各种物料，包括例如陈列台、陈列桌，用于直播产品的摆放和展示，黑板、海报、贴纸等用于展示商品营销信息的宣传用品；计时器、计算器等一系列用于炒热气氛激发用户兴趣的道具等。

二、各阶段直播间所需直播设备

各阶段直播间所需直播设备如表 2-24 所示。

表 2-24 各阶段直播间所需直播设备

时段	所需设备	用途
初期	手机、手机支架、桌椅、灯光	手机用于显示直播画面，手机支架用于固定直播手机，桌椅、灯光提供直播环境和光线
中期	相机、摄像头、三脚架、桌椅、灯光、高配置电脑、话筒、收音设备	相机、摄像头用于采集直播画面，三脚架用于固定拍摄设备，桌椅、灯光提供直播环境和光线，高配置电脑用于直播推流，话筒及收音设备用于输出直播声音
后期	相机、摄像头、三脚架、桌椅、灯光、高配置电脑、话筒、收音设备、采集卡、提词器、LED 屏	相机、摄像头、桌椅、灯光、高配置电脑、话筒及收音设备用途同上。采集卡用于采集相机信号，返送给电脑。提词器用于播放脚本。LED 屏放置主播身后，作为背景或展示产品信息

✱ 案例参考

案例参考内容见表 2-25、表 2-26。

表 2-25 电脑简易开播所需部分设备

设备名称	设备用途	设备价格（元）
桌椅	展示样品，主播休息	￥100～1000
美颜灯	补充光线，让直播间更明亮自然	￥100～3000
摄像头	直播间画面采集	￥500～2000
球形灯	补充光线，让直播间更明亮自然	￥1500～5000
摄像头支架	固定摄像头，避免晃动	￥20～100

表 2-26 手机简易开播所需部分设备

设备名称	设备用途	设备价格（元）
桌椅	展示样品，主播休息	￥100～1000
美颜灯	补充光线，让直播间更明亮自然	￥100～3000
手机支架	固定手机，避免晃动	￥20～100

案例来源：TikTok 平台。

任务操作

学习完上述知识，Peter 需完成如下操作。

☞ **步骤一　选择直播形式**

Peter 的直播团队选择使用 PC 端的形式进行直播。

☞ **步骤二　了解预算及要求**

StreamASEAN 直播电商公司期望 Peter 所在的直播团队搭建较为简易的直播间，预算控制在 10000 元以内，要求覆盖所有直播所需设备，同时保证直播画面及声音清晰、流畅。

☞ **步骤三　网上调研**

根据预算及公司对设备的要求，Peter 需要进行网上调研，通过购物网站，了解各类设备的型号、功能和价格，并形成设备调研表。

☞ **步骤四　选择直播设备**

在预算范围内选择直播设备，并将所选设备信息填写在表 2-27 中。

表 2-27　直播设备选择

设备类别	品牌型号	所需数量	价格	选择原因
总价				

☞ **步骤五　提交直播设备选择表**

说明设备选择原因及设备使用方法，选择的直播设备将根据表 2-28 进行评估。

表 2-28　设备选择评估标准

评估项目	评估标准
预算控制	预算控制在 10000 元以内
设备合理性	是否详细说明了设备选择的原因和使用方法
实际应用	是否能够将设备应用于实际直播中
演示效果	演示过程流畅，能够有效展示直播方案内容及亮点

Learning Process

1. Basic Equipment for the Live Streaming Room

1.1 Computer

Used for PC live stream, backend management, script design, photo editing, and video editing. Generally, a mainstream laptop configuration is sufficient, but it should have enough ports to connect external devices.

1.2 Video Equipment

Live Streaming Phone: Suitable for both indoor and outdoor live stream. It is recommended to choose a phone with a camera that supports 1080P or higher resolution and has at least 4GB of memory.

Camera: For PC live stream, choose an external camera that supports 4K resolution, and has autofocus and optical image stabilization to ensure clear and stable footage in various lighting conditions, as shown in Figure 2-3 (please see the Chinese section).

1.3 Stabilizing Equipment

The stabilizing equipment includes phone stands, tripods, and handheld gimbal stabilizers, which are used to stabilize phones, cameras, and microphones to ensure stable video, especially during mobile shooting or long recording sessions, as shown in Figure 2-4 (please see the Chinese section).

1.4 Audio Equipment

Audio Interface: Choose a professional external audio interface with multiple-channel input and high-quality audio output to meet the complex audio processing needs of live stream, as shown in Figure 2-5 (please see the Chinese section).

Radio Receiving Equipment: Used for capturing audio during the live stream, providing clear voice capture capabilities to accommodate activities in the studio, with excellent noise suppression technology.

Headphones: Allow the host to monitor their own voice during the live stream, enabling better control over pitch and discernment of the backing track.

Microphone: The quality of the microphone directly affects the quality of the live stream, so choosing the right microphone is crucial. Currently, common microphones are mainly divided into dynamic microphones and condenser microphones. Dynamic microphones provide clear and authentic sound but have less fullness in the captured audio. Condenser microphones have strong pickup capabilities, producing rich and smooth sound that is pleasant to listen to, without the harshness of sharp high frequencies, but they can easily cause "plosive" sounds. See Figure 2-6 (please see the Chinese section).

1.5 Network Equipment

A fast and stable network is crucial to avoid lag and ensure smooth live stream. It is recommended to upgrade the broadband to at least 30Mbps.

1.6 Lighting Equipment

Ring Light: Popular for its ability to provide even lighting and minimize shadows, enhancing the host's facial features. Commonly used in beauty photography, video blogs, and other shooting scenarios.

Softbox: Used to soften light, reduce shadow hardness, and ensure even light distribution. Different shapes are available, including rectangular, octagonal, and strip softboxes.

Soft Light Ball: Used to soften light to reduce shadows and highlights, improving video quality. Compatible with various light sources like flashlights and LED lights.

The types of lighting equipment are shown in Figure 2-7 (please see the Chinese section).

1.7 Teleprompter Equipment

A teleprompter helps hosts deliver content smoothly during live stream. It typically sits in front of the camera, reflecting text onto a transparent screen that the host can read without the camera capturing the text. Choose a teleprompter based on display clarity, compatibility, and mobility needs. Types include traditional teleprompters in front of lens, portable tablet teleprompters, and camera-mounted teleprompters, as shown in Figure 2-8 (please see the Chinese section).

1.8 Live Streaming Props

Live streaming props are various materials used to enhance the presentation of a live stream. These include display stands and tables for placing and showcasing products, blackboards, posters, stickers, and a series of promotional items used to display marketing information about the products. They also include props such as timers and calculators, which are used to create a lively atmosphere and stimulate user interest.

2. Required Live Streaming Equipment at Different Stages

The live streaming equipment for each stage is shown in Table 2-9.

Table 2-9: Live Streaming Equipment for Each Stage

Time Period	Required Equipment	Usage
Early-Stage	Phone, phone holder, tables and chairs, lighting	The phone is used to display the live stream; the phone holder is used to fix the live streaming phone; the table, chairs, and lighting provide the live streaming environment and light
Mid-Stage	Camera, webcam, tripod, tables and chairs, lighting, high-performance computer, microphone, audio recording equipment	The camera and webcam are used to capture the live streaming footage; the tripod is used to stabilize the shooting equipment; the table, chairs, and lighting provide the live streaming environment and light. The high-performance computer is used for live stream, while the microphone and audio recording equipment are used to capture the live audio
Late-Stage	Camera, webcam, tripod, tables and chairs, lighting, high-performance computer, microphone, audio recording equipment, capture card, teleprompter, LED screen	The camera, webcam, the table, chairs, lighting, high-performance computer, microphone, and audio recording equipment serve the same purposes as in the mid-stage equipment. The capture card is used to capture camera signals and send them to the computer. The teleprompter is used to display scripts. The LED screen is placed behind the host to serve as a background or to display product information

✽ Reference

For reference cases, please see Table 2-10 and Table 2-11.

Table 2-10: Partial Equipment Needed for Simple PC-Based Live Stream

Equipment Name	Equipment Use	Equipment Price
Desk and Chair	Display samples; rest area for host	¥100-1000
Beauty Light	Supplement lighting to make the live streaming room brighter and more natural	¥100-3000
Webcam	Capture live streaming video	¥500-2000
Spherical Light	Supplement lighting to make the live streaming room brighter and more natural	¥1500-5000
Webcam Stand	Stabilize the webcam to prevent shaking	¥20-100

Table 2-11: Partial Equipment Needed for Simple Mobile-Based Live Stream

Equipment Name	Equipment Use	Equipment Price
Desk and Chair	Display samples; rest area for host	¥100-1000
Beauty Light	Supplement lighting to make the live streaming room brighter and more natural	¥100-3000
Mobile Phone Stand	Stabilize the mobile phone to prevent shaking	¥20-100

Source: TikTok platform.

Task Operations

Step 1: Choose to Use a PC-Based Setup for the Live Stream
Step 2: Understand the Budget and Requirements

Set up a relatively simple live streaming studio with a budget controlled within ¥10,000, ensuring that all necessary equipment is covered while maintaining clear and smooth video and audio quality.

Step 3: Online Research

Based on the budget and the company's equipment requirements, conduct online research.

Using shopping websites, he should identify various equipment models, functions, and prices, and compile an equipment research table.

Step 4: Select Live Streaming Equipment

Select live streaming equipment within the budget.

Step 5: Submit the Live Streaming Equipment Selection Table

Explain the reasons for selecting the equipment and how it will be used. The selected live streaming equipment will be evaluated based on the Table 2-12 Criteria.

Table 2-12: Equipment Selection Evaluation Criteria

Evaluation Item	Evaluation Criterion
Budget Control	Budget controlled within ¥10,000
Equipment Rationality	Detailed explanation of the reasons and methods for selecting the equipment
Practical Application	Ability to apply the equipment in actual live stream
Presentation Effect	The presentation process is smooth and effectively showcases the content and highlights of the live streaming plan

子任务 2　布置直播间灯光

学习过程

直播间的灯光布置非常关键，它不仅能够影响视频的视觉质量，还能提升整个直播的专业度，使直播场景看起来更加专业和吸引人。在进行直播间灯光布置之前，Peter 对直播间灯光布置进行如下了解。

一、直播间光源类型

（一）主灯

主灯是直播间照明中最重要的光源，主要作用是为主体提供主要照明，确保主体面部和身体得到充足的光线。这种灯通常放置在摄像机的前方偏一侧，大约 45 度角，高于主体的头部，从而形成自然而有层次的光影效果。主灯的设置需要确保光线强度足够，同时避免产生过硬的阴影。

（二）辅助光

辅助光用来减少或软化主灯造成的阴影，它通常位于摄像机视线的另一侧，与主灯成对角放置。辅助光的亮度一般低于主灯，以确保能有效填充阴影而不产生额外的强烈阴影。这种灯的使用是为了平衡画面的光线，让主体的面部细节更加清晰可见。

（三）轮廓光

轮廓光又称为背光，它位于主体后方，作用是在主体的周围形成一种光晕，从而使主体从背景中脱颖而出，增加画面的立体感和深度。轮廓光通常比主灯和辅助光高，可以放置在主体头部的后上方，确保能够高亮主体的轮廓。

（四）顶光

顶光用于从上方直接照射主体，帮助增强主体的三维感，同时也能在某些情况下减少面部的阴影。顶光应该适度使用，以避免产生眼睛下方不自然的阴影。它的设置通常需要根据直播间的高度和主体的位置来调整。

（五）背景光

背景光用于照亮直播间的背景，使背景更加丰富或突出主体。通过使用不同颜色或强度的背景光，可以创建出吸引观众眼球的背景，或者为直播增添特定的氛围和风格。背景光的选择和布置应该与直播的主题和内容相协调。

二、直播间灯光设置原则

（一）注意光线均匀度

确保整个直播间内的光线分布均匀，避免出现局部过亮或过暗的情况。可以通过增加灯光数量或调整灯光位置来实现光线的均匀分布。

（二）控制光比

光比是指主灯与补光灯之间的亮度比例。合理的光比能够使画面更加自然、立体。一般来说，主灯的亮度应略高于补光灯，但不宜过高，以免画面过曝。

（三）色彩搭配

根据主播的个人风格和直播主题选择合适的灯光色彩，增加画面的美感和氛围。

（四）调整色温

色温对于直播间的整体色调有着重要影响。一般来说，暖色调的灯光能够营造温馨、舒适的氛围，适合温馨场景的直播内容；而冷色调的灯光则更加清新、明亮，适合活力四射的直播内容。根据直播内容选择合适的色温，使画面更加和谐统一。

三、直播间常见灯光布置方案

布置直播间灯光时，可通过使用不同型号的灯或不同类型的灯光，摆放在不同的位置，调整为不同的亮度，创造出不同的光线效果。

（一）直播间一灯方案

一灯方案是最基础的照明设置，适用于预算有限或空间较小的直播环境。主灯通常放置在主体前方偏一侧，提供足够的光线照亮主播，确保面部表情和细节清晰可见。常用的主灯包括LED环形灯或单个软箱灯，见图2-9。

图2-9 直播间一灯方案

图片来源：《自媒体直播间灯光布置图（一）——新手速成灯光师》，2021-11-12，https://zhuanlan.zhihu.com/p/432511727。

（二）直播间二灯方案

对角线布光的基本原理是将主光（主灯）和填充光（辅助灯）对角放置。通常，主灯被置于主体一侧的前方高处，形成主光源照射角度，在主体的对角线方向上，相对于主灯较低位置，放置填充光，用以平衡阴影，见图2-10。

图 2-10　直播间二灯方案

图片来源：《自媒体直播间灯光布置图（一）——新手速成灯光师》，2021-11-12，
https://zhuanlan.zhihu.com/p/432511727。

（三）直播间三灯方案

直播间要求空间的通透明亮，高调背景的低反差布光，因此灯光安排为：主光+辅助光+背景光。

1. 主光

主光在摄像机的前方偏一侧，大约30到45度角，并略高于主体的眼睛水平。

2. 辅助光

辅助光通常放置在与主光相对的另一侧，亮度要低于主光，以确保主体脸部的细节不会丢失。辅助光的距离和角度可根据所需的阴影软度进行调整。辅助光通常也通过扩散设备进行柔化，以避免产生第二个影子。

3. 背景光

背景光可以是定向的光源，也可以是柔和的光源，根据直播的主题和背景的具体需要进行设置，见图2-11。

图 2-11　直播间三灯方案

图片来源：《自媒体直播间灯光布置图（二）——新手速成灯光师》，2021-11-13，
https://zhuanlan.zhihu.com/p/432834134。

在短视频拍摄中，一般不以整体空间的明亮为目标，背景也以低调为主。视频创作汇总更追求光影的美感，光效更有层次和渐变过渡，三灯的安排多为：主光+辅助光+轮廓光。

主辅光的布光方式不变，背光设置在主体背后，创建主体周围的光晕，帮助主体从背景中突出，增加深度感和三维感，见图2-12。

（四）直播间四灯方案

在直播和视频制作中，四灯方案是一项非常有效的照明技术，它在传统的三灯方案

图 2-12 短视频三灯方案

图片来源：《自媒体直播间灯光布置图（二）——新手速成灯光师》，2021-11-13，https://zhuanlan.zhihu.com/p/432834134。

基础上添加了一个额外的灯光元素，从而提供更多的灵活性和控制。这种设置通常包括主光、辅助光、背景光和轮廓光。

主辅光的布光方式不变，背景光可以是一个聚光灯，位于主体的背后，对准背景上的某个特定区域或物体，或者使用彩色灯光以增添氛围。轮廓光通常位于主体的背后和上方，照射下来形成主体周围的轮廓光晕，见图 2-13。

图 2-13 四灯方案

图片来源：《自媒体直播间灯光布置图（二）——新手速成灯光师》，2021-11-13，https://zhuanlan.zhihu.com/p/432834134。

任务操作

学习完上述知识，Peter 需要进行直播间布光。在进行真实布光前，Peter 需要完成虚拟布光的练习，并根据练习结果进行布光，具体操作如下。

☞ **步骤一　创建项目**

下载并安装软件 set.a.light 3D STUDIO，启动软件后，创建新项目。输入项目的名称，并选择工作室空间的大小和形状等基本设置。

☞ **步骤二　选择模型**

在工具箱中选择模型（如摄影师、模特、道具等），并将其拖到工作区。调整模型的位置、姿势等，以符合拍摄需求。

☞ **步骤三　灯光布置**

从灯光库中选择所需的灯具类型，如闪光灯、持续光等。选择合适的灯光方案，将选中的灯具拖到工作区的适当位置。调整灯光的方向、强度、色温和其他参数，以达到预期的照明效果。

☞ **步骤四　选择相机模型**

选择相机模型，放置在适当的位置。根据需要调整焦距、光圈、快门速度和感光度等设置。点击相机图标进行虚拟拍摄。

☞ **步骤五　虚拟拍摄**

进行虚拟拍摄，检查最终效果和可能存在的问题。可以导出布局图、灯光列表和其他重要信息，用于现场实际拍摄时参考，见图2-14。

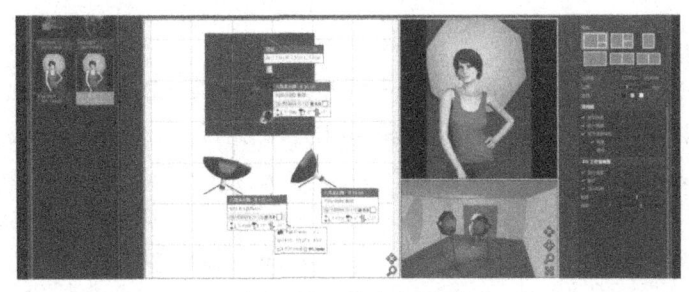

图 2-14　导出灯光图

☞ **步骤六　真实布光**

根据灯光图的指导，进行真实布光。

Learning Process

1. Types of Lighting in the Live Streaming Room

1.1 Key Light

Provides primary illumination, ensuring the subject's face and body are well-lit. It is typically placed in front of and slightly to the side of the camera.

1.2 Fill Light

Reduces or softens the shadows created by the key light, usually positioned on the opposite side of the camera's line of sight.

1.3 Back Light

Positioned behind the subject, creating a halo effect to make the subject stand out from the background.

1.4 Top Light

Illuminates the subject from above, enhancing the three-dimensionality of the subject.

1.5 Background Light

Lights up the background, adding depth and dimension to the scene.

2. Principles of Lighting Setup

(1) Ensure even distribution of light to avoid areas that are too bright or too dark.

(2) Control the light ratio to make the image more natural and three-dimensional.

(3) Choose appropriate light colors based on the theme of the live stream and the style of the host.

(4) Adjust the color temperature to create a suitable atmosphere for the live stream.

3. Common Lighting Arrangements

3.1 Single Light Setup

Uses the key light to provide basic illumination, as shown in Figure 2-9 (please see the Chinese section).

3.2 Two-Light Setup

Diagonal lighting with a key light and a fill light, as shown in Figure 2-10 (please see the Chinese section).

3.3 Three-Light Setup

Key light, fill light, and either a back light or background light, suitable for high-key backgrounds or short video shooting, as shown in Figure 2-11 and Figure 2-12 (please see the Chinese section).

3.4 Four-Light Setup

Adds a background light or back light to the three-light setup for more flexibility and control, as shown in Figure 2-13 (please see the Chinese section).

Task Operations

Step 1: Create a Project

Download and install the set.a.light 3D STUDIO software, and then create a new project.

Step 2: Select the Models

Select and adjust the positions and poses of the models.

Step 3: Arrange the Lighting

Choose the required lighting fixtures from the light library and place them in the appropriate positions, adjusting the light parameters.

Step 4: Place the Camera Model

Place the camera model and adjust the shooting settings.

Step 5: Perform Virtual Shooting

Perform virtual shooting, check the effect, and export the lighting diagram, as shown in Figure 2-14 (please see the Chinese section).

Step 6: Set up the Actual Lighting

Set up the actual lighting based on the lighting diagram.

子任务3　布置直播间场景

学习过程

搭建直播间场景是为直播创造一个具有视觉吸引力且功能性强的环境，这对于增强观众的观看体验和直播的专业感至关重要。在选择完直播设备后，Peter需要找到合适的直播场所，并进行直播间的布置。

一、选择直播空间

(一) 直播空间规划

直播间的大小应该根据直播的类型和内容进行规划。如果是小规模的一般性直播，场地大小控制在10~20平方米即可；如果是团队"带货"直播，则可以选择相对更大的场地，场地大小控制在20~50平方米即可；如果是个人美妆类直播，则可以选择更小的场地，8平方米左右的场地即可；如果是服装类的直播，选择15平方米以上的场地更为合适；等等。具体见表2-29。

表2-29 直播场地选择

直播规模	建议场地大小	可容纳人数	其他设施需求
小型（个人直播）	10~20平方米	1~3人	基本照明、稳定网络、声音设备
中型（工作室直播）	20~50平方米	3~10人	多角度摄像、专业照明、音频设备、布景
大型（活动直播）	50~200平方米	10人以上	广播级照明、高质量音响系统、多摄像机
特大型（演唱会）	200平方米至数千平方米	100人以上	大型LED屏、高级音响设备、安全控制设施

(二) 环境条件

室内场地可以选择一个隔音和收音效果良好的空间。窗户如果过多，应考虑使用窗帘来控制自然光。室内直播场地较为封闭，一般难以保证自然光充足，需要借助补光灯进行补光。

室外场地可以是工厂、超市、商场、专业直播间等，类型十分丰富。

二、直播间分区

直播间的分区主要是为了使空间的功能性最大化，同时保证直播过程的流畅和专业。

(一) 直播区

这是主播进行直播的主要区域，出现在观众手机屏幕里面的区域，通常离镜头很近，处于镜头画面的中间位置。直播区一般有5平方米左右，可以根据直播商品体积等来灵活调整。

(二) 陈列区

陈列区指商品摆放的区域。如果商品数量较多，则需要安排货架，将商品按照类别整齐地归置好，以便幕后工作人员在最短的时间内找到所需的商品。如果是在节假日、促销日，主播还可以在直播间适当布置一些和节日相关或者跟促销商品相关的道具。

(三) 后台区

后台区指直播幕后工作人员所在的区域，用来放置直播使用的计算机、摄像头设备，以及其他直播辅助工具。

(四) 其他区域

用于主播更换服装，或者放置其他搭配品。可以根据需要，灵活设置场地大小。

三、直播间背景布置

(一) 设置虚拟背景

虚拟场景直播是运用电影电视行业的色键抠像技术，将蓝、绿幕实时抠除，再实时置换成直播需要的理想场景的一种直播技术。通过这种技术，可以轻松创建多变的、具有高度视觉吸引力的背景，使得直播内容更加丰富和专业。虚拟场景直播不仅能够节省物理空间布置的成本，还可以根据需要灵活更换背景，提高观众的观看体验。虚拟场景对于实景直播来说，有着明显的优势。首先，无需进行实景搭建，仅需要虚拟场景加上电脑制作，便捷、成本低。其次，虚拟场景更容易更换场景。实景直播间搭建完成后，更换场景需要重新准备物料，布置直播间，而虚拟场景可以根据货品种类更换背景图，实现场景变换。

1. 绿幕技术

通过在直播区后方设置绿幕，可以在后期制作中替换任何虚拟背景。这种设置允许主播根据直播内容的需要快速更换背景，非常适合需要频繁变换场景的直播，如教学、游戏等。

2. 软件支持

使用专业的直播软件，例如 OBS Studio 直播软件，来处理虚拟背景，确保背景与实时视频流畅融合，无缝切换。OBS Studio 是一款免费且开源的直播软件，支持广泛的直播和录制功能，包括虚拟背景和绿幕效果。

（二）布置实体背景

直播间实体背景是指在实际物理空间内进行装饰和布置，以营造特定的直播氛围和效果。这种背景设置需要考虑到直播内容的特性和品牌形象，通过合理的道具摆放、灯光布置和背景设计，来实现最佳的展示效果。实体背景能够提供真实的物理互动感和环境氛围，适用于展示产品细节、烹饪、手工制作等需要实景拍摄的直播场景。常见直播间背景包括以下几种。

1. 纯色背景

这类背景一般以浅色为主，比如实木/深色/莫兰迪色等低饱和度的颜色，可用墙纸或背景布。使用背景布，可以经常更换，给买家带来新鲜感，成本不会很高。一般不用白色，因为白色不利于灯光布置。

2. 品牌标志布置直播间背景

用品牌的标志布置直播间的背景，背景直观简洁，可以增加品牌效应，适用于多种直播场景。

3. 产品摆放背景

一般将产品置于展示柜进行展示，产品的摆放数量根据展示柜的大小而定，但是不宜过多。

4. 与直播产品匹配的特色背景

背景应与直播的内容紧密相关，与品牌调性一致，或与直播主题相符合，例如使用图书架作为背景来做书评节目，或设置运动器材背景来进行健身教学。

四、规划直播间产品的陈列方式

通过合理规划和巧妙设计产品陈列方式，可以显著提升直播间的视觉效果和观众体验，从而达到更好的直播营销效果。直播间产品的陈列方式根据直播间的类型不同而有所不同，具体可以采用近景、中景和远景以及商品图组合贴片等方式进行展示。以下是具体建议。

（一）近景产品陈列建议

（1）商品高度搭配：如果展示台面较低，可以使用透明展台或盒子垫高商品，以便更好地展示产品细节。两边高、中间低，避免遮挡主播，使整体布局更加和谐。

（2）镜头角度：尽可能保持平视，避免俯视角度带来的不佳效果，确保产品和主播都能被清晰地看到。

（3）道具使用：利用不同材质和颜色的置物架与小道具，营造品牌氛围，增强视觉吸引力，见图2-15。

（二）中、远景产品陈列建议

（1）同色系/同种商品摆放：将同色系或同种类的商品摆放在一起，使视觉观感整洁有序。

（2）商品高度搭配：将较高的商品摆放在后侧，形成层次感，使整体展示更有深度。

（3）展台使用：利用展台使商品错落有致地摆放。对于软质包装产品，可放置在底层或透明置物架上，以确保它们稳定且可见，见图2-16。

图2-15 近景产品陈列
图片来源：抖音直播间截图。

图2-16 中、远景产品陈列
图片来源：抖音直播间截图。

（三）直播贴片

直播贴片具有良好的视觉效果，不受现场光线和角度影响，保证展示效果一致，且无需现场摆放实物，贴片与直播间背景有机融合，使得界面视觉统一，见图2-17。

【注意】贴片内容无法临时更改，需要事先确定产品内容并进行设计制作。

（四）背景实物货柜/实物场景

将前贴片与实物场景结合，提供多样的用户体验，见图2-18。

图2-17 使用直播贴片
图片来源：抖音直播间截图。

图2-18 实物场景与直播贴片结合
图片来源：抖音直播间截图。

【注意】真实布景成本较高,需要根据预算和实际需求进行选择。

任务操作

学习完上述知识,Peter 所在的直播团队选用虚拟背景进行直播,在 20 平方米以内的直播间内,完成直播间搭建。在本次直播任务中 Peter 将使用 OBS Studio 完成直播间虚拟背景的设置。需要完成如下操作。

☞ 步骤一　选择场地

Peter 的直播团队属于小规模的直播团队,选择 10~20 平方米的直播间即可。

☞ 步骤二　布置绿幕

直播间可使用实体背景及虚拟背景两种,在本次直播任务中 Peter 选用虚拟背景。因此 Peter 需要均匀、无褶皱地挂好绿幕,确保全幅覆盖摄像头的拍摄范围,见图 2-19。

【绿幕布置注意事项】

(1) 绿幕:需无褶皱、无暗角。

(2) 灯光:需要均匀照亮绿幕,无阴影。

(3) 距离:人物、物品需要与绿幕保持一定的距离,以无影子在绿幕上为标准。

图 2-19　绿幕布置

(4) 避免同色:不能穿着带有绿色、黄色、亮蓝色的服装,不能摆放上述颜色的物品。

(5) 速度:人物与物品需要避免快速移动。

☞ 步骤三　布置直播场景

完成摄像机、提词设备架设,灯光布置及商品陈列。调整好相机高度和角度,需要确保绿幕搭建在主播的背后,主播正对摄像头。

【提示】

(1) 建议主播穿着深色系的服装,衣服边缘清晰,抠像效果较好。

(2) 直播间的打光应提早进行测试和调整,以免灯光问题导致产品色彩出现偏差,使得产品被绿幕抠掉。

☞ 步骤四　完成直播间灯光布置

☞ 步骤五　安装软件

下载、安装 OBS Studio 直播软件。打开 OBS Studio,连接设备线路。

☞ 步骤六　设置直播视频采集

点击"来源(Sources)"左下角的"+"图标,在下拉列表中选择"视频采集设备(Video Capture Device)",进行直播视频采集。

☞ 步骤七　选择滤镜

右键点击"视频采集设备(Video Capture Device)",选择"滤镜(Filters)"。

☞ 步骤八　选择"色度键"

点击"+"号,选择"色度键(Chroma Key)",点击确定。

☞ 步骤九　进行色度抠图

应用色度键滤镜后,可以看到默认的绿色已被自动选择用于抠像。如果绿幕背景与默认的绿色略有不同,可以调整"相似性(Similarity)""平滑(Smoothness)"等滑块,以优化抠像效果。

☞ **步骤十　添加和调整背景**

再次点击源列表下的"+"号,选择"媒体源(Media Source)"或"图像(Image)"添加想要的直播背景图像或视频。除了背景图片之外还可以添加一些直播贴片等,丰富直播间背景。

【注意】确保背景图层位于视频捕获设备图层的下方。

☞ **步骤十一　开始直播或录制**

背景设置完成,并且通过预览确认没有问题,就可以连接直播平台,开始直播了。

Learning Process

1. Choosing a Live Streaming Space

1.1 Live Streaming Space Planning

Plan the size of the live streaming room based on the type and content of the live stream.

For small-scale live streams (personal live streams), choose a space of 10-20 square meters.

For medium-scale live streams (studio live streams), choose a space of 20-50 square meters.

For large-scale live streams, choose a space of 50-200 square meters or more.

For extra-large live streams (such as concerts), choose a space ranging from 200 square meters to several thousand square meters.

1.2 Environmental Conditions

When selecting an indoor venue, choose a space with good sound insulation and acoustics. If there are too many windows, consider using curtains to control natural light. Indoor live streaming venues are typically enclosed, making it difficult to ensure sufficient natural light, so supplementary lighting is often necessary.

Outdoor venues can include factories, supermarkets, shopping malls, professional live streaming rooms, etc. There is a wide variety of types to choose from.

2. Live Streaming Room Partitioning

2.1 Live Streaming Area

The main area where the host performs in the live stream, is typically very close to the camera, with a recommended area of about 5 square meters.

2.2 Display Area

The area for placing products. Organize the products neatly, and the area size depends on the number of products.

2.3 Backstage Area

The area for live streaming staff, where live streaming equipment and auxiliary tools are placed.

2.4 Other Areas

Areas for the host to change clothes or place other props. The size can be adjusted flexibly based on needs.

3. Live Streaming Room Background Setup

3.1 Virtual Background Setup

Virtual scene live stream is a technology that uses chroma-keying techniques from the film and television industry to remove blue or green screens in real time and replace them with ideal backgrounds for the live stream. This technology allows for the creation of dynamic and highly visually appealing backgrounds, making the live streaming content richer and more professional. Virtual scene live stream not only saves the cost of physical space setup but also allows for flexible background changes as needed, enhancing the viewers' experience.

Green Screen Technology: Use a green screen behind the live streaming area to replace it with any virtual background during post-production. This setup allows the host to quickly change backgrounds according to the live streaming content, suitable for streams that frequently change scenes, such as teaching or gaming.

Software Support: Use professional live streaming software (such as OBS Studio) to handle the virtual background, ensuring smooth integration with the real-time video.

3.2 Physical Background Setup

A physical background in a live streaming setup refers to the decoration and arrangement in a real physical space to create a specific atmosphere and effect for the live stream. This type of background setup needs to consider the characteristics of the live streaming content and brand image, using appropriate props placement, lighting arrangement, and background design to achieve the best display effect. Physical backgrounds provide a tangible sense of interaction and environmental ambiance, making them suitable for live streams that require real-world scenes, such as product detail showcases, cooking, and crafting.

Solid Color Background: Usually light colors with low saturation, such as wood or Morandi colors. Avoid using white as it is not conducive to lighting setup.

Brand Logo Background: Decorate the live streaming room with the brand logo to enhance brand effect, suitable for various live streaming scenarios.

Product Display Background: Place products in display cabinets, with the number of products depending on the size of the cabinets, but avoid overcrowding.

Themed Background Matching Live Streaming Products: The background should closely relate to the live streaming content and align with the brand tone or the live streaming theme. For example, use a bookshelf background for book review shows or exercise equipment background for fitness tutorials.

4. Planning Product Display Methods in the Live Streaming Room

By reasonably planning and cleverly designing product display methods, the visual effect and audience experience in the live streaming room can be significantly enhanced, achieving better live streaming marketing results. The product display methods in the live streaming room vary according to the type of live streaming room, and can specifically adopt close-up, medium, and long shots as well as product image collage patches for display. Here are specific suggestions.

4.1 Suggestions on Close-up Product Display

Product Height Arrangement: If the display surface is low, you can use a transparent display stand or a box to raise the product for better detail presentation. Place higher items on both sides and lower items in the middle to avoid blocking the host and make the overall layout more harmonious.

Camera Angle: Keep the camera as level as possible to avoid the poor effect of a bird's eye view, ensuring both the product and the host are clearly visible.

Use of Props: Use storage racks and small props of different materials and colors to create a brand atmosphere and enhance visual appeal, as shown in Figure 2-15 (please see the Chinese section).

4.2 Suggestions on Medium and Long Shot Product Display

Same Color/Type Product Placement: Place products of the same color or type together to make the visual perception neat and orderly.

Product Height Matching: Place taller products at the back to form a sense of hierarchy and make the overall display more profound.

Use of Display Stands: Use display stands to place products in a staggered manner. Soft-packaged products can be placed at the bottom or on transparent storage racks to ensure they are stable and visible, as shown in Figure 2-16 (please see the Chinese section).

4.3 Product Image Collage Patches

Visual Effect: Product image collage patches have a good visual effect and are not affected by on-site lighting and angles, ensuring consistent display effects, as shown in Figure 2-17 (please see the Chinese section).

Convenience: No need to place physical products on-site, and patches organically integrate with the bottom of the live streaming room, making the interface visually unified.

Note: The product content of the patches cannot be temporarily changed and needs to be determined and designed in advance.

4.4 Background Physical Cabinets/Real Scenes

Combination of Patches and Physical Scenes: Combine the front patches with physical scenes to provide a diverse user experience, as shown in Figure 2-18 (please see the Chinese section).

Note: The cost of real scenes is high and needs to be chosen based on budget and actual needs.

Task Operations

Step 1: Choose the Venue

Select a live streaming room of 10-20 square meters.

Step 2: Set up the Green Screen

Hang the green screen evenly and without wrinkles, ensuring it fully covers the shooting range of the camera, as shown in Figure 2-19 (please see the Chinese section).

Green Screen Guidelines:

(1) Green Screen: Ensure the green screen is smooth and free of wrinkles and dark spots.

(2) Lighting: Illuminate the green screen evenly without creating shadows.

(3) Distance: Maintain a sufficient distance between subjects or objects and the green screen to avoid shadows on the screen.

(4) Avoid Same Colors: Do not wear or place objects that are green, yellow, or bright blue in front of the green screen.

(5) Speed: Avoid quick movements of people or objects to prevent green blurring effects.

Step 3: Set Up the Live Streaming Scene

Complete the setup of the camera, teleprompter equipment, lighting arrangement, and product display. Adjust the camera height and angle. Ensure the green screen is set up behind the person who faces the camera.

Tips:

(1) It is recommended that the host wears dark-colored clothing. Clear edges of the clothing help achieve a better keying effect.

(2) The lighting in the live streaming room should be tested and adjusted in advance to avoid color distortion of the products caused by lighting problems and prevent the products from being keyed out by the green screen.

Step 4: Complete the Lighting Setup

Finish setting up the lighting for the live streaming room.

Step 5: Install OBS Software

Download and install OBS Studio, and then connect the equipment.

Step 6: Set Up Video Capture

Choose the "Video Capture Device" for live streaming video capture.

Step 7: Select Filters

Add a chroma key filter to key out the green screen.

Step 8: Select "Chroma Key"

Click the "+" sign, select "Chroma Key", and click "OK".

Step 9: Optimize the Keying Effect

After applying the chroma key filter, you can see that the default green has been automatically selected for keying. If the green screen background is slightly different from the default green, you can adjust the sliders for "Similarity" and "Smoothness" to optimize the keying effect.

Step 10: Add and Adjust the Background

Click the "+" sign under the source list again, and select "Media Source" or "Image" to add the desired live background image or video. In addition to the background image, you can also add some live streaming patches to enrich the background of the live streaming room.

Step 11: Start Live Streaming or Recording

Once the background is set and confirmed to be correct through preview, you can connect to the live streaming platform and start the live stream.

课后习题

1.（单选题）根据直播内容和规模选择合适的直播空间，以下哪种场地大小最适合工作室直播？

　　A. 8 平方米左右　　　　　　　　B. 10~20 平方米
　　C. 20~50 平方米　　　　　　　　D. 50~200 平方米

2. 请简要说明直播间的分区设置及其功能，并解释为什么分区设置对于直播的成功至关重要。

3.（单选题）在直播间照明中，哪个光源的主要作用是为主体提供主要照明，确保主体面部和身体得到充足的光线？

　　A. 辅助光　　　　　　　　　　　B. 轮廓光
　　C. 顶光　　　　　　　　　　　　D. 主灯

Exercises

1. (Single Choice) Based on the content and scale of the live stream, which venue size is most suitable for a studio live stream?

　　A. Around 8 square meters　　　　B. 10-20 square meters
　　C. 20-50 square meters　　　　　 D. 50-200 square meters

2. Please briefly describe the partitioning of the live streaming room and its functions, and explain why partitioning is crucial for the success of a live stream.

3. (Single Choice) In live streaming lighting, which light source primarily provides the main illumination for the subject, ensuring adequate lighting for the subject's face and body?

　　A. Fill light　　　　　　　　　　B. Back light
　　C. Top light　　　　　　　　　　 D. Key light

任务 5　开展直播预热

任务导入

直播预热，本质上是一场精心策划的宣传活动，旨在通过提前发布吸引眼球的文案、海报和短视频等内容，来提高公众对即将到来的直播的期待和参与意愿。在直播真正开始之前，StreamASEAN 直播电商公司向 Peter 下达任务：多渠道开展直播预热。

在这一任务中，Peter 负责创作引人入胜的预热文案、设计视觉冲击力强的海报以及制作内容丰富的预热视频，通过社交媒体、电子邮件、合作伙伴渠道等多种方式广泛传播，以吸引潜在观众的注意力，并有效引流到即将举行的直播，确保直播的高观看率和互动率。

任务目标

¤ 知识目标

1. 熟悉直播预热的方式

2. 了解直播视频、图文预热的方法
¤ 技能目标
1. 能够为直播间引流
2. 能够制作图文、短视频预热素材
¤ 素养目标
培养学生团结协作精神和组织协调能力

任务流程

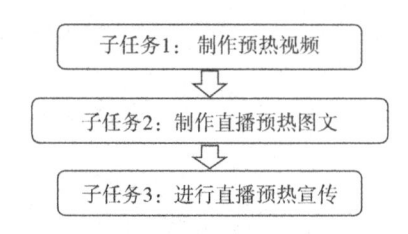

```
子任务1：制作预热视频
      ↓
子任务2：制作直播预热图文
      ↓
子任务3：进行直播预热宣传
```

子任务 1　制作预热视频

学习过程

预热视频是一种专为直播活动设计的宣传视频，旨在提升公众对即将到来的直播活动的认知与兴趣。这类视频精心挑选内容亮点，结合活动预告、特别嘉宾介绍以及其他相关吸引人的元素，有效地激发观众的期待并引发讨论。在Peter的直播团队开始制作预热视频之前，Peter对预热视频的知识做了如下了解。

一、直播预热视频的分类

（一）植入型预热

这种形式发布的预热视频在前半段输出和以往视频内容保持一致的内容，吸引固定粉丝观看，然后在后半段进行直播预热，通过设置悬念、透露直播亮点或介绍直播主题、内容、商品的形式，吸引粉丝的关注。

类似于新媒体软文的思路，在文章的开头按照往常的思路输出垂直领域的内容，只是在文尾结束的时候宣布直播的主题和时间。

（二）利益点预热

对于没有关注主播的用户来说，主播希望通过预热视频来吸引用户进入直播间，就需要在预热视频中添加利益点，来增强视频的诱惑力，从而激发观看视频用户的好奇心和兴趣，并采取行动，预约直播或者关注主播。

（三）直播亮点预热

可以将本场直播中的亮点内容作为预热视频的主题，直播亮点可以是特殊嘉宾、特色环节、特色场景等。例如某场直播邀请某个明星、某知名人物或者连线其他品牌直播间等。

（四）直播片段预热

有些重要的直播活动可以通过直播前发布直播筹备阶段花絮，或者以往直播活动发生过的一些有趣事情，为直播活动引流造势。

二、直播预热视频制作要求

(一) 原创竖屏

制作原创、首发的竖版短视频,会让平台认为是优质视频。视频封面要求清晰吸睛,主题突出,视频内容垂直,与以往主题一致。

(二) 内容优质

一个优质的短视频内容要考虑对目标顾客是否具有价值,可以是直播间的好物推荐、直播间优惠券领取方法、直播间嘉宾的互动等。优质有价值的视频内容可以提高视频点击率,从而达到引流目的。

(三) 推广效果好

短视频一般开播前两天开始发布,一开始可尝试小额付费推广,然后通过播放量、获客成本等数据分析短视频是否具有潜力,效果好则继续付费投放。衡量预热效果好坏,可通过直播开播后第一个小时内的观看数据来看。

三、制作直播预热视频的工具

直播视频素材的剪辑主要在手机端和 PC 电脑端进行,使用 Premiere、CapCut(剪映国外版)等视频剪辑工具完成直播视频素材的剪辑。可以为直播视频素材配上字幕、音效和旁白,制作出精美有趣的直播切片或短视频预告,上传至各平台,为直播引流推广。

任务操作

学习完上述知识,Peter 所在的直播团队将分工为即将进行的直播活动创建一个有吸引力的宣传视频。Peter 需要完成如下操作。

☞ 步骤一 拍摄直播预热视频

(一) 确定短视频选题

【提示】在拍摄短视频之前需要确定选题,一个具有创意、足够吸引人的选题能够在第一时间抓住用户的注意力。

(二) 策划短视频内容

在确定选题后,短视频创作者还需要策划短视频的具体内容。

Peter 首先应完成宣传短视频脚本撰写。脚本应包括以下内容:

(1) 一个吸引人的开头。

(2) 关于即将进行的直播活动的信息(日期、时间、平台)。

(3) 观众可以期待的亮点。

(4) 一个有力的行动号召(如"关注我们""不要错过"等)。

短视频拍摄脚本

场景:

人物:

道具:

镜头 1:

镜头 2:

镜头 3:

（三）准备拍摄设备及场地

准备拍摄设备，选择场地，并把相关内容填写在表 2-30 中。

表 2-30　拍摄场地及设备

项目	内容
场地选择	
拍摄工具	
辅助工具	

（四）短视频拍摄

以写好的脚本为依据，架设好相机或使用手机设备拍摄所需画面素材。

☞ **步骤二　使用 CapCut 制作直播宣传视频**

完成短视频拍摄后，Peter 选择使用 CapCut 对视频进行剪辑。具体操作步骤如下。

（1）下载适用于 Windows 或 macOS 的安装包。完成安装过程。打开 CapCut 应用。点击首页的"新建项目（New Project）"按钮，进入项目编辑界面。

（2）点击"媒体（Media）" ⇒ "导入（Import）"，导入需要编辑的视频文件和图片。可以拖放或使用导入按钮把媒体文件添加到时间轴上。

（3）原始视频素材通常需要经过裁剪处理。直播团队需要使用视频分割功能，对原始视频素材进行分割，以便进行后续的视频裁剪处理。

点击时间线上的分割按钮。点击时间轴上的视频，视频轨道中的视频画面即以时间轴为基点进行分割，分割后时间轴的左侧和右侧会显示分割标记。

（4）添加背景音乐有助于为视频渲染特定的氛围。点击"音频（Audio）"可选择合适的背景音乐及音效，并将音乐及音效拖动到时间轴上，对应视频需要添加音乐及特效的位置。

（5）在视频中添加合适的文字、字幕。点击"文字（Text）"进入文字选择页面，在画面上添加文字、字幕。

（6）根据实际需要点击"贴纸（Stickers）""特效（Effects）"和"转场（Transitions）"，增强视觉效果。

【提示】直播预告短视频时间不宜过长，最好保持在 30 秒以内。另外还要将直播地点、直播时间、直播主题展示在短视频显眼位置。

Learning Process

1. Types of Live Streaming Warm-up Videos

1.1 Embedded Warm-up

The warm-up video starts with content similar to previous videos to attract regular followers, and then transitions to live streaming promotion by creating suspense, revealing highlights, or introducing the live streaming topic and products.

1.2 Benefit-Based Warm-up

To attract users who do not follow the host, the warm-up video includes benefits (e.g., discounts or gifts) to enhance the video's appeal, spark curiosity and interest, and encourage users to book the live stream or follow the host.

1.3 Highlight-Based Warm-up

The warm-up video focuses on key highlights of the upcoming live stream, such as special guests, unique segments, or special scenes, to attract attention.

1.4 Segment-Based Warm-up

Important live streaming events can be promoted by releasing behind-the-scenes footage or interesting moments from previous live streams to generate interest and drive traffic.

2. Requirements for Making Live Streaming Warm-up Videos

2.1 Original Vertical Videos

Create original, first-release vertical short videos to be recognized as high-quality content by platforms. The video cover should be clear and eye-catching, with a prominent theme and consistent content.

2.2 High-Quality Content

Ensure the short video content is valuable to the target audience, such as product recommendations, voucher retrieval methods, or guest interactions. High-quality and valuable content can increase video clicks and drive traffic.

2.3 Good Promotion Effect

Post the short video two days before the live stream. Start with a small paid promotion, analyze the video potential through play rates and customer acquisition costs, and continue paid promotion if effective. Measure the warm-up effect by the number of viewers in the first hour of the live stream.

3. Tools for Making Live Streaming Warm-up Videos

Editing live streaming video mainly uses mobile and PC tools. On PC, tools like Premiere and CapCut can be used to edit live streaming video clips. Add subtitles, sound effects, and voiceovers to create attractive and interesting live streaming clips or short video previews, which can then be uploaded to various platforms for promotion.

Task Operations

Step 1: Shooting Live Streaming Warm-up Videos

1.1 Determine the Short Video Topic

Before shooting a short video, it is crucial to determine the topic. The topic is related to the target audience of the short video and influences the depth and breadth of the content. A creative and engaging topic can immediately capture the user's attention.

1.2 Plan the Short Video Content

After determining the topic, the short video creator needs to plan the specific content of the short video.

Complete the script writing for the promotional short video. Note that the script should include the following elements.

(1) An engaging opening.

(2) Information about the upcoming live event (date, time, platform).

(3) Highlights that viewers can look forward to.

(4) A strong call to action.

1.3 Prepare Shooting Equipment and Location

1.4 Shoot the Short Video

Based on the prepared script, set up the camera or use mobile devices to shoot the necessary footage.

Step 2: Using CapCut to Create Live Streaming Promotion Videos

(1) Download and install CapCut for Windows or macOS. Open the CapCut App and click "New project" to enter the editing interface.

(2) Click "Media" ⇒ "Import" to upload the video files and images to be edited.

(3) Use the video splitting function to divide the original video material for subsequent editing. Click the split button on the timeline to split the video at the desired points.

(4) Add background music to create a specific atmosphere. Click "Audio" to select suitable background music and sound effects, and drag them to the timeline.

(5) Add appropriate text and subtitles to the video. Click "Text" to enter the text selection page and add text and subtitles to the screen.

(6) Enhance the visual effects by adding "Stickers", "Effects", and "Transitions" as needed.

Tips: Keep the warm-up short video under 30 seconds. Highlight the live streaming location, time, theme, and other key details prominently in the video.

子任务2　制作直播预热图文

学习过程

直播团队可以利用图文编辑工具，设计直播预热图文宣传物料。如果直播活动的规格较高、影响力较大，则建议直播团队使用专业设计师设计的海报和封面图。在制作直播预热图文之前，Peter对直播预热图文的知识了解如下。

一、直播预热文案设计要点

广告大师大卫·奥格威说过这样一句话："阅读广告标题的人是阅读广告正文的5倍。"如果直播预热文案毫无吸引力，可能很大一部分用户就不会进入直播间观看主播对于具体产品的讲解。那么，直播预热文案怎么写吸引人？下面介绍几种文案写作技巧。

（一）借势型

目前，很多直播间会邀请当红明星到直播间做客，直接借"名人"的势来宣传造势，这样可以吸引大量明星粉丝关注，自然可以提高直播间关注度。

（二）抽奖型

借助一些平台的互动抽奖方式，让文案可以传播得更快。大部分人或多或少都会有"占便宜"的心理，物质上的或者是精神上的。

（三）价值包装型

给直播预热文案做一次价值包装，如果用户从你的文案中看到了"价值"，自然就会进入你的直播间。例如，助农直播预热文案。

（四）设置悬念型

设置悬念，勾起用户的好奇心。比如，用"欲语还休"的方式勾起用户的好奇心，让人产生进入直播间的欲望。

二、直播预热海报设计要点

图片能够直观地体现直播的内容和主题，直播之前要准备好预热需要的图片素材，一般图片形式有活动海报、直播产品清单。

（一）直播预热海报

直播预热海报设计的时候要考虑以下要点。

（1）体现直播活动主题。

（2）呈现活动要素，例如直播时间、直播渠道、直播产品、出镜主播等。如果是品牌专场活动，需体现品牌名称、品牌标志等信息。

（3）符合直播活动主题，配色和谐，排版合理，符合审美习惯。

（4）尺寸建议使用竖屏图，符合多数人阅读媒介手机的使用习惯。

（5）海报要从用户的角度考虑，吸引消费者的注意力。

（二）产品清单图

一般以长图形式呈现，可以在直播海报图的基础上增加本场直播的产品及活动信息，具体要求如下。

（1）可按照直播流程中产品发布的顺序依次排列，呈现产品。

（2）要有产品品牌、名称、图片、直播价格、促销内容、赠品等信息。

（3）产品清单图可以进行直播间价格与日常价格的对比，或标明折扣。

（4）在产品清单长图尾部建议增加引导用户关注直播的教学步骤。

任务操作

学习完上述知识，Peter 需与直播团队成员共同完成如下操作。

☞ **步骤一　设计预热文案**

参考预热文案设计的写作技巧，为即将开展的直播设计一段预热文案。

☞ **步骤二　制作预热海报**

（1）根据海报想要达到的视觉效果，拍摄所需图片素材。

【提示】确保素材拍摄清晰、具有吸引力，能够直观传达直播的主要卖点和吸引力。

（2）使用简单的图像编辑工具（如 Canva、Photoshop 或其他图像编辑工具）来编辑和组合图片，制作一张直播预热海报。

❋ **案例参考**

（1）访问 Canva 网站，登录或注册账号。

（2）搜索并选择合适的海报模板，部分模板需付费，模板中的图文元素可进行编辑和替换；也可以通过上传拍摄的图片素材进行海报设计，点击"上传（Uploads）"上传本地图，拖动到设计页面，调整大小和位置进行设计。

（3）根据需要选择预设尺寸，或者点击"自定义尺寸（Custom Size）"输入具体的宽度和高度。

（4）编辑文本和图片。点击左侧工具栏的"文本（Text）"按钮，选择并添加合适的文本框。点击左侧工具栏的"元素（Elements）"或"图片（Photos）"按钮，搜索并选择需要的图片或图形元素。

（5）添加装饰性图形、图标或插图，使海报更加生动和有吸引力。通过左侧工具栏的"元素（Elements）"选项，选择并调整装饰元素的位置和大小。

（6）保存和下载。点击"下载（Download）"按钮，选择合适的文件格式（如 PNG、JPEG 或 PDF）。保存并下载海报到本地计算机，或者直接分享到社交媒体或打印。

Learning Process

1. Key Points for Designing Live Streaming Warm-up Copy

Advertising master David Ogilvy once said, "Five times as many people read the headline as read the body copy." Similarly, if the live streaming warm-up copy is not attractive, most users will not enter the live stream to watch the host's product presentation. Here are several effective copywriting techniques.

1.1 Leverage-Based Warm-up Copy

Invite popular celebrities to the live stream. Using the celebrity effect can attract a large number of fans and increase the attention of the live stream.

1.2 Lottery-Based Warm-up Copy

Use interactive lottery methods on the platform to spread the copy faster, leveraging people's inclination to get something for free.

1.3 Value-Based Warm-up Copy

Highlight the value in the warm-up copy. If users see value, they are more likely to enter the live stream. For example, agricultural assistance live streaming warm-up copy.

1.4 Suspense-Based Warm-up Copy

Create suspense to arouse users' curiosity. For example, using a "hinting without revealing" approach to arouse curiosity and drive people to enter the live stream.

2. Key Points for Designing Live Streaming Warm-up Posters

Images can intuitively convey the content and theme of the live stream. Before the live stream, prepare the necessary image materials, such as event posters and live streaming product lists. Consider the following points when designing warm-up posters.

2.1 Event Posters

(1) Reflect the live streaming theme.

(2) Present key elements, such as live streaming time, channel, products, and host. For brand-specific events, they include the brand name and logo.

(3) Align with the live streaming theme. Ensure harmonious colors and reasonable layouts that conform to aesthetic habits.

(4) Use vertical images. This format is more suitable for most people's mobile reading habits.

(5) Consider the user's perspective to attract consumer attention.

2.2 Live Streaming Product Lists

Product lists are usually presented as long images and can include additional information about the products and activities of the live stream. Requirements are:

(1) Arrange products in sequence according to the order of product introduction during the live stream.

(2) Include product brand, name, image, live price, promotional content, and giveaways.

(3) Compare live streaming prices with regular prices or indicate discounts.

(4) Add steps at the end of the product list to guide users on how to follow the live stream.

Task Operations

Step 1: Design Warm-up Copy

Refer to copywriting techniques to design warm-up copy for the upcoming live stream.

Step 2: Design Warm-up Posters

(1) Capture the necessary image materials based on the desired visual effect of the poster.

Tip: Ensure the captured materials are clear and engaging, and able to visually convey the main selling points and appeal of the live stream.

(2) Use simple image editing tools (such as Canva, Photoshop, or other image editing tools) to edit and combine the images. Create a live streaming promo poster.

✽ Reference

(1) Visit the Canva website and log in or sign up for an account.

(2) Search for and select an appropriate poster template (some templates may require payment). The text and image elements in the template can be edited and replaced.

You can also upload the captured image materials for the poster design. Click "Uploads" to upload local images, drag them to the design page, and adjust the size and position.

(3) Select preset dimensions or click "Custom Size" to input the specific width and height.

(4) Edit the text and images. Click the "Text" button on the left toolbar, select, and add the appropriate text box. Click the "Elements" or "Photos" button on the left toolbar to search for and select the needed image or graphic elements.

(5) Add decorative graphics, icons, or illustrations to make the poster more vivid and attractive. Use the "Elements" option on the left toolbar to select and adjust the decorative position and size of elements.

(6) Save and download. Click the "Download" button, select the appropriate file format (e.g., PNG, JPEG, or PDF).

子任务3 进行直播预热宣传

学习过程

完成了直播预热的视频、图文素材的制作后，为了确保预热宣传的效果最大化，

Peter 将利用多种渠道广泛传播这些素材。在进行预热宣传前，Peter 对直播渠道的知识了解如下。

直播预热的主要渠道有两种：自有渠道和合作渠道，其中已关注的粉丝主要来自自有渠道，平台引流和平台外引流流量主要来源于合作渠道。

一、自有渠道

自有渠道包括企业的 Facebook、Twitter、TikTok 等社交媒体渠道，也可以使用 EDM（电子邮件营销）定期触达用户。自有渠道触达已关注的粉丝以及私域流量，目标性比较强，粉丝质量比较高。开播前几个小时在自有渠道进行多次预告，把直播的内容和优惠活动通过这些渠道传达给粉丝，吸引转化率高的粉丝进入直播间。

二、合作渠道

与行业 KOL（Key Opinion Leader，关键意见领袖）和其他自媒体平台合作，或使用平台的付费资源位。以 TikTok 平台为例，TikTok 可通过联盟渠道，找到合适的达人来推广，从而提高转化率。TikTok 的 Promote 投放将通过直播预览流的方式提高直播间的曝光，用户可在刷短视频时，看到直播间的预览卡片，并一键点击屏幕即可进入直播间。

任务操作

学习完上述知识，Peter 需要完成如下操作。

☞ **步骤一　列出推广渠道**

为完成预热宣传任务，Peter 首先需列出所有可以使用的宣传渠道，确定预热时间，并填写在表 2-31 中。

表 2-31　直播预热前准备

项目	内容
宣传渠道	
预热主题	
直播预热时间	
素材内容	

☞ **步骤二　发布预热内容**

在各大社交媒体、电商平台、内容平台和即时通信工具上发布预热内容。

以 TikTok 平台为例，具体操作如下。

（1）点击 TikTok 上的"+"，在相册中选择使用已存储的视频，点击"下一步（Next）"完成短视频发布。

（2）插入倒计时贴纸，添加推荐产品，点击"下一步（Next）"完成短视频上传。输入预热短视频标题及添加直播封面，点击"发布（Post）"，完成直播预热短视频的发布。

【提示】提前 3~7 天发布预热短视频。

（3）使用直播预约贴纸录制宣传视频。如果已经完成直播活动预约，则可以添加直播预约链接，然后点击"发布（Post）"，发布直播预热视频。

Learning Process

The main channels for live streaming warm-up are owned channels and partnership channels.

1. Owned Channels

Owned channels include the company's social media platforms such as Facebook, Twitter, TikTok, and EDM (Email Direct Marketing) to regularly reach users. These channels mainly target already subscribed followers and private traffic, making them highly targeted and of high quality. Several hours before the live stream, multiple announcements about the content of live stream and promotional activities are made through these channels to attract high-conversion followers to the live stream.

2. Partnership Channels

Collaborate with industry KOLs (Key Opinion Leaders) and other self-media platforms, or use the paid resources of the platform. For example, on the TikTok platform, suitable influencers can be found through affiliate channels to promote and increase conversion rates. TikTok's Promote feature boosts live streaming exposure through preview of live streams, allowing users to see preview cards while browsing short videos and click to enter the live stream with one tap.

Task Operations

Step 1: List Promotion Channels

List all available promotion channels, determine the warm-up schedule.

Step 2: Post the Warm-up Content

Post the warm-up content on main social media, e-commerce platforms, content platforms, and instant messaging tools.

Below is an example of specific operations on the TikTok platform.

(1) Click the "+" on TikTok, select the stored video from the album, and click "Next" to upload the short video.

(2) Insert a countdown sticker, add recommended products, click "Next" to upload, type the video title, add the live streaming cover, and click "Post" to complete the upload.

Note: Post the warm-up short video 3–7 days in advance.

(3) Use the live streaming reservation sticker to record a promotional video. If the live streaming event reservation is complete, add the live streaming reservation link and click "Post" to publish the warm-up video.

课后习题

1. （多选题）以下哪些选项是有效的直播预热文案设计技巧？

　　A. 借势型直播预热文案

　　B. 抽奖型直播预热文案

　　C. 悬念型直播预热文案

　　D. 无需设计文案，只需简单描述产品

2. （多选题）设计直播预热海报时需要考虑哪些要点？

　　A. 体现直播活动主题

B. 只使用横屏图

C. 呈现活动要素，例如直播时间和直播渠道

D. 配色和排版合理，符合审美习惯

3. 请简述直播预热视频的四种分类，并简要说明每种分类的特点。

Exercises

1. （Multiple Choice）Which of the following are effective techniques for designing live streaming warm-up copy?

A. Leverage-based warm-up copy

B. Lottery-based warm-up copy

C. Suspense-based warm-up copy

D. No need to design copy, just simply describe the product

2. （Multiple Choice）What factors should be considered when you design a live streaming warm-up poster?

A. Reflect the theme of the live streaming event

B. Only use horizontal images

C. Present elements such as live streaming time and channel

D. Harmonious color scheme and reasonable layout, in line with aesthetic habits

3. Briefly describe the four types of live streaming warm-up videos and explain the characteristics of each.

项目 3　使用 Shopee 平台进行直播

项目概述

Shopee Live 是 Shopee 平台的一项社交销售功能，可以与购物者进行优质互动，通过商品演示、折扣、赠品等来推动销售。消费者可以通过实时聊天进行互动，了解产品的更多信息，并在观看直播时直接购买。通过与消费者交谈，卖家可以更好地了解他们的需求，并为他们创造更好的购物体验。为了在 Shopee 平台上开展直播业务，StreamASEAN 直播电商公司向 Peter 所在的直播团队下达任务：在 Shopee 平台上完成直播设置，并开启直播。

在本项目中，Peter 将了解 Shopee 平台的开播流程及直播工具设置的知识，提前为开播做准备。

项目目标

¤ 知识目标
1. 熟悉 Shopee Live 直播规范
2. 学习 Shopee Live 开播流程
3. 了解 Shopee Live 直播工具设置

¤ 技能目标
1. 能够在 Shopee 平台进行直播
2. 掌握直播营销技巧

¤ 素养目标
传播积极内容和价值观，注重社会责任和道德价值

任务 1　学习 Shopee Live 的开播流程

学习过程

Shopee Live 的开播流程涉及准备直播内容、设置直播间信息、测试设备连接、确保库存充足、宣传预告等关键步骤。在开播前，直播团队需要在 Shopee Live 中完成直播标题、封面、描述、添加产品等信息设置，准备好要展示的商品，并确保设备正常工作，同时应提前宣传直播，吸引观众关注，为直播带来更多的流量。

Peter 了解到目前 Shopee Live 开播的方式有两种。一种是使用 App 端进行直播，优势在于直播灵活便捷，可以随时随地进行直播，适合于移动环境下的直播场景。一种是使用 PC 端进行直播，优势在于直播更加稳定，适合于需要更多功能和更高画质的直播场景。无论选择哪种方式，都需要确保直播设备和网络连接良好，以提供流畅的直播

体验。

一、Shopee Live 直播规范

在开播之前，Peter 应该先了解使用 Shopee Live 直播时需要遵守的规范。具体直播规范见表 3-1。

表 3-1　Shopee Live 直播规范

项目	内容	违规程度
未按排期开直播	预约 Shopee 排期直播，但却未按照指定的时间开始直播	轻度
直播内容不佳	产品展示不佳、音效不佳、图像不佳、背景杂乱、直播呈现效果不佳等	轻度
直播无真人解说	为确保高质量的直播，没有真人解说的直播将被警告	轻度
图像内容违规	可能引起焦虑或恐惧的令人不安的内容	轻度
有关动物虐待内容	任何形式的动物虐待、残忍行为、交易或动物剥削行为都将直接从平台上删除	中度
泄露个人信息	禁止有意或无意展示个人信息的内容	中度
粗俗内容	软色情、不当行为	中度
知识产权侵权	侵犯他人知识产权（版权和商标）的直播将被删除	中度
未成年直播	必须年满 18 周岁，才能在 Shopee 中创建直播	中度
误导/错误的信息	描述与直播内容不符、未经授权使用 Shopee logo	中度
无效内容/滥用平台功能	重复的直播（一景二机）静态展示、未与观众互动	中度
平台以外交易/信息	导向 Shopee 以外的信息、交易，引导买家到其他平台交易	重度
滥用优惠	既没有推广商品，也没有与观众进行适当的互动	重度
直播欺骗行为	使用多个账户同时直播相同的内容（重复直播）	重度
欺诈和诈骗	蓄意欺骗的行为，如网络钓鱼诈骗	重度
不当的商品	宣传/售卖违禁商品（包括原石等）	重度
不当的交易行为	涉及赌博性质的行为	重度
包含骚扰/网络霸凌	威胁、恐吓或使他人人身安全遭到威胁	重度
有害/伤害性内容	自杀和自残、暴力和犯罪活动、骚扰等	重度
敏感政治/宗教内容	宣扬暴力活动、讨论政治敏感内容、发表有关宗教的争议性言论	重度
包含色情内容	任何形式的色情或露骨内容	重度
包含性活动内容	裸体、性活动、性服务、性剥削和性虐待	重度

二、Shopee Live 开播流程

（一）App 端开播流程

1. 创建直播

通过 Shopee App "我（Me）"页面，选择"直播视频（Livestream）" ⇒ "创建直播（Create Stream）"。

2. 填写直播基本信息

填写/上传直播基本信息。

（1）直播标题：直播标题上限为 200 个字符，可输入表情符号。

（2）直播封面：可上传与直播主题或店铺有关、有吸引力的图。

（3）直播介绍：可填写店铺介绍、直播促销活动信息、主播身高体重信息（如有必要）等内容。

3. 添加商品

为直播添加相关商品。点击"新增相关商品（Add Related Products）"，最多添加 500 种商品，以便在直播中进行标记，然后点击"下一步（Next）"。

【提示】你可以通过右方的图标删除或重新排序直播商品。

4. 设置美颜和滤镜效果

点击"效果（Effect）"图标，开启直播美颜和滤镜功能。你可以调整主播的外观，包括磨皮、美白、脸部调整、眼部调整、小头等，也可以为直播间设置不同的视觉效果，如阴天效果、花朵效果等。在直播过程中可以随时调整美颜和滤镜效果。

5. 通知粉丝

选中"通知粉丝（Notify Followers）"，系统会在直播开始前 3 分钟内向你的粉丝发送直播通知。

6. 开始直播

上述步骤都确认完成后，点击"开始直播（Go Live）"，你的直播将于 3 秒后开始。

（二）PC 端开播流程

在本任务中，Peter 的直播团队将在 PC 端使用 Shopee 进行直播，具体步骤如下。

1. 创建直播

通过 Shopee "卖家中心（Seller Center）" ⇒ "营销中心（Marketing Center）"页面，选择"直播视频（Live Streaming）"，即可创建直播。

2. 填写直播基本信息

填写/上传直播基本信息。

（1）直播标题：建议不要超过 20 个字符。

（2）直播封面：图片尺寸建议 1∶1，否则将自动调整。

（3）直播介绍：可填写店铺介绍、直播促销活动信息、主播身高体重信息（如有必要）等内容。

（4）相关商品：选择商店商品，最多可添加 500 个。

（5）直播类型：包含普通直播和测试直播。

【提示】

（1）试播、重播会自动隐藏，你无法在商店页面展示试播、重播。

（2）在创建试播时，无论你是否点击"通知粉丝（Notify Followers）"，都不会触发推播通知。

（3）试播开始后，观众数量会变为 1（指卖家自身）。

3. 使用 OBS 软件进行直播

（1）前往网址 https：//obsproject.com/，下载并安装适用电脑系统的 OBS 软件。

（2）打开 OBS 软件，点击"设置（Settings）" ⇒ "直播"（Stream），选择服务为"自定义（Custom）"，复制"链接（URL）"到服务器；复制"钥匙（Key）"到推流码中，然后点击"OK"。

（3）点击"+"号，添加视频采集设备。选择"FaceTime 高清摄像头（FaceTime HD Camera）"视频采集设备，即可显示出你的摄像头。

【注意】不同的系统视频采集设备可能会不一样。

(4）按住方框上的圆点，可以拖动调整视频画面比例，以适应 720×1280 的画布，达到最佳的显示效果。点击"开始直播（Start Streaming）"。

（5）回到 Shopee "卖家中心（Seller Center）"，点击"开始直播（Go Live）"，勾选"通知粉丝（Notify Followers）"，即可完成开播。

【注意】结束直播时，请先到 OBS，点击"停止直播（Stop Streaming）"，再回到 Shopee Live 直播网页，点击"结束直播（End Live）"。

任务操作

学习完上述知识，Peter 所在的直播团队需要完成以下操作。

☞ **步骤一　确定直播产品**

选择一款直播产品：＿＿＿＿＿＿＿＿＿＿＿＿＿＿。

☞ **步骤二　进行模拟直播**

在完成了直播脚本策划、直播间搭建等直播前的准备之后，Peter 及其直播团队根据所确定的主题进行模拟直播，直播团队需要各司其职，在平台上完成模拟直播操作。

要求：

（1）使用 Shopee 平台进行模拟直播。

（2）完成模拟直播的时间限制在 5～10 分钟。

（3）结束模拟直播后，需要对直播表现进行评估，进行直播优化。

☞ **步骤三　模拟直播评估**

根据表 3-2，进行评估。

表 3-2　模拟直播评估标准

评估项目	评估标准
直播操作	直播开播步骤均已完成，操作合理
直播内容	话术讲解合理
	商品属性及卖点讲解准确到位
	销售促单具有吸引力
	主播礼仪得体，形象良好，人设鲜明

Learning Process

1. Shopee Live Streaming Regulations

Minor Violations: Examples include not starting the live stream as scheduled, poor live streaming quality, lack of real-person commentary, and inappropriate image content.

Moderate Violations: Examples include animal cruelty, leaking personal information, vulgar content, intellectual property infringement, and misleading information.

Severe Violations: Examples include off-platform transactions, abuse of promotions, fraudulent behavior, inappropriate products, harassment/cyberbullying, and other serious infractions.

2. Shopee Live Streaming Process

2.1 App Live Streaming Process

Create a Live Stream: Choose to create a live stream through the Shopee App.

Fill in Basic Information: Include live streaming title, cover image, and description.

Add Products: Display up to 500 products during the live stream.

Set Beauty and Filter Effects: Adjust the appearance of the host and visual effects.

Notify Followers: The system will notify followers 3 minutes before the live stream starts.

Start a Live Stream: Click "Go Live" to start the live stream after confirming the steps above.

2.2 PC Live Streaming Process

Creating a Live Stream: Create a live stream through the Shopee "Seller Center".

Fill in Basic Information: Fill in the live streaming title, cover image, and description.

Add Products: Select up to 500 shop products.

Use OBS Software for Live Stream: Set up video capture devices, adjust the screen ratio, and start streaming.

Notify Followers and Start a Live Stream: Complete the live settings, notify followers, and start the live stream.

Task Operations

Step 1: Select a Live Streaming Product

Choose one product for the live stream.

Step 2: Conduct a Mock Live Stream

After completing the live streaming script planning and setting up the live streaming room and lighting, the team will conduct a mock live stream based on the determined theme. Each team member should perform their specific roles and complete the mock live stream on the platform.

Step 3: Evaluate the Mock Live Stream

The evaluation criteria for mock live streams are shown in Table 3-1.

Table 3-1: Evaluation Criteria for Mock Live Streams

Evaluation Item	Evaluation Criterion
Live Streaming Operation	All steps for starting the live stream are completed and operations are reasonable
Live Streaming Content	Script and explanations are reasonable
	Product attributes and selling points are accurately explained
	Sales promotion is attractive
	Host's manners are appropriate, appearance is good, and persona is distinct

任务 2 学习 Shopee Live 直播营销工具

学习过程

在直播期间，可以使用许多工具来提高订单转化率，同时让直播更有趣，更吸引观众。创造有趣的直播活动可以帮助与买家建立良好的关系，吸引他们持续关注商店未来的直播。对此，Peter 了解到有以下几种直播营销工具可以有助于推动订单转化。

一、Shopee 币奖励

Shopee 币是平台的官方虚拟货币。对于卖家来说，Shopee 币也叫作卖家金币。卖家可以在 Shopee 直播、商店游戏和评论奖励中向买家赠送 Shopee 币。买家在 Shopee 的所有商店消费时，可以使用 Shopee 币抵现。

高效引流：有金币标识的直播更容易吸引观众。据统计，有金币发放的直播观看量是没金币的 2~6 倍。

增加留存：金币会每几分钟才发放一次，观众在等待金币发放的过程中会观看直播内容，观众停留时间越长，出单概率越大。

同时，Shopee 币对卖家有以下帮助：

（1）增加与买家的互动，提高粉丝黏性。

（2）为商店吸粉引流，提高商店流量。

（3）加强商品的曝光，优化商店转化率。

具体操作流程如下。

1. 充值 Shopee 币

通过 Shopee "卖家中心（Seller Center）" ⇒ "营销中心（Marketing Center）"页面，选择"卖家金币（Seller Coins）"，点击"充值（Top Up）"，选择你需要购买的金币数额，完成支付。

2. 在直播前设置金币发放规则

选择"促销活动（Promotion）"，点击"金币奖励（Coins Reward）"，再次点击"管理（Manage）"。

设置 Shopee 币的"预算（Budget）"，再设置每次 Shopee 币发放的频率，最后点击"保存（Save）"，即可完成 Shopee 币发放设置。

【提示】如果需要更多金币，也可以在设置金币奖励时点击"充值（Top Up）"直接充值。

二、直播促销

通过为产品提供直播独家价格来提高买家转化率，还可以为直播专享价格设置时间限制。观众将能够看到倒计时器和直播独家销售价格的剩余库存。

【注意】直播促销商品在你的购物袋列表的顶部显示。如果你的产品有超过一个变体选项，你可以为每个变体设置不同的流媒体价格，一次一个。当你设置有时间限制的直播促销价格时，促销价格适用于所选的生产变体选项，而计时器设置只能在产品级别进行不同的设置。

除了在直播前添加商品外，在直播期间也可以添加商品，点击添加/删除，然后选择更多商品。直播促销商品无法删除，需要取消直播促销价格后才可以删除。

【提示】如果某件商品恰好成为直播期间的热门话题，一定要把它添加到购物袋中，以提高即时转化率。如果你的直播吸引了其他类型的受众，那就即兴添加一些他们可能感兴趣的商品。

三、分享优惠券

在直播中持续提供优惠券期间，观看者将能在直播和整个应用程序中看到优惠券标签。使用优惠券将有助于增加浏览量和订单。你可以在直播期间出示商店优惠券，优惠券分为 30 秒优惠券和永久优惠券。

【注意】30 秒优惠券将向购物者展示 30 秒，并在全部认领后消失，你还可以随时关闭并删除优惠券标签。

具体操作流程如下。

1. 创建直播优惠券

通过 Shopee "卖家中心（Seller Center）" ⇒ "营销中心（Marketing Center）" 页面，选择 "优惠券（Vouchers）"，创建直播优惠券。

根据优惠券的内容，填写直播优惠券基本详情、奖励设置及可以优惠的商品，最后点击 "确认（Confirm）"，完成直播优惠券的创建。

2. 在直播中分享优惠券

选择 "促销活动（Promotion）"，点击 "优惠券（Vouchers）"，再次点击 "管理（Manage）"。

在直播期间，点击 "展示优惠券（Show Voucher）" 可以向观众分享优惠券；根据需要手动点击 "展示优惠券（Show Voucher）" 以鼓励参与者领取优惠券，优惠券旁边会有倒计时。点击 "填加优惠券（Add Voucher）" 添加创建的优惠券到优惠券展示页面。

【注意】优惠券弹出只有 30 秒。

四、竞拍

竞拍工具是 Shopee 平台提供的一种功能，允许主播在直播过程中举行拍卖活动。通过这个工具，主播可以展示商品并设置起始价格，然后观众可以通过出价来竞拍商品。竞拍工具通常包括计时器和价格跟踪功能，以便观众清楚了解拍卖的进展和当前价格。这种工具通常可以创造互动性和促进销售，增加直播的趣味性和吸引力，见图 3-1。

具体操作流程如下。

1. 创建竞拍

在直播中，点击 "活动（Activity）"，点击 "活动管理（Activity Management）"，选择 "开启竞拍（Start an Auction）"，设置直播互动拍卖功能，你可以在直播期间开始拍卖。

图 3-1 竞拍页面截图
图片来源：Shopee 直播间截图。

2. 竞拍设置

首先填写竞拍 "主题（Title）"，再填写竞拍 "价格（Price）"，选择竞拍 "规则（Rule）"。目前有两种规则：（1）最快手速（Fastest Finger），在这种模式下，最先参与拍卖的 X 位观众将获胜；（2）随机挑选参与者（Random），在此模式下，随机 X 名观众将获胜。

选择竞拍 "时长（Timer）"，最后点击 "开始（Start）" 即可完成竞拍创建。

五、投票

投票工具是 Shopee 平台提供的一种功能，允许主播在直播过程中进行投票互动。通过这个工具，主播可以创建投票问题，并在直播中邀请观众投票选择他们偏好的选项。观众可以通过点击相应的选项来参与投票，结果通常会实时显示在直播画面中，让观众了解投票结果。这种工具可以增加直播的互动性，让观众参与其中，增强直播的趣味性和吸引力。

【提示】投票功能分为限时投票与不限时投票，请根据需求设置。App 端和 PC 端都支持投票工具的使用。

具体操作流程如下。

1. 创建投票

在直播中，点击"活动（Activity）"，点击"活动管理（Activity Management）"，选择"开启投票（Start an Polling）"设置直播互动投票功能，你可以在直播期间开启投票活动。

2. 投票设置

填写投票的"主题（Theme）"，再设置投票的"时长（Timer）"以及投票的"选项（Options）"，让观众投票选出他们最喜欢的选项，最后点击"开始（Start）"即可完成投票设置。

六、幸运抽奖

Shopee 直播幸运抽奖功能是一种旨在提升直播互动性和观众参与度的游戏化工具。通过这一功能，直播主持人可以在直播过程中发起幸运抽奖活动，吸引更多观众积极参与和留在直播间，增加直播的趣味性和吸引力。

具体操作流程如下。

1. 创建幸运抽奖

在直播中，点击"促销活动（Promotion）"，在"幸运大转盘（Spin2Win）"处点击"重新开始（Start New）"，进入抽奖游戏设置页面。

2. 幸运抽奖设置

设置游戏"预算（Budget）"，还需要输入"获奖人数（Number of Winners）"和"最高奖金（Biggest Prize）"。系统将相应计算较小的奖金。

设置游戏"参与时间（Available to Play in）"，范围在 0~30 分钟。

最后点击"开始（Start）"，你可以在抽奖过程中查看抽奖结果并提前终止抽奖。

任务操作

学习完上述知识，Peter 所在的直播团队需要进行直播营销工具设置实操。

要求：

（1）为直播产品设置直播期间的优惠方案。

（2）在直播间完成优惠券创建。

Learning Process

1. Shopee Coin Rewards

Shopee Coins are the platform's official virtual currency. Sellers can give Shopee Coins to buyers during Shopee live streams, store games, and comment rewards. Shopee Coins effectively attract traffic and increase audience retention. By distributing coins, live viewership and audience retention time can be significantly improved. The specific steps include recharging Shopee Coins in the Shopee "Seller Center" and setting coin distribution rules.

2. Live Promotions

Improve buyer conversion rates by setting exclusive live streaming prices and adding time limits to display countdowns and remaining inventory. Live streaming promotion products will appear at the top of the shopping bag list and can be added during the live stream to enhance interactivity and immediate conversion rates.

3. Sharing Vouchers

Displaying voucher tags during live streams can increase views and orders. Sellers can create 30-second vouchers and permanent vouchers, visible to viewers during the live stream and throughout the App.

4. Auctions

Shopee's auction tool allows hosts to hold auction events during live streams. By showcasing products and setting starting prices, viewers can bid on items. This feature increases interactivity and the fun of sales, as shown in Figure 3-1 (please see the Chinese section).

5. Polling

The polling tool allows hosts to create poll questions during live streams and invite viewers to participate. Real-time displayed poll results can increase viewer engagement and the fun of the live stream.

6. Lucky Draw

The Shopee live lucky draw function attracts viewers to actively participate and stay in the live stream. By setting up lottery activities, it enhances the interaction and appeal of the live stream.

Task Operations

(1) Set discount schemes for live products during the live stream.

(2) Create vouchers in the live stream.

课后习题

1. （单选题）Shopee Live 直播提醒设置中的重要注意事项是什么？

A. 直播提醒需在直播开始前 60 天以内设置，且记录仅可保存 90 天。

B. 直播提醒需在直播开始前 30 天以内设置，且记录仅可保存 60 天。

C. 直播提醒需在直播开始前 90 天以内设置，且记录仅可保存 30 天。

D. 直播提醒需在直播开始前 120 天以内设置，且记录仅可保存 60 天。

2. （单选题）在 Shopee Live 开播过程中，以下哪项属于必填内容？

A. 直播背景音乐　　　　　　　　　B. 直播封面

C. 直播设备型号　　　　　　　　　D. 直播间布置照片

3. （单选题）使用 Shopee Live 直播时，以下哪种行为会被判定为中度违规？

A. 未按排期开直播　　　　　　　　B. 产品展示不佳

C. 知识产权侵权　　　　　　　　　D. 直播内容不佳

4. （单选题）在直播期间，通过使用 Shopee 币奖励功能可以带来的好处是什么？

A. 增加与买家的互动，提高粉丝黏性　　B. 提高直播视频的画质

C. 增加直播时长　　　　　　　　D. 提升直播间的背景音乐质量

5.（单选题）在 Shopee Live 中，如何设置优惠券来增加直播互动性？

A. 点击"活动管理"，选择"开启竞拍"，填写竞拍"主题"、竞拍"价格"、竞拍"规则"和竞拍"时长"

B. 点击"营销中心"，选择"优惠券"，创建直播优惠券，并在直播中分享

C. 点击"直播管理"，选择"创建优惠券"，设置优惠券内容和时间

D. 点击"促销活动"，选择"创建优惠券"，设置优惠券时长和数量

Exercises

1.（Single Choice）What are the important notes for setting up Shopee Live reminders?

A. Live reminders must be set within 60 days before the live stream starts, and records can only be saved for 90 days

B. Live reminders must be set within 30 days before the live stream starts, and records can only be saved for 60 days

C. Live reminders must be set within 90 days before the live stream starts, and records can only be saved for 30 days

D. Live reminders must be set within 120 days before the live stream starts, and records can only be saved for 60 days

2.（Single Choice）During the Shopee Live streaming process, which of the following is a required field?

A. Live background music　　　　B. Live cover

C. Live device model　　　　　　D. Live room layout photo

3.（Single Choice）When you use Shopee Live, which of the following behaviors is considered a moderate violation?

A. Not starting the live stream as scheduled　　B. Poor product display

C. Intellectual property infringement　　　　　D. Poor live content

4.（Single Choice）What are the benefits of using the Shopee Coin reward function during a live stream?

A. Increase interaction with buyers and enhance fan loyalty

B. Improve the video quality of the live stream

C. Increase the duration of the live stream

D. Enhance the quality of background music in the live stream

5.（Single Choice）How to set up vouchers in Shopee Live to increase interaction?

A. Click "Activity Management", select "Start an Auction", and fill in the auction title, auction price, auction rule, and auction

B. Click "Marketing Center", select "Vouchers", create live stream vouchers, and share them during the live stream

C. Click "Live Management", select "Create Voucher", and set the voucher content and time

D. Click "Promotion", select "Create Voucher", and set the voucher duration and quantity

项目 4　使用 TikTok 平台进行直播

项目概述

TikTok Live 是 TikTok 平台上提供的一项实时直播功能，旨在帮助用户与观众进行即时互动。通过 TikTok Live，主播可以在直播过程中展示商品、分享生活动态、进行才艺表演或回答观众提问，从而增加粉丝的参与度和互动性。为了在 TikTok 平台上开展直播业务，StreamASEAN 直播电商公司向 Peter 所在的直播团队下达任务：在 TikTok 平台上完成直播设置，并开启直播。

在本任务中，Peter 将提前了解 TikTok 平台的开播流程及直播工具使用方法，并学习直播技巧，为开播做准备。

项目目标

¤ 知识目标
1. 学习 TikTok Live 开播流程
2. 熟悉 TikTok Live 直播规范
3. 了解 TikTok Live 直播工具设置

¤ 技能目标
1. 能够通过小组合作，完成直播
2. 能够在直播间设置直播工具

¤ 素养目标
培养学生社会责任感、传播正面价值观

任务 1　开启 TikTok Live 直播

学习过程

在开启 TikTok Live 直播前，需要完成申请直播权限、设置直播间信息、测试设备连接、准备好展示的商品并发布宣传预告等步骤。目前 TikTok Live 的开播方式有移动端、PC 端两种直播方式。使用移动端进行直播的优势在于灵活便捷，可以随时随地进行直播，适合移动环境下的直播。使用 PC 端进行直播的优势在于更加稳定，适合需要更多功能和更高画质的直播场景。无论选择哪种方式，都需要确保直播设备和网络连接良好，以提供流畅的直播体验。

在开播之前，Peter 应先了解使用 TikTok 直播时应遵守的规范。具体直播权限及规范如下。

一、TikTok Live 直播间开通权限

开启 TikTok Live 直播权限，需要满足以下条件。

（1）拥有 TikTok 账号：在 TikTok 上注册账号并完成基本资料设置。
（2）年龄限制：要求年满 18 岁。
（3）有三种方式可以开通直播间权限。

①账号粉丝数量大于 1000 的商家可自动开通直播权限（该条件可能因地区而异）。

②拥有 TikTok Shop 的商家，在店铺后台绑定 TikTok 账号后，即使粉丝数量为 0，也可以实现开播。需注意 TikTok 账号归属地，只有归属地一致才能顺利绑定。

操作步骤：点击"我的账户（My Account）"⇒"绑定 TikTok 账户（Linked TikTok Accounts）"。

③与 MCN 机构合作，当卖家在 TikTok 上没有自己的店铺或者 TikTok 账号无法与 TikTok Shop 上的店铺绑定时，可以通过与 MCN 机构合作，开通电商达人权限，即可拥有电商权限与直播权限。

二、TikTok Live 直播规范

具体直播规范见表 4-1。

表 4-1　TikTok Live 直播规范

项目	内容
违法涉政	包括但不限于直播反党反政府或带有侮辱诋毁党和国家的行为、直播违反国家法律法规的内容等
衣着不当	包括但不限于裸露上身、大面积裸露文身等
色情低俗	包括但不限于一切色情、大尺度、带有性暗示的直播内容，其他低俗、违反公序良俗的行为等
辱骂挑衅	包括但不限于各种破坏社区氛围的言行等
违规广告	包括但不限于出售假冒伪劣和违禁商品、使用一些违反广告法的夸张和绝对化用语推销、以任何形式引导用户私下交易等
封建迷信	包括但不限于宣传封建迷信思想、直播迷信活动等
侵权行为	包括但不限于直播没有转播权的现场活动、录屏直播没有版权的视听内容等
对未成年人有害的行为	包括但不限于未成年人进行单独直播、未成年人进行消费或充值等
盗播录播	TikTok Shop 禁止商家达人通过录播盗播进行直播
其他不适合直播的行为	其他不适当的直播行为

三、TikTok Live 创建直播过程

（一）在 TikTok Live 创建直播预约

1. 创建一个直播预约并等待审核。

（1）入口 A：TikTok⇒个人资料（Profile）⇒点击直播预约图标。

（2）入口 B：TikTok⇒发布（Post）⇒LIVE⇒点击直播预约图标。

2. 点击直播预约，创建一个活动

输入预约名称，设置直播时间，为直播添加详细说明，提交申请，会看到已创建预约的提示。

（二）TikTok 的移动端开播流程

1. 申请直播权限

打开 TikTok 移动端，点击底部的"+"按钮，向左滑动，从相机切换到直播。

如果是第一次进行直播的卖家，需要申请直播权限，有资格开始直播的卖家，申请

按钮将变为红色,点击即可选择申请权限。

2. 直播间基本设置

(1) 设置直播封面:直播封面以缩略图的形式显示在"开始直播(Go Live)"按钮上方的小方块中,可以通过点击方块中显示的"添加封面(Add Cover)"选项来更新图片。

(2) 设置直播标题:卖家可输入直播标题,标题最长不超过 32 个字符。

(3) 镜头翻转:卖家可点击屏幕右侧"翻转(Flip)",选择翻转前后摄像头。

(4) 视频美颜:卖家可点击屏幕右侧"美颜(Enhance)",选择美颜和滤镜特效。

(5) 视频特效:卖家可点击屏幕右侧"特效(Effects)",选择不同的视频特效。

3. 直播间分享

卖家可点击"分享(Share)",分享直播间至 TikTok 好友或个人其他社媒主页,如 WhatsApp、Facebook 等。

4. 设置

卖家可点击"设置(Settings)",设置直播间礼物、开启直播间留言及直播间屏蔽关键词。

5. 开启直播

完成基础设置后,点击"开始直播(Go Live)"即可开启直播。

6. 添加商品

点击"管理店铺(Manage Shop)",卖家可添加 TikTok 店铺内商品或其他平台商品至直播间。

①商品名称:最长可输入 30 个字符(含空格),支持空格,不支持标点符号和表情包。

②添加商品时,会校验填入的商品链接是否有效,通过校验后才可添加商品。

【提示】在主播讲解商品的过程中,可以选择"置顶/取消置顶(Pin/Unpin)"商品。

7. 结束直播

直播结束后,点击关闭标志,确认结束直播。在直播结束后,您可以看到直播的数据统计,如直播间观看人数、新增粉丝、打赏观众及累计获得打赏。

(三) TikTok 的 PC 端开播流程

1. 创建直播

(1) TikTok Live Studio 是 TikTok 为 PC 端用户提供的官方直播工具。访问 www.tiktok.com 并登录。登录后,将光标悬停在页面右上角的个人资料照片上并选择"直播工作室(Live Streaming Studio)"。

(2) 点击"Windows 版免费下载(Downloaded for Windows for Free)",以获取 TikTok Live Studio。

(3) 安装/更新 Live Studio,登录 TikTok 账户,进入 TikTok Live Studio,开始设置直播间。

2. 进行直播设置

(1) 麦克风:可以使用内置麦克风或外部麦克风。

（2）摄像头：可以使用内置摄像头或外部网络摄像头。

（3）直播视频质量：默认视频质量为720P，可以根据自己的偏好进行调整。

（4）场景设置：可以自定义多达10个场景，每个场景包含多个来源。设置后，这些来源将显示在直播画布中，可以随时编辑和调整位置。

（5）直播信息设置：在直播间主页上，可以设置直播标题、封面照片、标签等，还可以选择是否允许观众在直播期间发送礼物或评论。

3. 添加商品到直播间

（1）使用TikTok账号登录主播工作台（https：//shop.tiktok.com/streamer/welcome），点击"直播商品（Livestream Products）"⇒"添加新商品（Add New Product）"⇒"展示商品（Showcase Products）"。

（2）点击"展示商品（Showcase Products）"⇒勾选商品⇒"添加商品（Add Product）"。

（3）复制"链接（URL）"，添加商品到直播。点击"展示商品（Showcase Products）"⇒复制"链接（URL）"⇒"添加商品（Add Product）"。

【提示】从"卖家中心（Seller Center）"⇒"商品管理（Manage Products）"中复制商品的"链接（URL）"。点击商品后方的眼睛图标，在新窗口中复制"链接（URL）"。

（4）添加商品到直播。点击"展示商品（Showcase Products）"⇒勾选商品⇒"添加商品（Add Product）"。

【建议】直播前将商品添加至直播间，然后调整商品顺序。

4. 使用TikTok Live Studio进行直播

（1）开始直播。点击"开始直播（Go Live）"就可以开启直播了。

（2）商品讲解。用电脑同时置顶或取消置顶商品卡片，帮助正在直播的商品进行讲解。

任务操作

学习完上述知识，Peter所在的直播团队需要完成以下操作。

☞ **步骤一　确定直播产品**

选择一款直播产品：＿＿＿＿＿＿＿＿＿＿＿＿＿。

☞ **步骤二　进行模拟直播**

在完成了直播脚本策划，直播间搭建等直播前的准备之后，Peter及其直播团队根据所确定的主题进行模拟直播，直播团队需要各司其职，在平台上完成模拟直播操作。

要求：

（1）使用TikTok平台进行模拟直播。

（2）完成模拟直播的时间限制为5~10分钟。

（3）结束模拟直播后，需要对直播表现进行评估及直播优化。

☞ **步骤三　评估直播**

根据表4-2的评估标准，对直播进行评估。

表4-2 直播评估标准

评估项目	评估标准
直播操作	直播开播步骤均已完成，操作合理
直播内容	话术讲解合理
	商品属性及卖点讲解准确到位
	销售促单具有吸引力
	主播礼仪得体，形象良好，人设鲜明

Learning Process

1. Enabling TikTok Live Permissions

To enable live stream on TikTok, the following conditions must be met.

(1) Have a TikTok Account: Register on TikTok and complete the basic profile setup.

(2) Age Requirement: Must be at least 18 years old.

(3) Three Methods to Enable Live Streaming Permissions:

①Merchant Account: If your TikTok merchant account has at least 1K followers, you can automatically enable live stream (may vary by region).

②TikTok Shop Merchants: Merchants with a TikTok Shop can go live even with zero followers by linking their TikTok account to the shop backend. Ensure the location of the TikTok account matches the shop location. Navigate to: My Account ⇒ Linked TikTok Accounts.

③MCN Partnership: Collaborate with MCN agencies to enable e-commerce and live streaming permissions if you don't have a TikTok Shop or if your TikTok account cannot be linked to the shop.

2. TikTok Live Streaming Guidelines.

The guidelines are shown in Table 4-1.

Table 4-1: TikTok Live Streaming Guidelines

Item	Description
Illegal Content	Includes but is not limited to content that is anti-government, defamatory to the state, or violates national laws and regulations
Inappropriate Attire	Includes but is not limited to topless streaming, or extensive tattoos
Sexual Content	Includes but is not limited to any sexual, explicit, or suggestive content
Abusive Behavior	Includes but is not limited to any disruptive or harmful behavior within the community
Unauthorized Ads	Includes but is not limited to selling counterfeit goods, exaggerated advertising, or encouraging private transactions
Superstition Promotion	Includes but is not limited to promoting superstitions or related activities
Infringement	Includes but is not limited to streaming copyrighted content without permission
Harmful to Minors	Includes but is not limited to minors streaming alone or making purchases
Replay Prohibition	TikTok Shop prohibits replaying or rebroadcasting content during live streams
Other Inappropriateness	Includes any other inappropriate live streaming behaviors

3. Steps to Go Live on TikTok (Mobile)

3.1 Request Live Permission

Open TikTok, tap the "+" button, and switch to Live mode by swiping left from the camera.

3.2 Set Up Your Live Stream

Cover Image: Tap "Add Cover" to update the live streaming cover image.

Title: Enter a live streaming title (up to 32 characters).

Flip Camera: Tap "Flip" to switch between front and back cameras.

Enhance Video: Tap "Enhance" to apply beauty filters and effects.

3.3 Share Live

Tap "Share" to share your live stream with TikTok friends or other social media platforms.

3.4 Settings

Sellers can click on the "Settings" button on the right to set live streaming room gifts, enable live streaming room messages, and block keywords in the live streaming room.

3.5 Go Live

Tap "Go Live" to start the live stream.

3.6 Add Products

Tap "Manage Shop" to add products from your TikTok shop or other platforms to the live stream.

3.7 End Live Stream

Tap the close icon to end the live stream. After the live stream review the data analysis such as viewers, new followers, and gifts received.

4. Steps to Go Live on TikTok (PC)

4.1 Create Live Stream

Visit www.tiktok.com, log in, and navigate to Live Streaming Studio to download TikTok Live Studio for Windows.

4.2 Live Streaming Settings

Microphone & Camera: Set up your internal or external microphone and camera.

Video Quality: Adjust the video quality (default is 720P).

Scene Setup: Customize up to 10 scenes with multiple sources.

4.3 Add Products

Log in to the streamer dashboard and add products by selecting "Showcase Products".

4.4 Start Live Stream

Click "Go Live" to begin live streaming.

Task Operation

Step 1: Select a Live Streaming Product

Choose a product to feature in the live stream.

Step 2: Conduct a Mock Live Stream

(1) Use TikTok for the mock live stream.

(2) Duration: 5-10 minutes.

(3) After the mock live stream, evaluate the performance and optimize the live stream.

Step 3: Evaluate the Live Stream

Evaluate the live stream according to the evaluation criteria in Table 4-2.

Table 4-2: Evaluation Criteria

Evaluation Item	Evaluation Criterion
Live Operation	All steps were completed reasonably
Content	Reasonable script delivery
	Accurate and detailed explanation of product attributes
	Attractive sales promotion
	Polite demeanor, good image, clear persona

任务 2　完成 TikTok Live 直播工具设置

学习过程

在直播期间，可以使用多种工具提高订单转化率，让直播更具有吸引力。有趣的直播活动可以帮助卖家与买家建立良好的关系，让买家持续关注商店的直播。Peter 了解到 TikTok Live 有以下直播工具可以有助于推动订单转化。

一、LIVE 赠品

（一）什么是 LIVE 赠品

LIVE 赠品（LIVE Giveaway）是一个由卖家资助的互动工具，允许卖家在 TikTok Shop 直播期间举办活动，并向观众提供免费奖品。卖家可以配置哪些产品以及他们想要赠送给观众的数量。观众可以通过直接参加比赛或完成卖家指定的任务来获得赠品。

（二）LIVE 赠品的作用

（1）提高实时参与度。

（2）增加实时流量。

（3）增加实时观看次数。

（4）增加平均观看时间。

以上内容见图 4-1。

图 4-1　LIVE 赠品的作用

图片来源：TikTok 学习中心。

(三) LIVE 赠品资格

要具备发放"LIVE 赠品"的资格，卖家必须符合以下要求：

(1) 成为 TikTok Shop 的注册卖家。

(2) 店铺体验评分（SES）大于等于 6.5。

(3) 店铺体验评分（SES）排名属于"良好"或"优秀"。

(4) 有官方 TikTok 账号（营销账号和创作者账号不符合）。

(四) 创建 LIVE 赠品活动的具体操作流程

(1) 首先，需要访问"卖家中心（Seller Center）"的"添加产品（Add New Products）"标签页，上传将用于直播赠送活动的产品。

(2) 填写列出产品所需的基本信息和产品详细信息。

(3) 创建一个 LIVE 赠品项目。在主播工作台（https://shop.tiktok.com/streamer/welcome），选择"直播（Livestreams）"选项，然后进入"LIVE 赠品（LIVE Giveaway）"页面。点击"项目（Item）"标签，然后点击"添加项目（Add Item）"。

通过选择产品并指定数量来添加一个 LIVE 赠品项目。如果所选产品有多种变体，请确保配置正确的项目。

【提示】在选择赠品时，只有卖家店铺中的产品（已成功上架且通过 TikTok Shop 产品上架政策的商品）可以被选择。LIVE 赠品的数量和卖家店铺的库存是分开管理的。

(4) 创建 LIVE 赠品活动。选择"LIVE 赠品（LIVE Giveaway）"标签，然后点击"创建赠品（Create a Giveaway Event）"按钮。

通过选择一个 LIVE 赠品项目并设定活动规则来创建 LIVE 赠品活动，如奖品数量和获奖者人数、任务以及 LIVE 赠品活动的持续时间。

【注意】对于单次 LIVE 赠品活动，单个赠品的 SKU 限量为 100 件。

(5) 发布 LIVE 赠品活动。

【提示】卖家必须先在 TikTok 应用中开始直播，然后才能发布 LIVE 赠品活动。

开始直播后，返回直播工作台界面。进入直播控制面板，选择之前步骤中配置的 LIVE 赠品项目和活动进行发布。可以点击 LIVE 赠品以检查赠品活动的状态、参与者和获奖者名单。

发布后，LIVE 赠品倒计时会开始。

【注意】一次只能运行一个 LIVE 赠品活动。

结果将在 LIVE 赠品倒计时结束时宣布。获奖者将在直播间内以及通过应用推送消息得到通知。观众在 LIVE 赠品活动结束后有 48 小时的时间来兑换奖品。

二、LIVE 广告牌

LIVE 广告牌是一种直播工具，可以实时显示关键销售点以吸引用户进入直播间并延长观看时间。卖家和创作者可以使用模板来设置他们自己的广告牌。

LIVE 广告牌是一种非常有效的工具，可推动直播观众采取行动，可以在不到五分钟内完成设置。

具体操作流程如下。

直播前，点击"产品（Products）"⇒"广告牌（Billboard）"来设置广告牌。直播时，点击"商店（Shop）"⇒"广告牌（Billboard）"来设置广告牌。

(1) 选择 LIVE 页面的"产品（Products）"选项，点击"广告牌（Billboard）"。

(2) 点击"模板（Templates）"，选择一个预设模板，检查、编辑、发布广告牌。

【提示】建议尝试不同的模板来突出显示商店的独特销售点。共有五个预设模板可以定制，以满足卖家独特的直播目标。

(3) 也可以点击"上传（Uploads）"，自定义模板，创建并上传自己的图片作为广告牌，并将其发布在 LIVE 广告牌中。

【注意】最多只能上传 100 张有效图片。

三、LIVE 精选

LIVE 精选是一个旨在录制 TikTok Shop 中表现最佳的直播内容的工具。这个工具对所有用户开放：无论是卖家、创作者、官方账号还是营销账号，都可以不受限制地使用此工具。直播流中的精彩瞬间会被平台自动录制成完美时长的片段，突出展示主播介绍不同产品的时刻。

系统将选择三个产品点击率最高的精彩片段作为"精选"。直播结束后 10 分钟内，这些片段将提供给主播。收到片段后，主播可以按照自己的意愿编辑 TikTok 视频，并发布带有产品链接的视频。

具体操作流程如下。

通过 LIVE 购物袋访问：在 TikTok 应用中点击"+"按钮，进入 LIVE 界面。选择"产品（Products）"按钮，打开"LIVE 购物袋（LIVE Shopping）"，点击"亮点（Highlight）"。

通过 LIVE 中心访问：在 TikTok 应用中点击"+"按钮，进入 LIVE 界面。选择"LIVE 中心（LIVE Center）"按钮，打开"回放（Replay）"。点击"查看更多"（See More），可以显示"回放（Replay）"部分。

选择任何三个精选发布为 TikTok 的短视频。根据实际需要编辑短视频，并点击"发布（Post）"。

【注意】只有点击表现最佳的三个精选会显示在精选模块中。

任务操作

学习完上述知识，Peter 所在的直播团队需要完成以下操作。

(1) 为直播间设置 LIVE 赠品。

(2) 在直播间设置 LIVE 广告牌。

(3) 在直播间设置 LIVE 精选。

Learning Process

1. LIVE Giveaway

1.1 What is a LIVE Giveaway

LIVE Giveaway is an interactive tool funded by the seller, allowing them to host events during a TikTok Shop live stream and offer free prizes to viewers. Sellers can configure which products and how many they want to give away. Viewers can participate by entering the contest directly or completing tasks specified by the seller.

1.2 Benefits of LIVE Giveaway

(1) Increase LIVE engagement.

(2) Increase LIVE traffic.

(3) Increase LIVE views.

(4) Increase average watch time.

The benefits are shown in Figure 4-1 (please see the Chinese section).

1.3 Eligibility for LIVE Giveaway

Must be a registered TikTok Shop seller, with a shop experience score (SES) $\geqslant 6.5$, have an official TikTok account, and meet other specific requirements.

1.4 Operation Process

(1) Visit the seller center to upload products for the giveaway.

(2) Fill in the basic and detailed information of the listed products.

(3) Create a LIVE Giveaway project, configuring the product and quantity.

(4) Create the LIVE Giveaway event, setting rules for participation.

(5) Publish the LIVE Giveaway event and start the live stream.

2. LIVE Billboard

2.1 Function

The LIVE Billboard tool displays key selling points in real time to attract users to the live stream and extend viewing time. Sellers and creators can use templates to set up their billboards.

2.2 Operation Process

(1) Set up billboard templates before the live stream.

(2) During the live stream, click "Shop" ⇒ "Billboard" to set up the billboard.

(3) Use preset or custom templates to highlight unique selling points.

3. LIVE Highlights

3.1 Function

LIVE Highlights is a tool designed to record the best-performing live content on TikTok Shop. It is available to all users: sellers, creators, official accounts, and marketing accounts. Highlight moments from the live stream are automatically recorded, emphasizing product introductions by the host.

3.2 Operation Process

Create short videos from LIVE Highlights via the LIVE Shopping or LIVE Center.

Select the best-performing highlights and publish them as TikTok short videos.

Task Operations

(1) Set up a LIVE Giveaway for the live stream.

(2) Configure a LIVE Billboard during the live stream.

(3) Set up LIVE Highlights for the live stream.

任务 3　开展 TikTok Live 直播推广

学习过程

为提升直播效果，StreamASEAN 直播电商公司要求 Peter 在一定的预算范围内，进行直播推广。为完成直播推广，Peter 对直播推广的有关知识进行如下了解。

一、私域推广

（1）在 Instagram/Facebook/YouTube 等其他社交媒体渠道，给自己的私域用户预告 TikTok 直播，告知私域用户可在 TikTok 应用内通过直播实时展示商品并完成购买，通过私域流量带动 TikTok 的公域流量，从而促进用户的转化。

（2）可用 EDM 定期触达用户，该部分用户可聚焦于曾经向商家下过订单的用户，商家可根据历史 EDM 的邮件打开高峰判断邮件发送时间。不建议轰炸式的 EDM，可能会影响邮件打开率。

（3）通过 Instagram Story 发布的 TikTok 直播预告示例。

二、付费推广

（一）Promote

Promote 是 TikTok 站内付费广告工具，可用于推广直播间和短视频。针对直播，Promote 通过直播预览流的方式提高直播间的曝光，用户可在刷短视频时，看到直播间的预览卡片，并一键点击屏幕即可进入直播间。

Promote 投放直播间可在直播前和直播期间创建计划，建议只勾选目标人群的年龄和性别，计划提交后需要 15~20 分钟的审核时间。审核通过后，系统才会推送付费流量至直播间。

（二）创建 Promote 的时机

参考历史直播间的分时段流量情况，判断流量一般在直播的哪个阶段开始下跌，可在该时段的前 15~20 分钟创建 Promote 计划。

（三）具体操作流程

（1）进入 TikTok Shop "卖家中心（Seller Center）"，点击"店铺广告（Shop Ads）"，选择"制作商品交易总额最大化的广告〔Create GMV Max Ads（BETA）〕"。

（2）选择直播购物的推广形式"LIVE 购物袋（LIVE Shopping）"，选择 TikTok Shop 和 TikTok 账户（用于播放直播购物广告的 TikTok 账户）。

（3）选择预算，选择与直播场次匹配的开始和结束日期、时间。

（4）选择优化目标，填写广告名称，发布后，即可完成直播推广。

任务操作

学习完上述知识，Peter 所在的直播团队需要完成以下操作。

☞ **步骤一　完成直播推广计划**

在进行 TikTok 平台上完成直播推广前，Peter 的直播团队需要完成直播推广计划，并填写在表4-3中。

表4-3 直播推广计划

项目	内容
直播主题	
直播时间	
目标受众	
推广预算	
推广方式	
预期效果	

☞ **步骤二 设置**

根据所学知识，在TikTok平台完成直播推广设置。

☞ **步骤三 评估**

根据表4-4评估标准，对直播推广设置进行评估。

表4-4 评估标准

评估项目	评估标准
操作设置	成功完成了直播推广设置
推广预算	合理规划了直播内容和推广预算
推广计划	推广计划清晰合理

Learning Process

1. Private Domain Promotion

（1）On Instagram/Facebook/YouTube and other social media channels: Announce the upcoming TikTok live stream to your private domain users, informing them that they can view the product showcase and complete purchases in real time via the TikTok App. Leverage private domain traffic to drive public domain traffic on TikTok, thereby enhancing user conversion.

（2）Use EDM: Regularly reach out to users, focusing on those who have previously placed orders with the merchant. The optimal time to send emails can be determined based on the peak open times of past EDMs. Avoid spamming users with frequent emails, as it may negatively impact the open rate.

（3）Example of a TikTok live streaming announcement via Instagram Story.

2. Paid Promotion

2.1 Promote

Promote is a paid advertising tool within TikTok that can be used to boost the visibility of live streams and short videos. For live streams, Promote increases exposure through the live preview stream, allowing users to see the preview card while browsing short videos and enter the live stream with a single click.

Set up a Promote campaign for live streams. Campaigns can be created before or during the live stream. It is recommended to only select the target audience's age and gender. After submitting the campaign, it takes 15-20 minutes for approval, after which the system will start pushing paid traffic to the live stream.

2.2 Timing for Promote

Based on the historical traffic patterns of previous live streams, identify when the traffic typically starts to decline and create a Promote campaign 15-20 minutes before this time.

2.3 Steps

(1) Go to the TikTok Shop "Seller Center", click on "Shop Ads", and select "Create GMV Max Ads (BETA)".

(2) Select "LIVE Shopping" as the promotion format and choose the TikTok Shop and TikTok account (the TikTok account that will play the live shopping ad).

(3) Set the budget and schedule to match the start and end dates and times of the live session.

(4) Choose the optimization goal, fill in the ad name, and then publish to complete the live streaming promotion.

Task Operations

Step 1: Finalize the Live Streaming Promotion Plan

Before completing the live streaming promotion on TikTok, finalize the live streaming promotion plan.

Step 2: Set Up

Based on the knowledge learned, set up the live streaming promotion on the TikTok platform.

Step 3: Evaluate

Evaluation criteria are shown in Table 4-3.

Table 4-3: Evaluation Criteria

Evaluation Item	Evaluation Criterion
Operation Setup	Completed the live streaming promotion setup
Promotion Budget	Reasonably planned the live streaming content and promotion budget
Promotion Plan	Clear and reasonable promotion plan

课后习题

1. （单选题）在 TikTok 平台上，以下哪项是开启直播权限的必要条件？

   A. 拥有 TikTok 账号必须年满 18 岁　　B. 拥有高级摄影设备

   C. 使用高级网络连接　　D. 有专业直播背景

2. （单选题）在 TikTok Live 开启直播前，需要完成的步骤有哪些？

   A. 设置直播间背景音乐　　B. 准备好展示的商品并发布宣传预告

   C. 购买高级直播设备　　D. 确定直播间色调

3. （单选题）在 TikTok Live 的直播中，以下哪种行为是被禁止的？

   A. 介绍新商品　　B. 直播反政府内容

   C. 分享个人生活动态　　D. 回答观众提问

4. （单选题）TikTok Live 的移动端开播流程中，以下哪项是设置直播间信息的一部分？

   A. 上传产品列表　　B. 设置直播封面

C. 购买直播广告　　　　　　　　D. 设置背景音乐

5.（单选题）使用 TikTok Live Studio 进行 PC 端直播时，可以自定义的场景数量最多是多少？

A. 5　　　　　　　　　　　　　B. 10

C. 15　　　　　　　　　　　　　D. 20

Exercises

1.（Single Choice）Which of the following is a required condition for enabling live stream on TikTok?

A. TikTok account holder must be at least 18 years old

B. Owning advanced photography equipment

C. Using a high-speed Internet connection

D. Having a professional live streaming background

2.（Single Choice）What are the necessary steps before starting a live stream on TikTok Live?

A. Setting up background music for the live stream

B. Preparing products for display and posting promotional previews

C. Purchasing advanced live streaming equipment

D. Deciding the color scheme of the live streaming room

3.（Single Choice）Which of the following behaviors is prohibited during a live stream on TikTok Live?

A. Introducing new products　　　　B. Broadcasting anti-government content

C. Sharing personal life updates　　　D. Answering audience questions

4.（Single Choice）In the TikTok Live mobile live streaming process, which of the following is part of setting up the live streaming room?

A. Uploading product lists　　　　　B. Setting up the live cover

C. Purchasing live ads　　　　　　　D. Setting background music

5.（Single Choice）When using TikTok Live Studio for PC live streaming, what is the maximum number of customizable scenes?

A. 5　　　　　　　　　　　　　B. 10

C. 15　　　　　　　　　　　　　D. 20

项目 5　直播数据分析与复盘

项目概述

直播数据分析与复盘是提高直播效果和销售业绩的重要环节。通过系统地收集和分析关键指标,直播运营人员能够全面了解每场直播的表现。这不仅有助于评估直播活动的成功与不足,还能发现改进点和优化方向。

首先,直播数据分析有助于全面了解观众的行为和偏好。通过分析观看人数、互动率和观众的停留时间,直播运营人员可以识别哪些内容最能吸引观众、哪些时段的观看率最高,从而总结直播中的成功经验和问题,不断改进直播策略。其次,直播数据分析有助于掌握营销活动的效果。复盘过程中,需要关注直播的各个环节,包括产品展示、互动方式、优惠活动等。通过对这些环节的详细分析,可以发现哪些做法能够提高观众的满意度和购买意愿、哪些方面需要进一步优化。最后,直播数据分析有助于优化选品定价策略。通过分析转化率和销售数据,评估不同产品的销售表现,确定最受欢迎的产品类别和价格区间,有助于直播运营人员在未来的直播中更好地选品和定价,提高整体销售业绩。

因此,掌握直播数据分析与复盘的技能对于任何希望在直播电商领域取得成功的企业来说都是必不可少的。

项目目标

¤ 知识目标
1. 了解直播数据获取的方法
2. 了解不同平台的直播关键数据指标
3. 了解直播数据分析的流程与方法
4. 了解直播复盘的意义及流程

¤ 技能目标
1. 能够通过 TikTok/Facebook/Shopee/Lazada 后台获取直播数据
2. 能够完成直播数据的统计和分析
3. 能够完成直播复盘

¤ 素养目标
1. 培养学生科学、系统地进行数据分析的能力
2. 培养学生精益求精的工匠精神

任务 1　获取平台直播数据

任务导入

直播数据收集是提升直播效果和优化营销策略的基础。通过系统地收集观看人数、

互动率、观众构成、转化率及产品表现等关键指标，商家可以全面了解直播的实际表现，为直播数据分析做准备。直播结束后，StreamASEAN 直播电商公司向 Peter 所在的直播团队下达任务：获取平台直播数据。

此次，Peter 分别在 TikTok、Facebook、Shopee、Lazada 上完成了直播任务，需要分别对此四个平台的数据进行收集整理。

任务目标

¤ 知识目标
1. 了解直播数据获取的方法
2. 了解不同平台的直播关键数据指标
¤ 技能目标
能够通过 TikTok/Facebook/Shopee/Lazada 后台获取直播数据
¤ 素养目标
培养科学、系统地进行数据分析的能力

任务流程

子任务1：获取TikTok平台直播数据
⇩
子任务2：获取Shopee平台直播数据

子任务 1　获取 TikTok 平台直播数据

学习过程

在进行直播数据分析之前，Peter 需要对 TikTok 平台直播数据进行收集，在此之前，Peter 对 TikTok 平台直播数据相关知识了解如下。

一、直播分析目标

帮助卖家实时了解全店、各账号的实时数据表现，并能够查看自有账号直播画面，进行直播监控。

二、获取直播数据的方法

方式一：查看全店或单个账号的直播汇总数据表现，可以对历史数据进行实时监控和分析，查看卖家产品的直播数据表现。TikTok 直播可通过数据罗盘和直播工作台两种方法查看数据。

方式二：查看实时直播页面，对于卖家自有账号，可以访问每场直播的直播画面，直播结束后进行实时数据跟踪和数据回放。

LIVE Board 是一个一站式中心，提供直播期间的流量和转化率综合分析，以及产品和推广工具分析。它还结合了实时操作调整。

三、TikTok 直播数据分析的功能

（一）重播直播的内容并寻找趋势

回放直播以分析交易发生的时间、观众进入和离开的时间点、观众互动、粉丝增长、产品点击和订单情况。分析这些数据并观察其随时间的变化，可以了解这些指标与直播内容的相关性。

（二）分析转化漏斗和流量

了解观众在每个用户旅程阶段的转化情况，从最初的直播印象、进入直播、产品印象、点击产品到购买。通过查看在漏斗的哪个阶段失去潜在买家，可以了解需要改进的地方，还可以查看广告流量（付费流量）和自然流量（免费流量）的趋势差异。

（三）下载并分析产品数据

下载添加到直播中的产品的印象、点击、交易和转化数据，分析每个产品的表现。识别收入最高或转化潜力最好的产品。

（四）分析观众

按年龄、性别、地区和购买力以及类别和产品偏好检查观众和买家的构成，帮助卖家更好地匹配产品/类别与观众/买家。

四、TikTok Shop 直播核心指标

TikTok Shop 直播核心指标如表 5-1 所示。

表 5-1 TikTok Shop 直播核心指标注释

指标	注释
GMV	总销售金额
GPM	每千次直播视频观看产生的 GMV，评估流量效率
PCU	直播间中的最高同时在线人数
买家数	通过短视频下单支付的单一用户数（包括退货退款订单）
浏览量	直播浏览量
平均观看时长	直播平均观看时长
CTR	商品链接点击次数
平均价格	卖出商品的平均价格

任务操作

学习完上述知识，Peter 的直播团队根据 TikTok Shop 直播后台，收集本场直播相关数据，具体步骤如下。

步骤一 TikTok Shop 数据罗盘获取汇总数据

（一）进入数据罗盘

登录 TikTok Shop "卖家中心（Seller Center）" ⇒ "数据罗盘（Data Compass）" ⇒ "直播和视频（Livestream & Video）" ⇒ "表现（Performance）" 获取直播核心数据。

（二）查看直播数据

（1）时间筛选：可以选择 7/28 天内的任何一天或过去 90 天内的一天。

（2）关键数据：在关键数据部分，可以查看收入、订单、买家、点击转化率、直播销量、点击率等指标。

（3）数据趋势比较：打开 "Trends（趋势）" 开关，即可查看显示过去 1/7/28 天数据（百分比）的上升或下降情况。

步骤二 使用实时仪表盘查看直播数据

（一）进入实时仪表盘

点击 "详情（Details）" ⇒ "实时仪表盘（Live Dashboard）"。

（二）查看直播数据

可以查看正在进行的直播和最近结束的直播的直播大屏数据。

（三）直播数据

界面上的三个主要选项卡是 GMV、流量效率、交易。每个选项卡都显示正在进行的直播的效果，切换到每个选项卡会显示特定的效果指标。

GMV 选项卡显示 GMV 总额、千次曝光成交金额、买家数、SKU 订单数、广告总收入、广告订单总数、直播间内广告收入、广告直播内订单、商品交易总额等。

流量效率选项卡显示观看次数、平均观看时长、流量人数、进房率、广告支出回报率、广告成本、广告直播观看次数、点赞数、分享次数、评论数等。

交易选项卡显示商品曝光次数、商品点击量、点击率、点击-成交转化率、广告商品点击率、广告直播商品点击量、广告点击-成交转化率等。

在界面的下半部分可查看其他指标。

浏览次数：可查看浏览来源、浏览次数、观看-商品点击率、点击-成交转化率。

商品浏览量：呈现商品浏览次数排行，卖家可查看访问量最大的商品。选择商品浏览次数高的商品，有助于提高直播间人气。

订单：查看最常购买的商品。

商品选项卡：可以查看商品的 GMV、点击率、点击订购、GPM 和 SKU 订单。还可以编辑或固定产品，编辑日期范围以及指标。

违规：违规行为按时间排序，滚动查看所有违规行为。

促销活动：查看促销活动在查看 UV、点击 UV 和加入 UV 中的效果。点击创建新的促销活动。

用户形象：切换至直播大屏基础版可以查看用户画像，查看包括用户性别、粉丝结构、年龄、国家和区域。

（四）分析数据

实时查看直播数据并根据直播数据进行分析，及时调整直播状态。

☞ 步骤三　使用直播工作台查看直播数据

（一）登录直播工作台

进入直播工作台（https：//shop.tiktok.com/streamer/compass），点击"LIVE 分析（LIVE Analytics）"，可查看一段时间内创作者所有直播的交易、流量、产品和互动数据概览。还可显示今天的直播和历史直播列表。正在进行的直播可以在直播屏幕/仪表盘上查看，直播结束后可以查看直播详情页面。

（二）获取直播数据

点击直播间列表后的直播"详情（Details）"，可获取直播间核心数据，包括内容分析、流量分析、商品分析和用户画像数据。

1. 内容分析

显示直播内容与观众行为之间的关系。这个页面显示了卖家在讲解某些产品和提供折扣或闪购时的数据情况，呈现了直播内容与交易、流量和观众互动趋势之间的关系。

2. 流量分析

展示观众在每个用户旅程阶段的转化情况：直播印象⇒进入直播⇒产品印象⇒点击

产品⇒付款下单。通过查看在漏斗的哪个阶段失去潜在买家,可以了解下次直播需要改进的地方,还可以查看广告流量和自然流量的趋势差异。

3. 商品分析

显示每1/5/15分钟内销售的商品、数量和销售排名。可以查看和下载所有商品的印象、点击、交易和转化数据。

4. 用户画像

提供按年龄、性别、地区和购买力划分的观众和买家信息,显示买家和观众的人口统计资料:年龄、性别、粉丝和非粉丝、国家和地区、城市、用户使用的设备、过去30天内在各种类别中的订单金额、用户类别偏好和产品偏好。

Learning Process

1. Live Streaming Analysis Goals

Help sellers understand real-time data performance for the entire store and individual accounts, and view their own accounts' live streams to monitor live streams.

2. Methods to Obtain Live Streaming Data

Method 1: View summary data for the entire store or a single account, enabling real-time monitoring and analysis of historical data. Check the live streaming data performance of the seller's products. TikTok live streaming can be analyzed through Data Compass and the Live Streaming Workbench.

Method 2: Access the live streaming page in real time for the seller's own account, view the live stream for each broadcast, track real-time data, and replay data after the live stream ends.

The LIVE Board is a one-stop center providing a comprehensive analysis of traffic and conversion rates during live streams, as well as product and promotional tool analysis, with real-time operational adjustments.

3. TikTok Live Data Analysis Functions

3.1 Replay Live Streams and Identify Trends

Replay live streams to analyze transaction times, when viewers enter and leave, viewer interactions, follower growth, product clicks, and orders. Analyze these data points, observe their changes over time, and correlate these metrics with live streaming content and spoken content.

3.2 Analyze Conversion Funnel and Traffic

Understand viewer conversions at each stage of the user journey, from initial live streaming impressions, entering the live stream, product impressions, clicking on products, to purchasing. By identifying at which funnel stage potential buyers are lost, determine areas for improvement. You can also observe the trend differences between ad traffic (paid traffic) and organic traffic (free traffic).

3.3 Download and Analyze Product Data

Download data on impressions, clicks, transactions, and conversions for products added to the live stream, and analyze each product's performance. Identify products with the highest revenue or best conversion potential.

3.4 Analyze Audiences

Check the composition of viewers and buyers by age, gender, region, purchasing power, category and product preferences, to help sellers better match products/categories with viewers/buyers.

4. TikTok Shop Live Streaming Core Metrics

The core metrics annotations are shown in Table 5-1.

Table 5-1: TikTok Shop Live Streaming Core Metrics Annotations

Metric	Annotation
GMV	Total sales amount
GPM	GMV generated per thousand live video views, evaluating traffic efficiency
PCU	Peak concurrent users in the live stream
Buyers	Number of unique users who placed orders via short videos (including return/refund orders)
Views	Live streaming views
Average Watch Time	Average watch time of the live stream
CTR	Click-through rate of product links
Average Price	Average price of sold products

Task Operations

Step 1: Accessing Summary Data on TikTok Shop Data Compass

1.1 Enter Data Compass

Log in to TikTok Shop "Seller Center", and then navigate to "Data Compass" ⇒ "Livestream & Video" ⇒ "Performance" to access core live streaming data.

1.2 View Live Streaming Data

Time Filter: You can select any day within the last 7/28 days or any day within the past 90 days.

Key Data: View metrics such as revenue, orders, buyers, click-through rates, live streaming sales, and click rates.

Data Trend Comparison: Toggle the Trends switch to view the increase or decrease percentage of data from the past 1/7/28 days.

Step 2: Using the Live Dashboard to View Real-Time Data

2.1 Use the Live Dashboard

Click "Details" ⇒ "Live Dashboard".

2.2 View Live Streaming Data

View data for ongoing and recently concluded live streams.

2.3 Live Streaming Data Tabs

GMV: Displays total GMV, GMV per thousand impressions, number of buyers, SKU orders, total ad revenue, and other metrics.

Traffic Efficiency: Displays view count, average view duration, room entry rate, ad return on investment, and other metrics.

Transaction: Displays product impressions, clicks, click-through rates, and conversion rates.

There are other detailed metrics on the Live Dashboard.

Views: Check sources, view counts, click rates, and conversion rates.

Product Views: Shows the ranking of the most viewed products.

Orders: View the most purchased products.

Product Tab: View GMV, click rates, GPM, and SKU orders for each product.

Violation: Violations are sorted by time, and you can scroll to see all violations.

Promotion: View the effect of promotions on UV views, UV clicks, and UV additions. Click to create a new promotion.

User Profile: View user demographics including gender, follower structure, age, country, and region.

2.4 Analyze Data

View live streaming data in real time, analyze the data and timely adjust the live streaming status.

Step 3: Using the Live Streaming Console to View Live Streaming Data

3.1 Log in to the Live Streaming Console

Log in to the live streaming console (https://shop.tiktok.com/streamer/compass) and click "LIVE Analytics" to view an overview of transactions, traffic, products, and interaction data for all live streams by the creator over a period of time.

3.2 Access Live Streaming Data

Click "Details" next to the live streaming list to access core data: content analysis, traffic analysis, product analysis, and user profile data.

Content Analysis: Shows the relationship between live streaming content and audience behavior.

Traffic Analysis: Understand conversion at each stage of the user journey: from live impressions to entry, product impressions, product clicks, and final purchase. View differences in trends between ad traffic and organic traffic.

Product Analysis: View sales and rankings of products every 1/5/15 minutes, and download data on impressions, clicks, transactions, and conversions.

User Profile: Provides demographic information of viewers and buyers by age, gender, region, and purchasing power. Displays demographic details and product preferences.

子任务 2　获取 Shopee 平台直播数据

学习过程

在进行直播数据分析之前，Peter 需要对 Shopee 平台直播数据进行收集，在此之前，Peter 所在的直播团队对 Shopee 平台直播数据相关知识了解如下。

一、Shopee 直播的核心指标注释

Shopee 直播的核心指标注释如表 5-2 所示。

表 5-2　Shopee 直播的核心指标注释

指标	注释
总直播次数	所有直播的次数
总直播时长	所有直播的时长
每次直播的平均时长	直播中观众的平均停留时长
销售额	所有直播期间下单（已付款和未付款）的订单价值，包括已取消、退货和退款订单的销售额
加入购物车总次数	直播中点击所有产品的"加入购物车"按钮次数
订单	所有直播期间下单（已付款和未付款）的订单数量，包括已取消、退货和退款订单
已售商品总数	直播中已下订单售出的商品数量
总观众数	直播中的观众数量
参与的观众数	观看直播超过 1 分钟的观众数量
总评论数	直播期间获取的评论数量
平均观看时长	观众平均观看直播时长
买家	直播中下单的不重复买家数
点击率	产品点击次数除以直播观看次数
点击下单率	直播中的产品订单数量除以直播中的产品点击数量
平均每单销售额	总销售金额除以已下订单总数
千次曝光成交销售额	每千次观看产生的销售金额
总浏览量	直播的观看次数
最高同时观看人数	直播期间的最高同时在线观众数量
总点赞次数	直播期间点击的"喜欢"数量
总分享次数	直播期间创建的分享数量
新增粉丝总数	直播期间获得的新粉丝数量
已领取的商店优惠券	领取的店铺优惠券数量
已领取的 Shopee 币	已领取的 Shopee 币数量

任务操作

学习完上述知识，Peter 所在的直播团队需要完成以下步骤。

步骤一　手机端直播数据获取

（一）直播中数据监控

开启直播，点击"仪表盘（Dashboard）"，进入数据大屏，查看实时直播数据，根据直播数据状况实时调整直播状态。

（二）直播后获取直播数据

（1）在手机端通过"我（Me）"标签⇒"直播（Livestream）"⇒"洞察（Insights）"，进入直播洞察。

（2）在关键指标板块，可查看直播的关键指标数据。

（3）在趋势板块可查看直播现场观众数量趋势、商品卡片点击次数、相关商品点击次数。

（4）查看产品排名。根据直播中的产品点击量、订单量和销售额，了解哪些产品最受买家欢迎。

☞ **步骤二　电脑端获取直播数据**

（一）直播中数据监控

（1）进入 Shopee 平台"卖家中心（Seller Center）"，点击"直播数据中心（Live Data Center）"⇒"直播列表（Livestreams List）"⇒"实时仪表盘（Live Dashboards）"，可以查看直播实时数据和最近结束的直播大屏。

（2）实时仪表盘分为五个选项卡：直播分析、趋势、直播画面、商品列表、违规提醒。

直播分析：提供当前直播活动的概览数据，包括总销售额、平均实时在线人数、总评论数、加入购物车次数、总浏览量、平均观看时长、评论率、千次曝光成交销售额、订单、平均客单价、总观众数、最高同时观看人数、点击率、点击下单率、买家、已售商品。

趋势：可以查看 GMV、流量、互动的实时趋势。

直播画面：可以在实时看板上查看直播画面。

商品列表：在此查看该直播活动中商品的详细表现。

违规提醒：违规按照严重程度进行分组，有轻度、中度、重度三个级别，根据违规的频率和严重程度，卖家可能会受到不同类型的处罚。

在顶部，可以查看收入、并发用户（CCU）、总浏览量、买家、平均观看时长、平均总成本（ATC）、销售总商品数、总订单数、产品点击率和点击订购率的实时数据。

（3）查看收入趋势的实时折线图，其中包括商品总价值、订单总额和售出商品总额，以及参与度趋势，其中显示查看者、并发用户、喜欢、评论、分享和新关注者的数量。

（4）产品见解：可以查看带有详细指标的产品列表，并使用各种过滤器，对产品进行排序。

（二）直播后获取直播数据

直播数据看板分为五个选项卡：数据概览、累积趋势、用户统计、直播列表、商品列表。

数据概览：可查看直播总时长、销售额、订单数、平均观看时长、转化率、参与度等直播数据。

累积趋势：卖家可以选择多个指标并显示折线趋势图（如果选择 XXX，则使用 XXX 作为 Y 轴），没有可选指标数量限制。

用户统计：统计直播用户的信息数据，包括年龄、性别、身份（粉丝或非粉丝）。

直播列表：显示直播过程相关数据，比如评论、加入购物车次数、平均观看时长、观众、订单数、销售金额和行动。

商品列表：展示商品列表数据，包括商品排名、产品点击次数、加入购物车次数、订单、已售商品数、销售金额。可以输入商品名称或商品编号进行搜索。

Learning Process

1. Shopee Live Core Metrics Annotations

The core metrics annotations are shown in Table 5-2.

Table 5-2: Shopee Live Core Metrics Annotations

Metric	Annotation
Total Number of Live Streams	The number of all live streams
Total Duration of Live Streams	The total duration of all live streams
Average Duration of Per Live Stream	The average duration of each live stream
Sales Amount	The value of orders placed during all live streams (both paid and unpaid), including sales from canceled, returned, and refunded orders.
Total "Add to Cart" Clicks	The number of times the "Add to Cart" button was clicked for all products during the live stream
Orders	The number of orders placed during all live streams (both paid and unpaid), including canceled, returned, and refunded orders
Total Number of Sold Items	The number of items sold in orders placed during the live streams
Total Number of Viewers	The number of viewers during the live streams
Engaged Viewers	The number of viewers who watched the live stream for more than one minute
Total Number of Comments	The number of comments received during the live stream
Average Watch Time	The average time viewers watched the live stream
Buyers	The number of unique buyers who placed orders during the live stream
Click-through Rate	The number of product clicks divided by the number of live stream views
Click-to-Order Rate	The number of product orders divided by the number of product clicks during the live stream
Average Sales Per Order	Total sales amount divided by the total number of orders placed
Sales Per Thousand Impressions	The sales amount generated per 1,000 views
Total Views	The number of views of the live stream
Peak Concurrent Viewers	The highest number of viewers online simultaneously during the live stream
Total Number of Likes	The number of "likes" clicked during the live stream
Total Number of Shares	The number of shares created during the live stream
Total Number of New Followers	The number of new followers gained during the live stream
Redeemed Store Vouchers	The number of store vouchers redeemed
Redeemed Shopee Coins	The number of Shopee coins redeemed

Task Operations

Step 1: Mobile Live Data Acquisition

1.1 Monitoring Live Data During the Stream

Start the live stream, click on "Dashboard" to enter the data dashboard, and monitor real-time live data. Adjust the live streaming status based on the data.

1.2 Accessing Live Data After the Live Stream

(1) On the mobile App, go to "Me" ⇒ "Live" ⇒ "Insights" to enter the live insights.

(2) In the "Key Metrics" section, you can view key metrics data for the live stream.

(3) In the "Trends" section, you can see trends for the number of live viewers, product card clicks, and related product clicks.

(4) Product Rankings: Understand which products were most popular based on clicks,

orders, and sales value during the live stream.

Step 2: Accessing Live Data on Desktop

2.1 Monitoring Live Data During the Stream

(1) Go to the Shopee "Seller Center", and click on "Live Data Center" ⇒ "Livestreams List" ⇒ "Live Dashboards" to view real-time live data and the dashboard for recently ended live streams.

(2) The live dashboard consists of five tabs: Live Analysis, Trends, Live Screen, Product List, and Violation Alerts.

Live Analysis: Provides an overview of the current live activity, including total sales, average real-time online users, total comments, add-to-cart actions, total views, average watch time, comment rate, sales per thousand impressions, orders, average order value, total viewers, peak concurrent viewers, click rate, click-to-order rate, buyers, and sold items.

Trends: View real-time trends for GMV, traffic, and interactions.

Live Screen: View the live stream on the real-time dashboard.

Product List: Check the detailed performance of products during the live stream.

Violation Alerts: Violations are grouped by severity into mild, moderate, and severe levels. Based on the frequency and severity of violations, sellers may face different types of penalties.

At the top, monitor real-time data for revenue, concurrent users (CCU), total views, buyers, average watch time, average total cost (ATC), total sold items, total orders, product click rate, and click-to-order rate.

(3) View real-time line charts for revenue trends, including total product value, total order value, and total sold product value and engagement trends showing the number of viewers, concurrent users, likes, comments, shares, and new followers.

(4) Product Insights: View a list of products with detailed metrics and sort the products based on various filters.

2.2 Accessing Live Data After the live Stream

The live data dashboard is divided into five tabs: Data Overview, Cumulative Trends, User Statistics, Live List, and Product List.

Data Overview: View the data of live streaming activities.

Cumulative Trends: Sellers can select multiple metrics and display them in line trend charts (if selecting XXX, use XXX as the Y-axis), with no limit on the number of selectable metrics.

User Statistics: Displays user information, including age, gender, and identity (fans or non-fans).

Live List: Shows data related to the live process, such as comments, add-to-cart actions, average watch time, viewers, order numbers, sales amount, and actions.

Product List: Displays the product list, including product rankings, product click times, add-to-cart actions, orders, sold item numbers, and sales amount. You can search by the product name or product number.

课后习题

1. （单选题）哪个指标显示了直播期间观看直播的总人数？
   A. 订单量　　　　　　　　　　　　B. 观众
   C. GMV　　　　　　　　　　　　　D. 商品查看量

2. （单选题）在 Shopee 直播中，哪个指标显示了在直播期间点击"加入购物车"按钮的次数？
   A. 订单　　　　　　　　　　　　　B. 买家数
   C. 加入购物车总次数　　　　　　　D. 总观看次数

Exercises

1. （Single Choice）Which metric shows the total number of viewers who watched the live stream?
   A. Order Volume　　　　　　　　　B. Viewers
   C. GMV　　　　　　　　　　　　　D. Product Views

2. （Single Choice）In a Shopee live stream, which metric shows the number of times the "Add to Cart" button was clicked during the stream?
   A. Orders　　　　　　　　　　　　B. Number of Buyers
   C. Total Add to Cart Clicks　　　　D. Total Views

任务 ② 进行数据分析与直播复盘

任务导入

直播数据分析与复盘是通过系统化的方法，对直播活动产生的各类数据进行处理与分析，从而评估直播的表现，找出成功因素和需要改进的方面，并优化未来的直播策略。StreamASEAN 直播电商公司向 Peter 所在的直播团队下达任务：进行数据分析与直播复盘。

Peter 此次需要全面了解直播数据分析的流程与方法，进行本次直播的数据统计和分析，完成直播复盘。

任务目标

¤ 知识目标
1. 了解直播数据分析的流程与方法
2. 了解直播复盘的意义及流程

¤ 技能目标
1. 能够完成直播数据的统计和分析
2. 能够完成直播复盘

¤ 素养目标
培养学生精益求精的工匠精神

任务流程

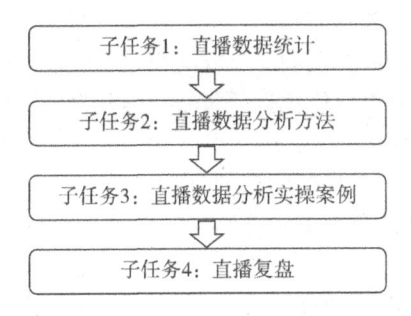

```
子任务1：直播数据统计
        ↓
子任务2：直播数据分析方法
        ↓
子任务3：直播数据分析实操案例
        ↓
子任务4：直播复盘
```

子任务1 直播数据统计

学习过程

一、确定直播数据分析目标

（一）寻找直播间数据波动的原因

直播间数据波动可能由内容质量、主播表现、外部因素和平台算法等多种因素引起。内容新颖、互动性强的直播吸引更多观众，而高峰期竞争和平台算法调整也会影响数据。此外，节假日和特定时段的选择可能导致观众数量变化。综合考虑这些因素，有助于理解数据波动原因。

（二）通过数据分析寻找优化直播内容、提升直播效果的方案

通过数据分析，可以确定观众偏好的内容和最佳直播时段，识别出最畅销的产品并优化推荐策略。分析观众的反馈和满意度，发现直播中的不足并进行改进。通过A/B测试不同策略，找到最有效的直播形式，提高观众参与度和销售转化率，持续优化直播效果。

（三）通过数据规律推测平台算法，然后从算法出发对直播进行优化

分析数据规律，了解平台算法偏好的内容和形式，有针对性地优化直播。通过提高互动率、观看时长和留存率等关键指标，增加直播被推荐的概率。观察平台推荐机制的变化趋势，提前调整直播策略，提高曝光度和观众参与度，显著提升直播效果。

二、分析直播效果关键数据指标

（一）分析用户画像数据指标

用户画像数据指标的分析旨在了解观众的基本特征和行为习惯，以便为直播内容和营销策略提供依据。首先，分析用户的年龄、性别、地理位置和兴趣爱好等人口统计学特征，可以帮助确定目标观众群体的具体属性。其次，关注用户的观看习惯，例如平均观看时长、观看频次和活跃时间段，能够了解观众的行为模式。此外，分析用户的消费习惯，包括购买频次、偏好产品类别和购买力等，可以为产品推荐和促销活动提供指导。通过综合这些数据，能够构建出详细的用户画像，优化直播内容和营销策略，提升观众的参与度和满意度。

（二）分析流量数据指标

流量数据指标反映了直播间的访问情况和观众规模。首先，关注总观看人数和独立观

看人数，了解整体流量和独立访客情况。其次，分析流量来源，如通过短视频平台、社交媒体、搜索引擎等渠道进入直播间的观众比例，能够识别最有效的引流渠道。此外，监测流量变化趋势，包括高峰期和低谷期的流量波动情况，可以帮助调整直播时间和内容策略。通过对流量数据的深入分析，可以优化推广策略，提升直播间的曝光度和吸引力。

（三）分析互动数据指标

互动数据指标是衡量观众参与度的重要标准。首先，分析观众的互动行为，例如弹幕、评论、点赞和分享的数量及频率，能够评估观众的活跃程度和参与意愿。其次，关注互动内容的质量和情感倾向，例如正面评价和负面反馈的比例，以此了解观众的满意度和后续工作需要改进的方向。此外，监测观众在直播中的提问和关注点，可以识别观众最感兴趣的话题和需求。通过提升互动数据指标，可以增强观众的参与感和黏性，提升直播效果和观众满意度。

（四）分析转化数据指标

转化数据指标反映了观众的购买行为和实际转化效果。首先，关注销售转化率，即观看直播的观众中实际购买的比例，评估直播带货的效果。其次，分析购买行为，如购买频次、平均订单金额和购买产品类别，了解观众的消费习惯和偏好。此外，监测促销活动的效果，例如优惠券使用率和限时抢购的参与度，评估促销策略的有效性。通过优化转化数据指标，可以提高直播的销售业绩和观众的购买意愿，增加收益。

任务操作

完成了直播数据的收集后，Peter 所在的直播团队需要对直播数据进行整理和分析，主要步骤如下。

☞ **步骤一　分类数据**

导出以下数据，并将数据记录在表格中。

用户画像数据：包括观众的性别、年龄、地域等数据。

流量数据：包括在线观众人数和粉丝增长等数据。

互动数据：包括评论数、点赞数和分享次数等数据。

转化数据：包括商品点击和购买等数据。

☞ **步骤二　整理数据**

记录并整理数据，填写在表 5-3 中。

表 5-3　平台数据分析表

数据类型	数据指标	数据值
用户画像数据		
流量数据		
互动数据		
转化数据		

Learning Process

1. Live Streaming Data Analysis Goals

1.1 Analyzing the Causes of Live Streaming Data Fluctuations

Data fluctuations in live streams can be caused by various factors such as content quality, host performance, external factors, and platform algorithms. Novel and interactive content attracts more viewers, while peak time competition and platform algorithm adjustments also affect data. Additionally, choosing specific holidays and time periods can lead to changes in viewer numbers. Considering these factors helps understand the reasons behind data fluctuations.

1.2 Finding Ways to Optimize Live Streaming Content and Improve Effectiveness through Data Analysis

Through data analysis, you can determine the content and best live streaming times that viewers prefer, identify the best-selling products, and optimize recommendation strategies. Analyzing viewer feedback and satisfaction helps identify shortcomings in the live stream and make improvements. By conducting A/B testing on different strategies, you can find the most effective live streaming formats, increase viewer engagement, and improve sales conversion rates, thereby continuously optimizing live streaming effectiveness.

1.3 Inferring Platform Algorithms through Data Patterns and Optimizing Live Streams Based on These Algorithms

Analyzing data patterns helps understand the content and formats preferred by platform algorithms, allowing targeted live streaming optimization. By improving key metrics such as interaction rate, watch time, and retention rate, you can increase the chances of the live stream being recommended. Observing changes in the platform recommendation mechanism trends helps adjust live streaming strategies in advance, enhancing exposure and viewer engagement, thereby significantly improving live streaming effectiveness.

2. Key Data Metrics for Live Streaming Effectiveness Analysis

2.1 Analyzing User Profile Data Metrics

The analysis of user profile data aims to understand the basic characteristics and behavior patterns of viewers to provide a basis for live streaming content and marketing strategies. First, analyzing demographic characteristics such as age, gender, geographic location, and interests helps determine the specific attributes of the target audience. Next, paying attention to viewing habits, such as average watch time, viewing frequency, and active time periods, helps understand viewer behavior patterns. Additionally, analyzing consumption habits, including purchase frequency, preferred product categories, and purchasing power, provides guidance for product recommendations and promotional activities. By combining these data points, detailed user profiles can be constructed to optimize live streaming content and marketing strategies, and enhance viewer engagement and satisfaction.

2.2 Analyzing Traffic Data Metrics

Traffic data metrics reflect the access situation and viewer scale of the live streaming room.

First, paying attention to total viewership and unique viewers helps understand overall traffic and unique visitor situations. Next, analyzing traffic sources, such as viewers entering the live stream through short video platforms, social media, and search engines, helps identify the most effective channels for attracting viewers. Additionally, monitoring traffic trends, including peak and low traffic periods, helps adjust live streaming times and content strategies. By thoroughly analyzing traffic data, promotional strategies can be optimized to increase the exposure and appeal of the live streaming room.

2.3 Analyzing Interaction Data Metrics

Interaction data metrics are key indicators of viewer engagement. First, analyzing viewer interaction behaviors, such as the number and frequency of comments, likes, and shares, helps assess viewer activity levels and participation willingness. Next, paying attention to the quality and emotional tone of interactions, such as the proportion of positive and negative feedback, helps understand viewer satisfaction and areas for improvement. Additionally, monitoring viewer questions and focal points during the live stream helps identify topics and needs that interest viewers the most. By enhancing interaction data metrics, viewer engagement and loyalty can be increased, thereby improving live streaming effectiveness and viewer satisfaction.

2.4 Analyzing Conversion Data Metrics

Conversion data metrics reflect viewers' purchasing behaviors and actual conversion effects. First, paying attention to sales conversion rates, i.e., the proportion of viewers who make purchases, helps assess the effectiveness of the live stream in driving sales. Next, analyzing purchasing behaviors, such as purchase frequency, average order value, and preferred product categories, helps understand viewers' consumption habits and preferences. Additionally, monitoring the effectiveness of promotional activities, such as voucher usage rates and participation in limited-time offers, helps evaluate the effectiveness of promotional strategies. By optimizing conversion data metrics, sales performance and viewers' purchase intentions can be improved, thereby increasing revenue.

Task Operations

Step 1: Categorize Data

Export the following data and record it in a table.

User Profile Data: Includes viewer gender, age, region, etc.

Traffic Data: Includes online viewer numbers and follower growth, etc.

Interaction Data: Includes the number of comments, likes, and shares, etc.

Conversion Data: Includes product clicks and purchase data, etc.

Step 2: Organize Data

Record and Organize Data.

子任务2 直播数据分析方法

学习过程

数据统计结束后,Peter及其直播团队需要根据本次直播数据展开数据分析,Peter

对直播数据分析的常用方法了解如下。

一、对比分析法

对比分析法即通过比对找出异常数据。"异常"不是指有偏差的数据，而是指离平均线偏差较大的数值。如某主播每天增粉长期维持在50~100人这个区间，某天增粉量突增到200人，虽然这是令人惊喜的事，但也属于异常数据，需要密切关注，查找出粉丝增加的原因，以便改进运营方案。这就是进行数据统计的原因，只有把一段时间以来的数据放在一个表格里，才能发现数据的异常。在数据多的情况下，建议使用Excel的数据透视功能。

二、特殊事件法

大部分数据出现"异常"都会关联某个特殊事件，如平台首页或者频道改版、标签变化、开播时段更改等，这就要求直播运营人员在日常记录数据时，一定要同步记录这些特殊事件，然后进行对比分析。

三、曲线分析法

曲线通常能够代表数据的走势，可以挑选三类相关性高的数据放在一起对比分析走势，使用曲线分析法可以判断趋势。

数据分析就是运用量化方法，帮助直播运营人员从中找到问题并解决问题。因此，根据数据分析得出的结论，对直播具有重要的指导意义。直播运营团队要养成观察数据、分析数据的好习惯。

任务操作

根据上述知识，Peter所在的直播团队需要对本场直播进行直播数据分析，Peter分别使用对比分析法、特殊事件法和曲线分析法三种方法对此次直播进行分析，具体操作步骤如下。

☞ **步骤一　对比分析法**

使用Excel或其他数据分析工具将数据进行对比，找出异常数据点，深入分析其原因，并填写在表5-4中。

表5-4　对比分析法分析

数据类型	数据值	异常原因

☞ **步骤二　特殊事件法**

收集特定事件期间的详细数据，如促销活动期间的观看人数和销售额。评估特定事件对数据的影响，并总结经验，填写在表5-5中。

表5-5　特殊事件法分析

事件	数据类型	数据值	影响

☞ **步骤三　曲线分析法**

通过绘制单场直播的数据变化趋势图，分析直播效果和后续工作需要改进的方向。

（1）记录以下数据指标：例如在线观众人数、粉丝增长、评论数、点赞数、分享次数、商品点击、购买数据等不同时间段的数据。

（2）整理数据：将数据整理为可视化表格。

（3）使用 Excel 或其他数据分析工具。

（4）绘制趋势图。

· 打开 Excel，选择数据区域，插入折线图。

· 设置图表标题、轴标签等，确保图表清晰易读。

（5）分析与总结，分析直播数据变化趋势，总结直播问题和改进建议。

Learning Process

There are three common methods for analyzing live streaming data.

1. Comparative Analysis Method

Comparative Analysis Method involves identifying outlier data through comparison. "Outlier" does not mean erroneous data but refers to values significantly deviating from the average. For example, if a live streamer's daily follower increase consistently ranges between 50 to 100, and suddenly one day it jumps to 200, this surge, although positive, is considered outlier data. It requires close attention to determine the cause of the follower increase to improve the operational plan. This is the purpose of data statistics—only by compiling data over a period into a table can one identify anomalies. When you deal with large datasets, Excel's pivot table function is recommended.

2. Special Event Method

Most "anomalies" in data are associated with specific events, such as homepage or channel redesigns, changes in tags, or adjustments in broadcast times. This requires live streaming operators to keep track of these special events while recording daily data and then perform comparative analysis.

3. Curve Analysis Method

Curves usually represent the trend of the data. Selecting three highly related data points for comparison can help analyze trends. Curve analysis helps determine trends and patterns. Data analysis involves using quantitative methods to help live streaming operators identify and solve problems. Therefore, conclusions drawn from data analysis have significant guiding importance for live stream. The live streaming operations team should cultivate the habit of observing and analyzing data.

Task Operations

Step 1: Comparative Analysis Method

Use Excel or other data analysis tools to compare data and identify outlier data points. Conduct an in-depth analysis to determine the causes of these anomalies.

Step 2：Special Event Method

Collect detailed data during specific events, such as the number of viewers and sales during promotional periods. Evaluate the impact of these events on the data and summarize the findings.

Step 3：Curve Analysis Method

Analyze the trend of data changes during a single live stream to evaluate the effectiveness and identify areas for improvement.

（1）Record Data Indicators：For example, record data on the number of online viewers, fan growth, comments, likes, shares, product clicks, and purchase data at different time intervals.

（2）Organize Data：Arrange the data into a visual table format.

（3）Use Excel or Other Data Analysis Tools：Utilize these tools to analyze the data.

（4）Draw Trend Charts：

Open Excel, select the data range, and insert a line chart.

Set the chart title, axis labels, etc., to ensure the chart is clear and easy to read.

（5）Analyze the trend of live streaming data changes, summarize live streaming issues and propose improvement suggestions.

子任务 3　直播数据分析实操案例

学习过程

在直播完成后，Peter 及其直播团队将深入分析直播数据，并根据数据制定优化策略，以提升直播效果和销售转化率。

Peter 及其直播团队将对该场直播的数据进行整理分析，见图 5-1。

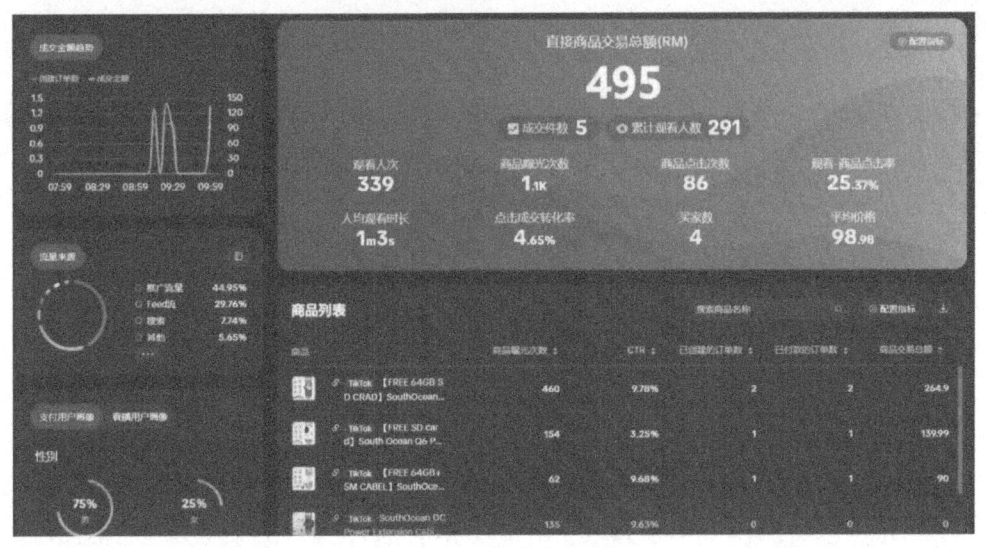

图 5-1　TikTok 直播数据

一、数据解读
(一) 观看人次与观看时长
观看人次 (339 次): 这是直播间总观看人数。观看人次越多, 说明直播间的吸引力越强。

人均观看时长 (1 分 3 秒): 观众平均观看直播的时间。这个指标可以反映观众对直播内容的兴趣程度。如果平均观看时长较短, 可能意味着内容不够吸引人, 或者观众的注意力容易被分散。

(二) 商品展示与点击率
商品曝光次数 (1100 次): 商品在直播中的展示次数。这个指标显示了商品在直播过程中被展示给观众的频率。

商品点击次数 (86 次): 观众点击商品链接的次数。这个指标反映了观众对商品的兴趣。

点击-成交转化率 (4.65%): 点击商品链接后最终购买的转化率。这个指标用于评估商品的销售效果。如果转化率较低, 可能需要优化商品描述或展示方式。

(三) 销售数据
直接商品交易总额 (495 RM): 直播期间商品总销售金额。这个指标直接反映了直播的销售成果。

成交件数 (5 件): 直播期间销售的商品总数。这个指标用于评估销售效率。

买家数 (4 人): 完成购买的独立用户数。这个指标体现了购买用户的数量。

平均价格 (98.98 RM): 每件商品的平均售价。这个指标用来分析商品的定价策略和市场接受度。

(四) 流量来源
推广流量 (44.95%): 通过推广活动获取的观众比例。这个指标用来评估推广活动的效果。

Feed 流 (29.76%): 通过信息流内容获取的观众比例。这个指标反映自然流量的获取情况。

搜索流量 (7.74%): 通过搜索功能获取的观众比例。这个指标用来分析观众的搜索行为。

(五) 观众性别
男性 (75%): 观看直播的男性观众比例。这个指标用来了解观众群体的性别分布。

女性 (25%): 观看直播的女性观众比例。这个指标用来了解观众群体的性别分布。

二、数据整理
数据清洗: 检查数据的完整性和一致性, 去除重复数据和错误数据。

重复数据处理: 使用 Excel 中的"删除重复项"功能, 确保每条数据都是独立的。

错误数据处理: 手动检查并修正数据中的错误, 如异常值和数据格式不一致的问题。

数据格式化: 统一数据格式, 确保数据字段名称一致, 方便后续分析。

字段名称统一: 确保所有数据表中的字段名称一致, 如"观看人次""商品点击次数"等。

三、数据分析

（一）观看人次和时长分析

使用 Excel 或 Google Sheets 中的折线图功能，展示观众人数变化趋势，找出观看高峰和低谷时段。

方法：在 Excel 中选择"插入（Insert）"选项卡，点击"折线图（Line Chart）"。选择数据范围，生成折线图。标记出观看高峰时段，分析其原因。

（二）时长分布分析

分析观众的观看时长分布，找出平均观看时长和较长观看时长的观众比例。

方法：使用数据透视表，计算每个观众的观看时长。在 Excel 中生成柱状图或饼图，展示观看时长的分布情况。

（三）商品点击率和转化率分析

点击率计算：点击次数/曝光次数，用于评估商品的吸引力。

方法：在 Excel 中新增一列，输入公式=点击次数/曝光次数。计算每件商品的点击率。

转化率计算：成交次数/点击次数，用于评估商品的销售效果。

方法：在 Excel 中新增一列，输入公式=成交次数/点击次数。计算每个商品的转化率。

（四）比较分析

比较不同商品的点击率和转化率，找出表现最佳和最差的商品，分析其原因。

方法：在 Excel 中生成对比图表，展示每个商品的点击率和转化率。标记出表现最佳和最差的商品，分析其特点。

（五）销售数据分析

使用柱状图展示不同商品的销售额和成交件数，找出销售最佳的商品。

方法：在 Excel 中选择"插入（Insert）"选项卡，点击"柱状图（Bar Chart）"。选择数据范围，生成柱状图。标记出销售额和成交件数最高的商品。

（六）平均价格分析

计算每件商品的平均价格，分析商品的定价策略和市场接受度。

方法：在 Excel 中新增一列，输入公式=销售金额/成交件数。计算每件商品的平均价格。

（七）流量来源分析

使用饼图展示不同来源的流量比例，找出主要的流量来源。

方法：在 Excel 中选择"插入（Insert）"选项卡，点击"饼图（Pie Chart）"。选择数据范围，生成饼图。标记出各个流量来源的比例。

（八）转化效果

分析不同来源的观众转化率，评估各个流量渠道的效果。

方法：在 Excel 中新增一列，计算各个流量来源的转化率。生成对比图表，展示各个流量来源的转化效果。

（九）观众性别分析：使用饼图展示观众的性别比例，了解主要观众群体的性别分布。

方法：在 Excel 中选择"插入（Insert）"选项卡，点击"饼图（Pie Chart）"。选择数据范围，生成饼图。标记出男性和女性观众的比例。

（十）性别偏好：分析不同性别观众的观看和购买行为，制定针对性策略。

方法：在 Excel 中生成性别分布图表。分析男性和女性观众的购买行为，找出性别偏好的商品和内容。

四、优化策略制定

（一）优化内容和互动

高峰时段优化：根据观看高峰时段，调整直播时间，确保在观众最多的时候进行直播。

示例：分析观看高峰时段，确定最佳直播时间。调整直播计划，在高峰时段进行重点内容展示。

（二）提高内容丰富度

增加观众平均观看时长，优化直播内容，增加互动环节，提升观众参与度。

示例：增加互动环节，如问答、抽奖等，吸引观众参与。优化直播内容结构，确保内容丰富有趣，保持观众注意力。

（三）提高商品吸引力

优化商品展示，对点击率高但转化率低的商品，优化展示方式，增加详细介绍和用户评价。

示例：增加商品详细介绍，突出商品特点和优势。邀请用户留下评价，增加商品的可信度和吸引力。

（四）组合销售策略

推广点击率高且转化率高的商品，设计优惠套餐，增加连带销售。

示例：设计优惠套餐，将高点击率商品和高转化率商品组合销售。在直播中推广优惠套餐，吸引观众购买。

（五）提升销售转化率

精准推广：针对推广流量，分析推广活动的效果，优化广告投放策略，提高观众转化率。

示例：分析不同推广渠道的效果，选择效果最好的渠道进行重点推广。优化广告投放策略，增加针对性强的广告内容，吸引更多目标观众。

（六）优化搜索策略

提高搜索流量转化率，通过优化商品标题和标签，提高商品在搜索结果中的排名。

示例：优化商品标题和标签，增加相关关键词，提高商品在搜索结果中的曝光率。通过 SEO（Search Engine Optimization，搜索引擎优化），提高商品页面的排名和点击率。

（七）拓展观众群体

根据观众性别比例，调整直播风格和互动方式，迎合主要观众群体的偏好。

示例：根据男性观众的偏好，增加科技类、运动类等男性感兴趣的内容。根据女性观众的偏好，增加美妆、时尚等女性感兴趣的内容。

（八）多渠道推广

结合不同流量来源的效果，拓展新的推广渠道，提高整体流量和转化率。

示例：分析各个流量来源的效果，找出最有效的渠道。拓展新的推广渠道，如社交媒体、合作伙伴等，增加流量来源。

任务操作

学习完上述知识，请帮助 Peter 的直播团队完成以下任务操作。

☞ **步骤一　数据整理和分析**

从下面的 TikTok 直播数据中选择一个数据进行数据整理和分析，演示如何根据分析结果制定优化策略，见图 5-2、图 5-3。

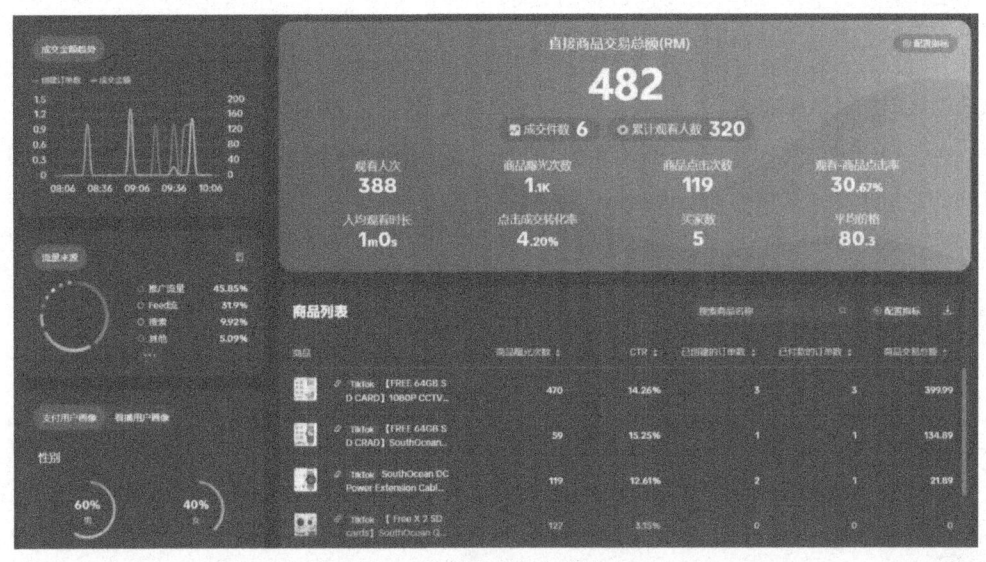

图 5-2　TikTok 直播数据

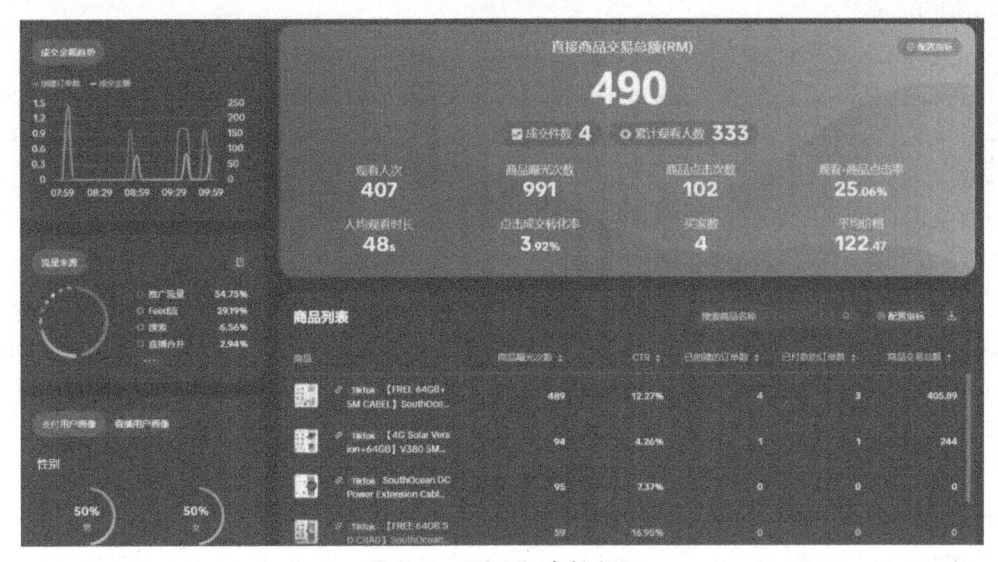

图 5-3　TikTok 直播数据

☞ **步骤二　小组讨论**

分组讨论各自直播的数据分析结果，交流分析方法和策略，分享优化经验。
（1）将学员分成小组，分配不同的分析任务。
（2）各组学员讨论并分析自己的直播数据，找出存在的问题和需要改进的方面。

（3）各组学员分享分析结果和优化策略，相互学习和借鉴。

☞ **步骤三　反馈与改进**

根据反馈，进一步改进数据分析的方法和策略，提升直播效果，制定更加精准的优化方案。

（1）收集对课程内容和实操环节的反馈。

（2）根据反馈，调整和改进数据分析的方法和策略。

（3）制定更加精准和有效的优化方案，提升直播效果。

Learning Process

After the live stream, the operation team will conduct an in-depth analysis of the live streaming data and develop optimization strategies based on the data to improve the effectiveness and conversion rates of their live stream. The team will organize and analyze the data from this live stream, as shown in Figure 5-1 (please see the Chinese section).

1. Data Interpretation

1.1 View Count and Average Watch Time

View Count (339 times): This is the total number of views for the livestream. The higher the number of views, the more attractive the live stream is.

Average Watch Time (1 min 3 sec): The average time viewers spend watching the live stream. This metric can reflect the audiences' interest in the live content. If the average watch time is short, it may mean that the content is not engaging enough, or the audience's attention is easily distracted.

1.2 Product Display and Click-through Rate

Product Exposure (1.1k times): The number of times the product is displayed during the live stream. This metric shows how frequently the product is presented to the audience during the live stream.

Product Clicks (86 times): The number of times viewers click on the product link. This metric reflects the audience's interest in the product.

Click-to-Conversion Rate (4.65%): The conversion rate of clicks on the product link to final purchases. This metric is used to evaluate the sales effectiveness of the product. If the conversion rate is low, the product description or display method may need to be optimized.

1.3 Sales Data

Sales Amount (495 RM): The total sales amount of products during the live stream. This directly reflects the sales results of the live stream.

Number of Transactions (5 items): The total number of products sold during the live stream. This is used to evaluate sales efficiency.

Number of Buyers (4 people): The number of unique users who completed purchases. This metric measures the number of purchasing users.

Average Price (98.98 RM): The average price per item. This helps analyze the product's pricing strategy and market acceptance.

1.4 Traffic Sources

Promotional Traffic (44.95%): The proportion of viewers acquired through promotional activities. This metric evaluates the effectiveness of promotional activities.

Feed Traffic (29.76%): The proportion of viewers acquired through Feed content. This reflects the acquisition of natural traffic.

Search Traffic (7.74%): The proportion of viewers acquired through the search function. This metric analyzes the search behavior of viewers.

1.5 Audience Gender

Male (75%): The proportion of male viewers of the live stream. This helps understand the gender distribution of the audience.

Female (25%): The proportion of female viewers of the live stream. This helps understand the gender distribution of the audience.

2. Data Organization

Data Cleaning: Check the completeness and consistency of the data, and remove duplicate and erroneous data.

Duplicate Data Handling: Use the "Remove Duplicates" function in Excel to ensure each data entry is unique.

Error Data Handling: Manually check and correct errors in the data, such as outliers and inconsistent data formats.

Data Formatting: Standardize data formats to ensure data field names are consistent, facilitating subsequent analysis.

Field Name Standardization: Ensure that field names in all data tables are consistent, such as "View Count" and "Product Clicks".

3. Data Analysis

3.1 View Count and Watch Time Analysis

Use the line chart function in Excel or Google Sheets to show the trend in audience numbers, identifying peak and low viewing times.

Method: In Excel, select the "Insert" tab and click "Line Chart". Select the data range and generate the line chart. Mark peak viewing times and analyze the reasons.

3.2 Watch Time Distribution Analysis

Analyze the distribution of audience watch times to find the average watch time and the proportion of viewers with longer watch times.

Method: Use a pivot table to calculate the watch time for each viewer. Generate a bar chart or pie chart in Excel to display the distribution of watch times.

3.3 Click-through Rate and Conversion Rate

Click-through Rate Calculation: Calculate the click-through rate using the formula "clicks/exposures" to evaluate product attractiveness.

Method: In Excel, add a new column and enter the formula =clicks/exposures. Calculate the click-through rate for each product.

Conversion Rate Calculation: Calculate conversion rate using the formula "transactions/clicks" to evaluate product sales effectiveness.

Method: In Excel, add a new column and enter the formula = transactions/clicks. Calculate the conversion rate for each product.

3.4 Comparative Analysis

Compare the click-through and conversion rates of different products to identify the best and worst-performing products and analyze their characteristics.

Method: Generate comparison charts in Excel to display the click-through and conversion rates for each product. Mark the best and worst-performing products and analyze their features.

3.5 Sales Data Analysis

Use bar charts to display the sales amounts and transaction counts for different products, identifying the best-selling products.

Method: In Excel, select the "Insert" tab and click "Bar Chart". Select the data range and generate the bar chart. Mark the products with the highest sales amounts and transaction counts.

3.6 Average Price Analysis

Calculate the average price per item by using the formula "sales amount/transaction" count to analyze the product's pricing strategy and market acceptance.

Method: In Excel, add a new column and enter the formula = sales amount/transaction count. Calculate the average price for each product.

3.7 Traffic Source Analysis

Use pie charts to display the proportion of different traffic sources, identifying the main traffic sources.

Method: In Excel, select the "Insert" tab and click "Pie Chart". Select the data range and generate the pie chart. Mark the proportions of each traffic source.

3.8 Conversion Effectiveness

Analyze the conversion rates of viewers from different sources to evaluate the effectiveness of each traffic channel.

Method: In Excel, add a new column to calculate the conversion rate for each traffic source. Generate comparison charts to display the conversion effectiveness of each traffic source.

3.9 Audience Gender Analysis

Use pie charts to display the gender distribution of the audience, understanding the main audience groups.

Method: In Excel, select the "Insert" tab and click "Pie Chart". Select the data range and generate the pie chart. Mark the proportions of male and female viewers.

3.10 Gender Preference Analysis

Analyze the viewing and purchasing behaviors of viewers of different genders to develop targeted strategies.

Method: Generate gender distribution charts in Excel. Analyze the purchasing behaviors of male and female viewers, and identify products and content preferred by different genders.

4. Strategy Development

4.1 Optimize Content and Interaction

Peak Time Optimization: Adjust the live stream time based on peak viewing times to ensure the live stream occurs when there are the most viewers.

Example: Analyze peak viewing times, determine the best live streaming time, and adjust the live streaming schedule to showcase key content during peak times.

4.2 Content Richness: Increase the average watch time of viewers by optimizing live streaming content and adding interaction segments to enhance audience engagement.

Example: Add interactive segments such as Q&A and giveaways to attract audience participation. Optimize the live streaming content structure to ensure it is rich and engaging, maintaining audience attention.

4.3 Increase Product Attractiveness

Optimize Product Display: For products with high click-through but low conversion rates, optimize the display method, add detailed descriptions, and include user reviews.

Example: Add detailed product descriptions, highlighting product features and advantages. Invite users to leave reviews to increase the product's credibility and attractiveness.

4.4 Bundling Sales Strategy

Promote products with high click-through and conversion rates by designing discount bundles to increase cross-selling.

Example: Design discount bundles by combining high click-through products with high conversion rate products. Promote discount bundles during the live stream to attract audience purchases.

4.5 Increase Sales Conversion Rate

Targeted Promotion: Analyze the effectiveness of promotional activities for promotional traffic, optimizing advertising strategies to increase audience conversion rates.

Example: Analyze the effectiveness of different promotional channels, selecting the most effective channel for targeted promotion. Optimize advertising strategies to include highly targeted content to attract more target audiences.

4.6 Optimize Search Strategy

Increase the conversion rate of search traffic by optimizing product titles and tags to improve product ranking in search results.

Example: Optimize product titles and tags to include relevant keywords, improving the product exposure in search results. Improve product page ranking and click-through rate through SEO optimization.

4.7 Expand Audience Groups

Gender Preference Adjustment: Adjust the live stream style and interaction method based on the gender distribution of the audience to cater to the preferences of the main audience groups.

Example: Increase tech and sports content to cater to male viewers. Increase beauty and fashion content to cater to female viewers.

4.8 Multi-channel Promotion

Expand new promotion channels based on the effectiveness of different traffic sources to increase overall traffic and conversion rates.

Example: Analyze the effectiveness of each traffic source to identify the most effective channels. Expand new promotion channels such as social media and partners to increase traffic sources.

Task Operations

After learning the above knowledge, please help the live streaming team complete the following task operations.

Step 1: Data Organization and Analysis

Select actual TikTok live data from the options below, perform data organization and analysis, and demonstrate how to develop optimization strategies based on the analysis results, as shown in Figure 5-2 and Figure 5-3 (please see the Chinese section).

Step 2: Group Discussion

Divide participants into groups, assign different analysis tasks, discuss and analyze each group's live streaming data, and identify issues and improvement points.

(1) Divide participants into groups and assign different analysis tasks.

(2) Each group discusses and analyzes its live streaming data, identifies problems, and finds improvement points.

(3) Each group shares its analysis results and optimization strategies, and learn from each other.

Step 3: Feedback and Improvement

Based on feedback, further improve data analysis methods and strategies, enhance live streaming effectiveness, and develop more precise optimization plans.

(1) Collect feedback on course content and practical sessions.

(2) Adjust and improve data analysis methods and strategies based on feedback.

(3) Develop more precise and effective optimization plans to enhance live streaming effectiveness.

子任务4　直播复盘

学习过程

直播复盘是一个系统性的回顾和分析过程，用于评估直播活动的各个方面，从主播的表现、内容的安排到观众的互动和反应。在复盘的过程中可以分析直播表现，从而优化未来的直播策略和提升观众体验。在进行直播复盘前，Peter所在的直播团队需要对直播复盘的知识进行如下了解。

一、直播复盘类型

（一）单场复盘

单场复盘指的是对一场直播进行复盘，一般是在下播后进行。

（二）主题复盘

主题复盘指的是以某个主题内容进行复盘，一般是在直播一段时间后，对多个场次的直播进行复盘。

二、参与复盘人员

（一）主播

主播主要复盘直播脚本、话术问题、产品卖点掌握度和控场能力。

（二）场控人员

场控人员重点关注直播中的实时目标、直播间热度变化、突发事件预警能力，以及与主播的配合度。

（三）运营人员

运营人员重点复盘预热/引流环节，以及投放操盘等问题。

（四）选品人员

选品人员主要复盘评估品牌和商品的筛选是否合理，利润款、引流款、爆款产品的设置是否合适。

（五）客服

客服人员主要复盘活动福利说明及可能存在的售后问题，以及直播过程中回答粉丝提问的质量。

三、复盘的思路

直播复盘有一个大前提：透过现象看本质，本质上其实都是"人""货""场"的问题。

（一）人

话术：借助回放录屏，找出高光时刻前后的话术，分析话术调整对互动数据的影响。

互动：通过互动数据分析，找出互动频繁的时段和话题。

用户画像：分别分析看播用户和成交用户的画像，了解观众和买家的特征。

（二）货

选品能力：通过交易数据分析选品的转化效果。

排品能力：通过商品的属性、定价、销量、销售额等数据综合分析排品的合理性。

（三）场

场景吸引力：通过点击转化率来评估场景的吸引力。

场景匹配度：结合账号定位、商品定位、人群定位来评估场景匹配度。

四、复盘前的准备工作

（一）录屏

将一场完整直播录制下来，方便后续拆解分析。登录直播中控后台，选择本场直播回放进行下载，复盘阶段可投屏至电视进行分析拆解。

（二）表格

每天下播后第一时间填写数据表格，进行同比、环比分析，判断每项指标的变化。

（三）工具

通过第三方数据工具，补充分析各维度数据。例如，一场具体直播的流量数据，进场人数、在线人数及留存率。

任务操作

根据上述知识，Peter 及其团队成员需要对本场直播进行单场直播复盘，具体操作步骤如下。

☞ **步骤一　归纳直播问题**

（一）直播团队成员主观发现问题

直播团队成员可以凭借自身的经验和参与直播活动的经历，快速地发现整场直播活动中哪个环节或哪个方面存在不足。

（二）通过数据分析客观发现问题

直播团队成员的主观判断能够快速找到直播活动存在问题的方向，但不足以准确地发现问题。此时，直播团队可以借助数据分析将直播活动中存在的问题具体化、量化。

☞ **步骤二　分析直播问题**

（一）总结主播状态

分析主播是否重视本场直播，开播前是否做好了充足准备，是否充分了解商品的卖点信息，是否熟悉直播脚本与话术，妆容及穿着是否适宜；分析直播过程中主播的精神状态是否饱满，注意力是否集中，是否与用户积极互动，并填写完成表 5-6。

表 5-6　主播自检表

自检内容	是/否
是否体现商品卖点信息、产品价格、直播间价格	
是否熟悉直播脚本与话术	
是否话术趋于单一，情绪没有起伏	
是否缺少拉关注、分享直播间的场景	
妆容及穿着是否适宜	
精神状态是否饱满集中	
是否与观众积极互动	
是否全程使用英文/东南亚其他国家语言直播	
是否中英文夹杂，或英文不流利	
其他：	

（二）总结团队配合情况

1. 副播

分析副播是否存在与主播配合不佳、商品细节展示不清晰、用户问题回复或解决不及时等问题，并填写完成表 5-7。

表 5-7　副播自检表

自检内容	是/否
是否存在与主播配合不佳的情况	
是否存在商品细节展示不清晰	
是否存在用户问题回复或解决不及时	
其他：_____	

2. 助理

分析助理是否存在道具准备错误、与主播的互动不及时、声音不够洪亮等问题，并填写完成表 5-8。

表 5-8 助理自检表

自检内容	是/否
是否提前准备好直播所需的所有物品和道具	
是否协助主播熟悉商品卖点和直播流程	
是否在直播前检查商品展示效果（如光线、角度等）	
是否及时提供主播需要的信息和资料	
是否存在商品、道具、资料错误或缺失	
是否协助维护直播间秩序、处理观众的问题、与观众互动	
是否监控直播间弹幕和评论，及时反馈给主播	
是否在直播结束后整理和收纳所有物品	
其他：	

3. 场控人员

分析场控人员是否存在商品上下架操作失误、优惠券发放不及时、库存数量修改错误等问题，并填写完成表 5-9。

表 5-9 场控人员自检表

自检内容	是/否
是否确保直播设备（摄像头、麦克风、灯光等）正常工作	
是否检查网络连接的稳定性和速度	
是否准备并检查直播间布景、背景和道具	
是否协调和安排直播团队的各项工作，确保流畅进行	
是否存在上下架、优惠券等平台操作不及时或失误	
是否及时处理直播过程中出现的技术问题	
是否监控直播进程，确保按计划进行	
是否监控并记录直播数据，以便后期分析	
其他：	

4. 运营人员

分析运营人员是否存在商品要点归纳不足、预估直播数据出现偏差、直播突发状况未做出有效判断等问题，并填写完成表 5-10。

表 5-10 运营人员自检表

自检内容	是/否
是否明确直播目标和 KPI	
是否进行详细的直播前期策划与准备	
是否有效协调主播、产品和技术团队	
是否熟悉直播平台的操作和功能	
是否实时监控并分析直播数据（流量、互动、转化等）	
是否制定并执行推广和引流策略	
是否实时解决直播中的突发问题	
其他：	

【注意】从人、货、场三个角度，对本场直播存在问题进行自检分析。

（三）分析销售数据

1. 记录销售数据

为了解商品及定价的合理性，Peter 需对销售数据进行分析，并填写在表 5-11 中。

表 5-11 销售数据

商品	点击数	购买数	销售额

2. 分析选品和定价策略

分析高销量商品，记录其特点和策略，并填写在表 5-12 中。

表 5-12 选品定价分析

高销量商品	特点	选品策略	定价策略

3. 根据上述记录，写下商品选品和定价优化策略

（四）汇总直播间用户评论

通过汇总直播间用户的评论，可以了解用户感兴趣的话题，以便在下次直播时"对症下药"。因此 Peter 需要将直播间用户评论进行收集，并填写在表 5-13 中。

表 5-13 直播间评论汇总

评论内容	相关商品	反馈类型	建议

（五）总结热门话题及商品

把总结的内容填写在表 5-14 中。

表 5-14 热门话题汇总

热门话题	热门商品	改进建议

（六）回顾变化

回顾直播间人气变化，并填写在表 5-15 中。

表 5-15 直播间人气变化

时间段	进场人数	在线人数	离开原因

（七）分析变化，找出原因

分析不同时间段人气变化，找出高峰低谷原因，并填写在表 5-16 中。

表 5-16 峰值变化分析

高峰时间段	低谷时间段	原因分析

（八）整理直播内容

记录直播中的话术和脚本，并填写在表 5-17 中。

表 5-17 直播内容整理

内容类型	脚本/话术	直播间效果	改进建议

（九）分析用户弹幕互动

分析互动积极和不足的部分，并填写在表 5-18 中。

表 5-18 用户弹幕分析

时间段	弹幕内容	互动积极	互动不足	改进建议

☞ 步骤三 形成直播优化方案

直播团队根据直播后台数据，分析相关数据，评估直播的整体效果，提炼直播的亮点及不足，形成一份直播优化方案。

文档格式：使用 PPT 或 PDF 格式提交。

☞ 步骤四 复盘汇报

直播团队针对数据分析与复盘结果进行汇报。

Learning Process

1. Types of Live Streaming Review

1.1 Single Session Review

Reviewing a single live streaming session, typically conducted after the live stream ends.

1.2 Thematic Review

Reviewing multiple live streaming sessions based on a specific theme, usually conducted after a period of time.

2. Participants in the Review

2.1 Host

Review live streaming script, speaking skills, product knowledge, and control abilities.

2.2 Field Controller

Monitor real-time goals during the live stream, changes in popularity, ability to handle unexpected events, and coordination with the host.

2.3 Operation Staff

Review warming up before the live stream and traffic-driving stages, and advertising management.

2.4 Product Selection Team

Evaluate the rationality of brand and product selection, and the suitability of profit products, traffic products, and bestsellers.

2.5 Customer Service Representative

Review explanations of promotional benefits, potential after-sales issues, and responses to fan questions during the live stream.

3. Review Approach

Live streaming reviews focus on understanding the underlying issues of "people", "goods", and "scenes" through observed phenomena.

3.1 People

Speech: Use playback recordings to identify key moments and analyze the impact of speech adjustments on interaction data.

Interaction: Analyze interaction data to identify periods and topics with frequent interactions.

User Profiles: Analyze the profiles of viewers and buyers to understand their characteristics.

3.2 Goods

Product Selection: Analyze transaction data to assess the effectiveness of product selection.

Product Arrangement: Evaluate the rationality of product arrangement based on attributes, pricing, sales volume, and revenue data.

3.3 Scenes

Scene Attractiveness: Assess scene attractiveness through click-through rates.

Scene Compatibility: Evaluate scene compatibility with account positioning, product positioning, and audience targeting.

4. Preparation for Review

4.1 Recording

Record the entire live streaming session for subsequent detailed analysis. Log in to the live streaming control panel, select the session replay for download, and use it for screen projection analysis during the review.

4.2 Data Tables

Fill out data tables immediately after the live stream ends, conduct year-on-year and month-on-month analyses, and evaluate changes in each metric.

4.3 Tools

Use third-party data tools to supplement and analyze data from various dimensions. For example, analyze traffic data for a specific live streaming session, including the number of entrants, online viewers, and retention rates.

Task Operations

Step 1: Summarize Live Streaming Issues

1.1 Subjective Issue Identification by Team Members

Live streaming team members can quickly identify areas of improvement in the live stream based on their experience and involvement.

1.2 Objective Issue Identification through Data Analysis

While subjective judgments help in quickly pinpointing issues, data analysis is needed to accurately identify and quantify these issues.

Step 2: Analyze Live Streaming Issues

2.1 Summary of Host's Performance

Analyze whether the host was well-prepared, understood product features, followed the script, maintained a professional appearance, and engaged actively with the audience.

2.2 Summary of Team Coordination

Co-host: Analyze if the co-host had issues coordinating with the main host, clearly presenting product details, or responding to user queries promptly.

C. 特殊事件法 D. 数据整理法

2. （单选题）在直播数据分析过程中，哪种数据指标反映了观众的参与度？
A. 流量数据指标 B. 用户画像数据指标
C. 转化数据指标 D. 互动数据指标

3. （单选题）在进行直播复盘时，哪一项内容不属于主播的自检内容？
A. 了解商品卖点信息 B. 监控直播进程
C. 是否积极与观众互动 D. 妆容及穿着是否适宜

4. （单选题）哪个步骤不属于直播复盘前的准备工作？
A. 录屏 B. 填写数据表格
C. 分析销售数据 D. 使用第三方数据工具

5. （单选题）哪种分析方法主要用于评估特定事件对直播数据的影响？
A. 曲线分析法 B. 对比分析法
C. 特殊事件法 D. 数据整理法

Exercises

1. （Single Choice） Which method identifies outlier data by comparison?
A. Curve Analysis Method B. Comparative Analysis Method
C. Special Event Method D. Data Organization Method

2. （Single Choice） Which data metrics reflects viewer engagement in live streaming data analysis?
A. Traffic Data Metrics B. User Profile Data Metrics
C. Conversion Data Metrics D. Interaction Data Metrics

3. （Single Choice） Which item is not part of the host's self-check during live streaming review?
A. Knowing product features B. Monitoring the live streaming process
C. Actively interacting with viewers D. Having appropriate makeup and attire

4. （Single Choice） Which step is not part of the preparation for live streaming review?
A. Recording the live stream B. Filling out data tables
C. Analyzing sales data D. Using third-party data tools

5. （Single Choice） Which analysis method is primarily used to evaluate the impact of specific events on live streaming data?
A. Curve Analysis Method B. Comparative Analysis Method
C. Special Event Method D. Data Organization Method

课后习题答案

项目1 认识东南亚直播电商

任务1 调研东南亚直播市场
课后习题

1. 答案：ABCD   2. 答案：D

3. 答案：市场趋势可以提供有关当前和未来市场发展方向的关键信息。了解这些趋势有助于预测市场潜在的增长领域、消费者偏好的变化，以及新兴技术的影响。通过对趋势的了解，企业可以更好地调整其产品和营销策略，以符合市场的发展，从而抓住更多的商机。（言之有理即可。）

Exercises

1. Answer：ABCD   2. Answer：D

3. Answer：Understanding market trends provides key information about the current and future directions of market development. This knowledge helps predict potential growth areas, changes in consumer preferences, and the impact of emerging technologies. By understanding these trends, companies can better adjust their products and marketing strategies to align with market developments, thereby seizing more business opportunities. (Any reasonable explanation is acceptable.)

任务2 选择直播平台
课后习题

1. 答案：C   2. 答案：A   3. 答案：略

Exercises

1. Answer：C   2. Answer：A   3. Answer：Omitted

任务3 选择直播商品
课后习题

1. 答案：ABCD   2. 答案：B   3. 答案：B

Exercises

1. Answer：ABCD   2. Answer：B   3. Answer：B

项目2 进行直播前的准备

任务1 组建直播团队
课后习题

1. 答案：C   2. 答案：B

3. 答案：在直播团队的初始阶段，团队结构通常较为简单，资源和人手有限，因此运营人员需要具备全能型的技能。

这种全能型的要求对团队运营的影响主要体现在提高了操作的灵活性和成本效率。然而，这也可能带来一定的风险，如个别运营人员的过载可能导致工作质量的不稳定，或者在专业技能深度上的不足。因此，随着团队逐渐发展，适时地扩展团队规模和引入专职人员，以平衡效率和专业性，是直播团队发展的必要策略。（言之有理即可。）

Exercises

1. Answer：C　　2. Answer：B

3. Answer：In the initial stage of a live streaming team, the structure is usually simple, and resources and personnel are limited, thus requiring operation staff to have versatile skills. This versatility improves operational flexibility and cost efficiency. However, it may also pose risks such as overloading individual operation staff, leading to inconsistent work quality, or a lack of depth in professional skills. Therefore, as the team develops, it is necessary to expand the team size and introduce specialized roles to balance efficiency and professionalism, which is essential for the growth of the live streaming team. (Reasonable explanations are acceptable.)

任务2　策划直播活动

课后习题

1. 答案：ABCD　　2. 答案：C

3. 答案：

在策划直播主题时，有效结合当前热点的关键步骤包括以下内容。

（1）深入研究热点背景。首先，了解热点的背后故事和核心内容，这包括热点的起源、相关人物、发展过程以及社会影响等。

（2）挖掘热点的核心价值。识别热点的核心价值和观众关注的焦点，分析这些内容如何与直播产品或服务相关联。

（3）设计互动环节。在直播中设计与热点相关的互动环节，例如讨论、问答或观众投票，以增强观众的参与感和活动的互动性。

（4）二次开发热点内容。即使热点的高关注期已过，依旧可以通过创造性的方式继续利用其影响力，例如通过回顾、深度解析或与其他主题的结合，来维持观众的兴趣。

（5）选择与直播内容相关的热点。确保所选的热点与直播内容有自然的结合点，避免生硬地蹭热点，这样才能更自然地吸引目标观众，避免负面评价。

（言之有理即可。）

Exercises

1. Answer：ABCD　　2. Answer：C

3. Answer：Key steps to effectively incorporate current hot topics into live streaming themes include：

(1) In-depth Research on Hot Topics：Understand the background story and core content of the hot topic, including its origin, key figures, development process, and social impact.

(2) Identify Core Values：Recognize the core values and focal points of the hot topic that attract audience attention and analyze how these relate to the live streaming product or service.

(3) Design Interactive Segments：Create interactive segments related to the hot topic during the live stream, such as discussions, Q&A sessions, or audience polls to enhance

engagement and interactivity.

(4) Reutilize Hot Topic Content: Even after the peak interest period, continue to creatively leverage the hot topic's influence through retrospectives, in-depth analysis, or by combining it with other themes to maintain audience interest.

(5) Choose Relevant Hot Topics: Ensure the selected hot topic naturally aligns with the live streaming content to attract the target audience more effectively and avoid negative feedback from forced associations.

(Reasonable explanations are acceptable.)

任务 3　创作直播内容

课后习题

1. 答案：C　　2. 答案：ACD　　3. 答案：略

Exercises

1. Answer: C　　2. Answer: ACD　　3. Answer: Omitted

任务 4　搭建直播间

课后习题

1. 答案：B　　2. 答案：略　　3. 答案：D

Exercises

1. Answer: B　　2. Answer: Omitted　　3. Answer: D

任务 5　开展直播预热

课后习题

1. 答案：ABC　　2. 答案：ACD

3. 答案：

（1）植入型预告。在预热视频的前半段输出与以往视频内容一致的内容，吸引固定粉丝观看，然后在后半段进行直播预热，通过设置悬念、透露直播亮点或介绍直播主题内容来吸引粉丝关注。

（2）利益点预热。通过在预热视频中添加利益点来吸引没有关注主播的用户，例如优惠活动或赠品，增强视频的诱惑力，激发用户的好奇心和兴趣，促使他们预约直播或关注主播。

（3）直播亮点预热。将本场直播中的亮点内容作为预热视频的主题，例如邀请特殊嘉宾、设置特色环节或展示特色场景等，以此吸引用户的关注。

（4）直播片段预热。通过发布直播筹备阶段的花絮或以往直播活动中的有趣片段，预先为直播活动引流造势。

Exercises

1. Answer: ABC　　2. Answer: ACD

3. Answer:

(1) Embedded Warm-up: The first half of the warm-up video outputs content consistent with previous videos to attract regular followers, and the second half introduces the live stream by creating suspense, revealing highlights, or introducing the theme to attract followers.

(2) Benefit-Based Warm-up: Adds benefits (e.g., discounts, gifts) in the warm-up video

to attract users who do not follow the host, enhancing the video's appeal and stimulating users' curiosity and interest, prompting them to book the live stream or follow the host.

（3）Highlight-Based Warm-up: Uses the highlight content of the upcoming live stream as the warm-up video theme, such as special guests, unique segments, or special scenes, to attract users' attention.

（4）Segment-Based Warm-up: Publishes behind-the-scenes footage or interesting moments from previous live streams as warm-up videos to generate interest and drive traffic to the live stream.

项目3　使用 Shopee 平台进行直播

课后习题

1. 答案：A　　2. 答案：B　　3. 答案：C　　4. 答案：A　　5. 答案：B

Exercises

1. Answer: A　　2. Answer: B　　3. Answer: C　　4. Answer: A　　5. Answer: B

项目4　使用 TikTok 平台进行直播

课后习题

1. 答案：A　　2. 答案：B　　3. 答案：B　　4. 答案：B　　5. 答案：B

Exercises

1. Answer: A　　2. Answer: B　　3. Answer: B　　4. Answer: B　　5. Answer: B

项目5　直播数据分析与复盘

任务1　获取平台直播数据

课后习题

1. 答案：B　　2. 答案：C

Exercises

1. Answer: B　　2. Answer: C

任务2　进行数据分析与直播复盘

课后习题

1. 答案：B　　2. 答案：D　　3. 答案：B　　4. 答案：C　　5. 答案：C

Exercises

1. Answer: B　　2. Answer: D　　3. Answer: B　　4. Answer: C　　5. Answer: C

参考文献

［1］ 王美英．跨境电商理论与实训［M］．成都：西南财经大学出版社，2018．
［2］ 李琦．跨境电商营销（第2版 慕课版）［M］．北京：人民邮电出版社，2023．
［3］ 韩红梅，王佳．数字营销基础与实务（微课版）［M］．北京：人民邮电出版社，2023．
［4］ 汪新兵．跨境电商选品维度与技巧［M］．重庆：重庆大学出版社，2023．
［5］ 郑延，刘祎．直播运营管理：微课版［M］．北京：人民邮电出版社，2023．
［6］ 吴娟，赖启军．新媒体运营（慕课版）［M］．北京：人民邮电出版社，2023．
［7］ 陶俪蓓，王晓宇，李文川．直播销售实务（慕课版）［M］．北京：人民邮电出版社，2023．
［8］ 彭军．直播电商基础［M］．重庆：重庆大学出版社，2021．
［9］ 7点5度，万字研究：东南亚在线直播［EB/OL］．7点5度，2022-08-02．
［10］ Momentum. Live Commerce in Southeast Asia［EB/OL］．Momentum，2022-09．
［11］ Ninja Van. Live Selling in Southeast Asia［EB/OL］．Ninja Van，2024．